NEW National Curriculum Mathematics

K. M. Vickers
M. J. Tipler
H. L. van Hiele

First published in 1991 by Canterbury Educational Ltd
Revised edition published in 1995 by:
Stanley Thornes (Publishers) Ltd
Ellenborough House, Wellington Street
CHELTENHAM Glos. GL50 1YW
England

98 99 00 / 10 9 8 7 6 5 4 3

A catalogue record for this book is available from the British Library.

ISBN 0-7487-3768-5
ISBN 0-7487-3769-3 (with answers)

Printed and bound in Italy by
STIGE, TURIN

PREFACE

"National Curriculum Mathematics" by K.M. Vickers and M.J. Tipler is a complete course carefully designed and now updated to ensure full coverage of the revised National Curriculum.

In the 1995 revised National Curriculum, the Level Descriptions describe the performance that pupils working at a particular level should demonstrate. This book covers all the material in **Level 6** of the National Curriculum in four separate sections: Number; Algebra; Shape, Space and Measures; and Handling Data. Using and Applying Mathematics is integrated throughout the book. The material is presented in this order to enable pupils, or a group of pupils, to work across the different areas of mathematics at different levels.

Each section begins with revision from previous levels, printed on pink paper for ease of identification. Each section ends with a review chapter which contains revision questions on the material developed in this book. In each of the other chapters, every skill developing exercise finishes with review questions.

With the exception of the Review chapters, all chapters begin with "Discover, Discuss, Do" which encourages the pupils to relate the topic to their everyday experiences; and finish with "For Your Interest" which encourages the pupils to relate the topic to other areas of the school curriculum and to people and careers which use the mathematics. Throughout each topic, relevance to everyday life is emphasised. The acquisition of knowledge and skills is integrated with the use and application of these skills and this knowledge.

This book does not replace the teacher. Rather, it is a resource for both the pupil and the teacher. The teacher can be flexible about what is taught and when.

Throughout the book there is a variety of activities: skill developing exercises, investigations, practical work, problem solving activities, discussion exercises, puzzles and games. All the activities are related to the topic being studied. Whenever possible, activities and exercises have been written as open rather than closed tasks.

There is a good balance between tasks which develop knowledge, skills and understanding, and those which develop the ability to tackle and solve problems. Many activities do both. There is a thorough and careful development of each topic. Questions within each exercise or activity are carefully graded to build pupil confidence.

This book takes into consideration:
    pupils' needs
    pupils' interests
    pupils' experiences
    the need for pupils to explore mathematics
    the use of technology
    both independent and co-operative work habits

This book encourages pupils to:
- use a wide range of mathematics
- discuss mathematical ideas
- undertake investigations
- participate in practical activities
- use reference material
- relate mathematics to everyday life
- select appropriate methods for a task
- analyse and communicate information
- discuss difficulties
- ask questions

It is hoped that the pupil who uses this book will:
- develop a real interest in mathematics
- become well motivated
- gain much enjoyment from mathematics
- develop a fascination with mathematics
- develop an ability to use mathematics in other subjects
- become confident in the use of the calculator and computer
- gain a firm foundation for further study
- become proficient at applying mathematics to everyday life
- develop both independent and co-operative work habits
- become aware of the power and purpose of mathematics
- develop an ability to communicate mathematics
- develop an appreciation of the relevance of mathematics
- develop an ability to think precisely, logically and creatively
- become confident at mathematics
- gain a sense of satisfaction

Calculator keying sequences are for the Casio *fx–82LB*. Some slight variation may be needed for other models and makes.

The version of LOGO used is LOGOTRON—standard LOGO for the BBC. The version of BASIC used is BBC BASIC.

K.M. Vickers
1995

Acknowledgements

The author wishes to thank all those firms and enterprises who have so kindly given permission to reproduce tables and other material. A special thanks to S.M. Bennett, S. P. R. Coxon, J.A. Ogilvie and S. Napier for their valuable contributions; to F. Tunnicliffe for the illustrations and J. McClelland for the photographs.

Every effort has been made to trace all the copyright holders. If any have been inadvertently overlooked the publishers will be pleased to make the necessary arrangement at the first opportunity.

Contents

ALGEBRA

SHAPE, SPACE and MEASURES

HANDLING DATA

Level Descriptions for Level 6

Attainment Target 1: Using and Applying Mathematics

■ Level 6

Pupils carry through substantial tasks and solve quite complex problems by breaking them down into smaller, more manageable tasks. They interpret, discuss and synthesise information presented in a variety of mathematical forms. Pupils' writing explains and informs their use of diagrams. Pupils are beginning to give a mathematical justification for their generalisations; they test them by checking particular cases.

Attainment Target 2: Number and Algebra

■ Level 6

Pupils order and approximate decimals when solving numerical problems and equations such as $x^2 = 20$, using trial-and-improvement methods. Pupils are aware of which number to consider as 100 per cent, or a whole, in problems involving comparisons, and use this to evaluate one number as a fraction or percentage of another. They understand and use the equivalences between fractions, decimals and percentages, and calculate using ratios in appropriate situations. When exploring number patterns, pupils find and describe in words the rule for the next term or nth term of a sequence where the rule is linear. They formulate and solve linear equations with whole number coefficients. They represent mappings expressed algebraically, interpreting general features and using graphical representation in four quadrants where appropriate.

Attainment Target 3: Shape, Space and Measures

■ Level 6

Pupils recognise and use common 2-D representations of 3-D objects. They know and use the properties of quadrilaterals in classifying different types of quadrilateral. They solve problems using angle and symmetry properties of polygons and properties of intersecting and parallel lines, and explain these properties. They devise instructions for a computer to generate and transform shapes and paths. They understand and use appropriate formulae for finding circumferences and areas of circles, areas of plane rectilinear figures and volumes of cuboids when solving problems. They enlarge shapes by a positive whole-number scale factor.

Attainment Target 4: Handling Data

■ Level 6

Pupils collect and record continuous data, choosing appropriate equal class intervals over a sensible range to create frequency tables. They construct and interpret frequency diagrams. They construct pie charts. Pupils draw conclusions from scatter diagrams, and have a basic understanding of correlation . When dealing with a combination of two experiments, pupils identify all the outcomes, using diagrammatic, tabular or other forms of communication. In solving problems, they use their knowledge that the total probability of all the mutually exclusive outcomes of an experiment is 1.

NUMBER

Number from Previous Levels

REVISION

ORDER of OPERATION

Calculation without the Calculator

If $14 - 2(5 + 1)$ is worked out without the calculator we must
work out the brackets first
then do $\times$ and $\div$
finally do $+$ and $-$
For instance, $14 - 2(5 + 1) = 14 - 2 \times 6$
$$= 14 - 12$$
$$= 2$$

Calculation with the Calculator

The scientific calculator does operations in the correct order. A calculation such
as $14 - 2(5 + 1)$ is keyed in as $\boxed{14}\ \boxed{-}\ \boxed{2}\ \boxed{\times}\ \boxed{(}\ \boxed{5}\ \boxed{+}\ \boxed{1}\ \boxed{)}\ \boxed{=}$ to get the
correct answer of 2. Some calculators do not need the $\boxed{\times}$ pressed before the $\boxed{(}$.
We sometimes need to insert **brackets** or use the **memory**.

For instance, $\frac{29+6}{4+3}$ can be worked out in one of the following ways.

Either **Key** $\boxed{(}\ \boxed{29}\ \boxed{+}\ \boxed{6}\ \boxed{)}\ \boxed{\div}\ \boxed{(}\ \boxed{4}\ \boxed{+}\ \boxed{3}\ \boxed{)}\ \boxed{=}$
or **Key** $\boxed{29}\ \boxed{+}\ \boxed{6}\ \boxed{=}\ \boxed{\div}\ \boxed{(}\ \boxed{4}\ \boxed{+}\ \boxed{3}\ \boxed{)}\ \boxed{=}$
or **Key** $\boxed{29}\ \boxed{+}\ \boxed{6}\ \boxed{=}\ \boxed{\text{Min}}\ \boxed{4}\ \boxed{+}\ \boxed{3}\ \boxed{=}\ \boxed{\text{SHIFT}}\ \boxed{X \leftrightarrow M}\ \boxed{\div}\ \boxed{\text{MR}}\ \boxed{=}$

ROUNDING

27 is closer to 30 than to 20.   327 is closer to 300 than to 400.
27 rounded to the nearest 10 is 30.   327 rounded to the nearest 100 is 300.

45 is halfway between 40 and 50.
45 rounded to the nearest 10 is 50.

To the nearest whole number 2·631 is 3.
To the nearest whole number 2·361 is 2.

continued . . .

. . . from previous page

PLACE VALUE

Place value is given by this chart.

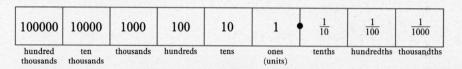

100000	10000	1000	100	10	1	$\frac{1}{10}$	$\frac{1}{100}$	$\frac{1}{1000}$
hundred thousands	ten thousands	thousands	hundreds	tens	ones (units)	tenths	hundredths	thousandths

In 372468, the digit 3 means 3 hundred thousands
the digit 7 means 7 ten thousands
the digit 2 means 2 thousands
the digit 4 means 4 hundreds
the digit 6 means 6 tens
the digit 8 means 8 units (or 8 ones)

In 305·607, the digit 3 means 3 hundreds
the digit 5 means 5 ones
the digit 6 means 6 tenths
the digit 7 means 7 thousandths

We say 372468 as "three hundred and seventy-two thousand, four hundred and sixty-eight."
We say 305·607 as "three hundred and five point six zero seven."

Place value may be used to multiply and divide numbers by 10, 100, 1000 etc.
For instance, $24 \times 1000 = 24000$, $2·4 \div 100 = 0·024$.
For instance to multiply 23×90, first multiply 23 by 10 to get 230, then multiply 230×9 to get 2070.

LONG MULTIPLICATION and DIVISION

One method for long multiplication and one for long division is shown.
There are several others.

895×41

	800	90	5
40	32000	3600	200
1	800	90	5

$$895 \times 41 = 32000 + 3600 + 200$$
$$+ 800 + 90 + 5$$
$$= 36695$$

$895 \div 41$

```
            41
        ┌──────────
        │      895
10  410 │  − 410
        │  ──────
        │      485
10  410 │  − 410
        │  ──────
        │       75
 1   41 │  −  41
        │  ──────
   21           34
    ↑            ↑
 answer      remainder
```

continued . . .

. . . from previous page

ESTIMATING ANSWERS using APPROXIMATION

We can check that the answer to a calculation such as 895×41 is about the right size by **approximating.**

We can approximate 895 as 900 and 41 as 40.

$$900 \times 40 = 900 \times 10 \times 4$$
$$= 9000 \times 4$$
$$= 36000$$

So we estimate 895×41 to be about 36000.

FRACTIONS and PERCENTAGES

$\frac{5}{6}$ is read as "five-sixths" and means 5 parts out of every 6.

24% is read as "twenty-four percent" and means 24 out of every 100.

The word "of", used in calculation, means "multiply".

For instance, $\frac{5}{6}$ of 42 means $\frac{5}{6} \times 42 = 35$

24% of 42 means $\frac{24}{100} \times 42 = 10 \cdot 08$.

NEGATIVE NUMBERS

The $\boxed{+/-}$ key on the calculator is pressed to display a **negative number.**

Positive numbers, such as +2, may be written without any sign.

Negative numbers, such as –2, are always written with a negative sign.

The negative numbers are shown on a number line, or scale, as numbers that are less than zero.

On a number line, the further to the right a number is, the larger it is. The further to the left it is, the smaller it is.

The **integers** include both the negative and positive whole numbers and also zero. Zero is neither positive nor negative.

continued . . .

. . . *from previous page*

INDEX NOTATION

3^4 is read as "three to the power of four" and means $3 \times 3 \times 3 \times 3$.

The **square numbers** are 1^2, 2^2, 3^2, 4^2, . . . That is 1, 4, 9, 16, . . .
The **cube numbers** are 1^3, 2^3, 3^3, 4^3, . . . That is 1, 8, 27, 64, . . .
The answer to "what number squared gives 9" is 3. 3 is called the **square root** of 9. This is written as $\sqrt{9} = 3$.
The answer to "what number cubed gives 8" is 2. 2 is called the **cube root** of 8. This is written as $\sqrt[3]{8} = 2$.

On a **calculator** 26^2 is keyed as $\boxed{26}$ $\boxed{\text{SHIFT}}$ $\boxed{x^2}$
 $\sqrt{169}$ is keyed as $\boxed{169}$ $\boxed{\sqrt{}}$
 $\sqrt[3]{216}$ is keyed as $\boxed{216}$ $\boxed{\text{SHIFT}}$ $\boxed{\sqrt[3]{}}$

INVERSE OPERATIONS

Inverse operations "undo" each other. Some inverse operations are: adding and subtracting, multiplying and dividing, squaring and finding a square root, cubing and finding a cube root.

REVISION EXERCISE

1. 345   435   3542   3452   4523   354   453   4235   4253   3425

    Write these numbers in order, from the smallest to the largest.

2. Sue has two dogs, Saint and Jake.
    Saint weights 33kg. Jake is 7kg lighter than Saint.

    How much do both these dogs weigh altogether?

3. What is the place value of the 2 in these?

   (a) 123   (b) 24591   (c) 32·61   (d) 0·012   (e) 14·23

4. What is the missing number?

   (a) $18 + 5 - \ldots = 18$ (b) $23 \times 5 \div \ldots = 23$ (c) $43 - \ldots + 19 = 43$

5. Out of every 100 books sold in a sale, 17 are hardcover.
   What percentage of books sold in this sale are hardcover?

6. (a) Copy this chart.

H											
−3	−5	3		−4	−2	−4		4	−5	−1	
										−4	−5

   (b) Use the number line below to find the letter that represents each number.
   Complete your chart.
   H is done for you.

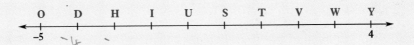

7. Write these in figures.

   (a) two thousand and forty

   (b) one hundred and two thousand, four hundred and seventy six point three

   (c) zero point zero nine zero

8. Which of 10, 100 or 1000 goes in the box?

   (a) $8·2 \times \square = 820$ (b) $2·68 \div \square = 0·00268$

   (c) $231 \div \square = 23·1$ (d) $24 \div \square = 0·24$

   (e) $0·059 \times \square = 59$

9. When Rashid was taken to hospital his temperature was 2·1° above normal.

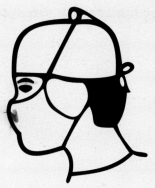

   (a) After one day it had risen another 0·8°. What was Rashid's temperature then?

   (b) The next day it fell 3·7°. How far below normal was his temperature then?

10. (a) The water level in a dam was –1m. The water level rose 2m. What is the water level now?

   (b) The water level in a dam was –1m. The water level fell 2m. What is the water level now?

   (c) The water level in a dam was 2m. The water level fell 5m. What is the water level now?

11.

$$\boxed{4593.627}$$

This calculator display shows the answer to a calculation.
Rob rounded this answer to the nearest 10. Dean rounded it to the nearest hundred. Amanda rounded it to the nearest whole number.
What answers should Rob, Dean and Amanda get?

12. How many times larger is the first 7 than the second 7?

   (a) 77   (b) 237574   (c) 37·74   (d) 273·07

13. Use place value to find the answer to these.

   (a) 28 × 1000   (b) 4·06 × 10   (c) 0·49 ÷ 100   (d) 70 × 60

   (e) 2·64 ÷ 4   (f) 21·2 × 0·04

14. At a Secondary Schools' athletics competition, a cup is awarded to the school with the best overall results in 20 events. The system of points used is shown.
This year, Harrowdale School won the cup. They gained 29 points in the 20 events. How many 1st, 2nd and 3rd placings did this school have?
Is there more than one answer to this problem?

1st	3 points
2nd	2 points
3rd	1 point

15. Which 1-digit number is neither a prime nor a square nor a cube?

16. Heanside School set aside £1500 to buy calculators.
    They bought 50 at £7·99, 80 at £8·95 and 20 at £15·99.

    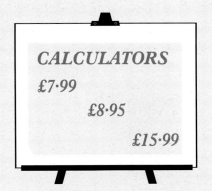

    (a) How much of the £1500 did the school have left?

    (b) How many more of the cheapest sort could they buy?

17. Choose the best estimate for the answer to each calculation.

    (a) 221 × 86   A. 20000   B. 30000   C. 2000

    (b) 888 ÷ 21   A. 400   B. 450   C. 45

18. 340 articles are auctioned. Of these, 20% do not reach the reserve price.

    How many do not reach the reserve price?

19. (a) What addition could you do to check the answer to 234 − 59 = 175?

    (b) What calculation could you do to check the answers to 207 ÷ 9 = 23 and $\sqrt{196} = 14$?

20. Gavin got $\frac{3}{4}$ of the possible marks in his maths. aural test.
    He got $\frac{2}{3}$ of the possible marks in his investigation. The aural test was out of 28 and the investigation was out of 30.
    Which did Gavin get more marks in?

21. Cameron changed 334 dollars into pounds. The exchange rate was 58p for each dollar.

    (a) Estimate the number of pence Cameron got.

    (b) Use long multiplication to calculate the amount Cameron got. Give your answer in pounds. Use your estimate from (a) as a check.

22.(a) Write these in index notation: $5 \times 5 \times 5$, $2 \times 2 \times 2 \times 2 \times 2 \times 2$

   (b) Find the value of 2^5 and 5^2.

23. Give the answers to the nearest penny.

   (a) $\frac{2}{3}$ of £26·50   **(b)** $\frac{4}{9}$ of 82p   **(c)** 65% of £2·49

24. Copy and complete these addition squares.

+	99			
	251			
124	360			
213			368	
			391	402

+		−2		
1				0
			− 4	2
			−3	
− 4	−2			

25. Without using your calculator, find:

   (a) 37×400 **(b)** $4\,(3 + 2)$ **(c)** $8 + 2 \times 4$ **(d)** $15 - 6 \div 3$

   (e) $4530 \div 30$ **(f)** $\frac{2}{5}$ of 45   **(g)** $17 - 3\,(4 + 1)$ **(h)** 3^4

   (i) $\sqrt[3]{64}$ **(j)** $\sqrt{64}$.

26. A school has a roll of 1213.

   All of these students travelled by bus to a special sports event.

   (a) **Estimate** the number of buses needed if each bus seats 37 students.

   (b) Use long division to **calculate** the number of buses needed.

27. Are these true or false?

   (a) $\frac{4}{7} < 40\%$ **(b)** $1000 > 999$ **(c)** $-8 > -1$

28. Last year, the Aviemore Tennis Team played 35 matches. It won $\frac{3}{5}$ of these and drew $\frac{2}{7}$.

    How many games did this team   (a) win

    (b) draw

    (c) lose?

29. Calculate.   (a) $2\cdot7 + 0\cdot2 \times 3\cdot6$ (b) $14 - 0\cdot4\,(2\cdot4 - 1\cdot92)$

30.

WRAGGS WINTER SALE

SHIRTS
20% off

JEANS
30% off

Kylie bought a shirt and a pair of jeans at this sale. Before the sale began the shirt cost £29·95 and the jeans cost £19·50.

(a) How much did Kylie save on the shirt?

(b) Did she save more on the jeans than on the shirt?

31.

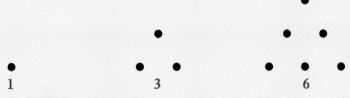

1   3   6

1, 3 and 6 are the first three triangular numbers.

(a) How many dots are on the bottom row of dots in the "picture" for the fourth triangular number? How many for the tenth triangular number?

(b) What is the tenth triangular number?

32. Insert $+, -, \times, \div$ and brackets to make these true. You may use any of the operations more than once or not at all.

    (a) 6   2   3   4 = 8   (b) 6   2   3   4 = 34   (c) 6   2   3   4 = 15

19

33. In a game this spinner is spun twice. The smaller number is subtracted from the larger.
The answer gives the number of spaces to be moved.

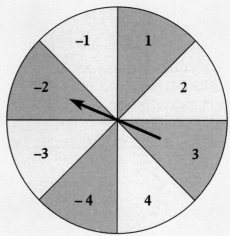

   (a) Melanie spins – 4 and –2 when it is her turn. How many spaces does Melanie move?

   (b) Scott spins 3 and –1. How many spaces does Scott move?

   (c) What is the greatest number of spaces a player can move?

   (d) At his turn, Abel got –2 and –2.
   Write another rule for this game to tell Abel how to move.

DISCOVER, DISCUSS, DO

- Winstone is trying on shoes.
  He first tries the size 8 which are too large.
  He next tries the size $5\frac{1}{2}$ which are too small.
  Which size should Winstone try next?
  Discuss.

- Rebecca is planting a shrub.
  She digs a hole which is too deep.
  How will she get the hole just the right depth?
  Discuss.

- Think of some other situations for which you would use the same method of estimating and trying, then making a better estimate and trying again and so on. Think about cooking, playing sport etc.
  Discuss with your neighbour or group or class.

- Make a cube as accurately as you can without actually *measuring* any of the lengths.

TRIAL and IMPROVEMENT

The method that Winstone used when finding shoes of the right size, and Rebecca used when planting a shrub (see above) is called **Trial and Improvement Method**. This method is described below.

Guess a likely answer. Check to see if this answer fits the given facts. If it doesn't, guess another answer and repeat this guessing and checking until the correct answer is found.
Guessing and checking a likely answer is a **trial** of a likely answer.

If the first guess was too large, you will trial a smaller answer next. If the first guess was too small, you will trial a larger answer next. By working in this way, each guess will be an **improvement** on the previous guess.

Worked Example   A shop bought a number of dictionaries at £6 each and five times that number of novels at £2 each. The total cost of all these dictionaries and novels was £1088. How many dictionaries did the shop buy?

Answer *1st trial*   100 dictionaries and 500 novels.
Total cost = 100 × £6 + 500 × £2
            = £1600   which is too much.

Next trial   50 dictionaries and 250 novels.
Total cost = 50 × £6 + 250 × £2
            = £800   which is too small.

Next trial   Since the actual cost of £1088 is closer to £800 than to £1600, try a number for the dictionaries that is closer to 50 than to 100. Try 70 dictionaries and 350 novels.
Total cost = 70 × £6 + 350 × £2
            = £1120   which is just a little too much.

Next trial   67 dictionaries and 335 novels.
Total cost = 67 × £6 + 335 × £2
            = £1072   which is just a little too small.

Next trial   68 dictionaries and 340 novels.
Total cost = 68 × £6 + 340 × £2
            = £1088   which is correct.

The shop bought 68 dictionaries.

EXERCISE 1:1

1.

Arrange the numbers 1 to 12 in the corners of these squares. Use the following rules:

1.   There must be just one number in each corner.
2.   The four numbers in each square must add to 26.

Is there more than one answer?

2. On a quiz show, Sarah earned £25 for each correct answer and lost £15 for each incorrect answer (or for questions she couldn't answer). After 20 questions had been asked, Sarah had £20.
   How many questions had she answered correctly?

3. When two numbers are multiplied the answer is 437. Both of these numbers are greater than 1.
   Find these two numbers.

4. When two numbers are multiplied the answer is 312.
   Find these two numbers.

   Is there more than one answer? If so, find as many answers as you can.

5.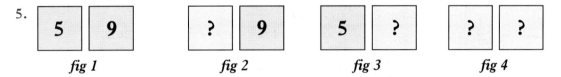

   | **fig 1** | **fig 2** | **fig 3** | **fig 4** |

   The two cards in *fig 1* have different numbers on their reverse sides. When the cards have the front sides showing as in *fig 1* they total 14.

   One or both cards may be turned over as in *fig 2, fig 3, fig 4*.
   No matter which two sides are showing, the only possible totals are 9, 10, 14, 15.

   What numbers are on the reverse sides?

6. In Alexandra's family each child has at least one brother and one sister. What is the smallest possible number of children in Alexandra's family?

7. Bonny counted the number of emus and elephants in a zoo. Her friend Ines counted the number of legs of these emus and elephants. Altogether Ines counted 70 legs. How many emus and how many elephants did Bonny count?

   Is there more than one answer? If so, how many answers are there?

   What if Ines counted 70 legs and 24 heads?

8. Philippa has £2·50 worth of coins.
   Some are 10p coins, some are 20p coins and the rest are 50p coins.
   She has twice as many 10p coins as 50p coins.
   She has one more 50p coin than 20p coins.
   How many 50p coins does Philippa have?

9.

"David is 11" said Dianne.
"I'm 13" said David.
"David is older than me" said Michael.

Dianne sometimes tells the truth, Michael always tells the truth and David never tells the truth.
One of them is 11, another 12 and the other 13.
How old is each person?

10. Ten years from now, Sarah will be three less than twice her present age. How old is Sarah now?

11.

Number on the die	1	2	3	4	5	6
Number of times	3	4	3	4	3	1

John, Ravi and Kate each tossed a die six times.
They each scored a total of 19.
The table shows how many times each number came up
(e.g. the number 5 came up 3 times).
Ravi scored all the 4's.
Kate scored more 2's than anyone else.
John scored more 5's than Kate.

Who scored the only 6?

Review 1 Oni has 18 pen-friends. Last weekend she
wrote to all of them. She wrote 4-page letters
to some and 3-page letters to the others.
Altogether she wrote 61 pages.
To how many of her pen-friends did Oni
write 3-page letters?

Review 2 In the Singh family each boy has as many sisters as brothers. Each girl in
this family has twice as many brothers as sisters.
How many children are there in this family?

FOR YOUR INTEREST

- Discuss fully, the following statements. Find examples to support your point of view.

  The only way to solve some problems is by trial and improvement.

  Trial and improvement should only be used as a last resort.

  You could make a summary of your discussion.
  You may like to join with another group and debate one of the statements.
  If you do this, one group should give arguments to support the statement and the other group should give arguments against the statement.

- Builders, engineers, clothing manufacturers, painters, artists, writers, pilots, teachers, accountants.

  Discuss the following statement in relation to one or more of these people.

  Some people should never use trial and improvement in their job.

  Make a summary of your discussion.

DISCOVER, DISCUSS, DO

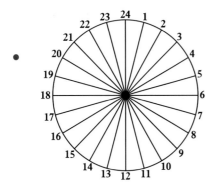

Draw a large circle, radius 10cm, and divide it into 24 parts like the one shown.
Each part represents one hour of a day.
Fill in what you do each hour of a typical day.
Work out what fraction of the day you spent in class, watching TV, sleeping and so on.

- Artists use fractions to help them draw in proportion. Study lots of pictures and paintings.
What fractions do artists use often? For instance, is the sky usually about one-third of the picture?

- Our money system is a decimal system. (100p make one pound.) Are all money systems decimal systems? Find out about as many systems as you can. What units are used in these systems? **Discuss** what you found out with your group.

- Engineers avoid decimals by always working in mm rather than cm or m. Who else might avoid using decimals? How might they do this? **Discuss.**

| £4·32 | 10·32 sec | Pethadine – 1·5m*l* |

Pounds always have two numbers after the decimal point.
Times for running 100m have no more than two numbers after the decimal point.
Medicine measured in m*l* has no more than 1 number after the decimal point.

Why? **Discuss.** Think of other similar examples. **Discuss.**

6 for £1·87   6 for £1·89   6 for £1·90

For each pack, work out how much one bun would cost. **Discuss.**

EQUIVALENT FRACTIONS

DISCUSSION EXERCISE 2:1

●

The diagrams above show the fractions $\frac{1}{2}$, $\frac{2}{4}$, $\frac{8}{16}$, $\frac{32}{64}$.

Are these fractions equal?

Discuss how to draw diagrams to show the fractions $\frac{1}{2}$, $\frac{3}{6}$, $\frac{5}{10}$, $\frac{6}{12}$.

What can you say about the fractions $\frac{1}{2}$, $\frac{2}{4}$, $\frac{3}{6}$, $\frac{4}{8}$, $\frac{5}{10}$, $\frac{6}{12}$?

●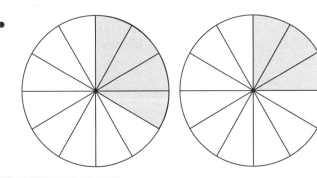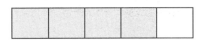

What fractions are shown in the above diagrams?

Discuss how to draw diagrams to show that the fractions in each of the following lists are equal.

List A $\frac{2}{5}$, $\frac{4}{10}$, $\frac{6}{15}$, $\frac{8}{20}$
List B $\frac{1}{4}$, $\frac{2}{8}$, $\frac{3}{12}$

List C $\frac{1}{3}$, $\frac{4}{12}$
List D $\frac{16}{20}$, $\frac{4}{5}$

- $$12 \div 3 = 4$$
  $$24 \div 6 = 4$$

In the second calculation the 12 has been doubled.
We need to double the 3 as well to get the same answer of 4.

$$8 \div 4 = 2$$
$$24 \div 12 = 2$$

In the second calculation the 8 has been multiplied by 3.
We need to multiply the 4 by 3 as well to get the same answer of 2.

Do these work for just the given calculations or do they work for others as well?
Discuss.

Use calculations such as the following in your discussion.
$6 \div 3 = 2 \quad 12 \div 4 = 3 \quad 15 \div 3 = 5 \quad 10 \div 5 = 2 \quad 8 \div 2 = 4 \quad 18 \div 3 = 6$

- $\left.\begin{array}{l} 60 \div 6 = 10 \\ 20 \div 2 = 10 \end{array}\right\} \quad \left.\begin{array}{l} 24 \div 8 = 3 \\ 12 \div 4 = 3 \end{array}\right\} \quad \left.\begin{array}{l} 48 \div 8 = 6 \\ 6 \div 1 = 6 \end{array}\right\} \quad \left.\begin{array}{l} 5 \div 10 = 0{\cdot}5 \\ 1 \div 2 = 0{\cdot}5 \end{array}\right\} \quad \left.\begin{array}{l} 2 \div 8 = 0{\cdot}25 \\ 1 \div 4 = 0{\cdot}25 \end{array}\right\}$

Discuss how the second calculation in each of the above is obtained from the first calculation.

Write down some more pairs of calculations similar to these.
Discuss with your neighbour or group or class.

- The fraction $\frac{12}{4}$ means $12 \div 4$.

  Discuss why the fraction $\frac{12}{4}$ is equal to $\frac{6}{2}$ and is also equal to $\frac{24}{8}$.

  The fraction $\frac{3}{6}$ means $3 \div 6$.

  Discuss why the fraction $\frac{3}{6}$ is equal to $\frac{1}{2}$ and is also equal to $\frac{30}{60}$.

In the fraction $\frac{5}{8}$, 5 is called the **numerator,**

8 is called the **denominator.**

The numerator is the number on the top, the denominator is the number on the bottom.

Equal fractions are called **equivalent fractions.**

For instance, $\frac{3}{4}$, $\frac{6}{8}$, $\frac{15}{20}$, $\frac{30}{40}$ are equivalent fractions.

Equivalent fractions may be formed by multiplying (or dividing) both the numerator and denominator by the same number.

For instance $\frac{5}{8} = \frac{5 \times 3}{8 \times 3} = \frac{15}{24}$. $\frac{5}{8}$ and $\frac{15}{24}$ are equivalent fractions.

For instance, $\frac{24}{32} = \frac{24 \div 2}{32 \div 2} = \frac{12}{16}$. $\frac{24}{32}$ and $\frac{12}{16}$ are equivalent fractions.

A fraction is written in its **lowest terms,** or as the simplest fraction, if the numbers in the fraction are the smallest possible whole numbers.

Worked Example Write $\frac{24}{32}$ in its lowest terms.

Answer The largest number that divides into both 24 and 32 is 8.

$$\frac{24}{32} = \frac{24 \div 8}{32 \div 8} = \frac{3}{4}$$

Then, $\frac{24}{32}$ in its lowest terms is $\frac{3}{4}$.

Worked Example What is x if $\frac{3}{5} = \frac{18}{x}$?

Answer To find x, write the fraction equivalent to $\frac{3}{5}$ that has 18 as the numerator.

Since $3 \times 6 = 18$, $\frac{3}{5} = \frac{3 \times 6}{5 \times 6} = \frac{18}{30}$.

Then x = 30.

EXERCISE 2:2

1. Which of these is *not* true?

   A. $\frac{2}{10}$ is shaded   **B.** $\frac{2}{5}$ is shaded   **C.** $\frac{1}{5}$ is shaded

2. Choose the two fractions that are equivalent in each of the following.

   (a) $\frac{2}{4}$, $\frac{3}{5}$, $\frac{1}{2}$ (b) $\frac{1}{2}$, $\frac{5}{10}$, $\frac{2}{5}$ (c) $\frac{1}{3}$, $\frac{1}{5}$, $\frac{5}{15}$ (d) $\frac{3}{5}$, $\frac{3}{4}$, $\frac{6}{10}$

   (e) $\frac{4}{5}$, $\frac{8}{10}$, $\frac{3}{4}$ (f) $\frac{40}{100}$, $\frac{4}{10}$, $\frac{3}{5}$ (g) $\frac{7}{10}$, $\frac{70}{100}$, $\frac{10}{100}$

3. Complete these equivalent fractions.

   (a) $\frac{3}{10} = \frac{\cdots}{30}$ (b) $\frac{2}{3} = \frac{\cdots}{12}$ (c) $\frac{4}{5} = \frac{\cdots}{15}$ (d) $\frac{3}{4} = \frac{6}{\cdots}$

   (e) $\frac{3}{8} = \frac{15}{\cdots}$ (f) $\frac{4}{8} = \frac{\cdots}{4}$ (g) $\frac{25}{100} = \frac{1}{\cdots}$ (h) $\frac{1}{1} = \frac{5}{\cdots}$

4. Find the value of x in each of the following.

   (a) $\frac{x}{5} = \frac{8}{.10}$ (b) $\frac{4}{10} = \frac{x}{5}$ (c) $\frac{7}{x} = \frac{70}{100}$ (d) $\frac{2}{4} = \frac{1}{x}$ (e) $\frac{4}{x} = \frac{20}{35}$

   (f) $\frac{x}{25} = \frac{3}{5}$ (g) $\frac{30}{x} = \frac{3}{4}$ (h) $\frac{1}{5} = \frac{x}{50}$

5. Write these fractions in their lowest terms.

   (a) $\frac{24}{40}$ (b) $\frac{32}{50}$ (c) $\frac{16}{30}$ (d) $\frac{18}{24}$ (e) $\frac{15}{45}$

   (f) $\frac{30}{48}$ (g) $\frac{12}{72}$ (h) $\frac{20}{75}$

6. In a book, 10 of the 150 pages are illustrated.
   What is the fraction of pages that are not illustrated?

7. Rachel was absent from school 4 days out of the last 30.
   What fraction of days was Rachel absent?

8. Copy and complete.

   (a) $\frac{2}{5} = \frac{4}{\cdots} = \frac{10}{\cdots} = \frac{16}{\cdots}$

   (b) $\frac{3}{8} = \frac{\cdots}{16} = \frac{\cdots}{24} = \frac{\cdots}{40} = \frac{\cdots}{80}$

   (c) $\frac{2}{3} = \frac{\cdots}{9} = \frac{12}{\cdots} = \frac{\cdots}{12}$

   (d) $\frac{4}{5} = \frac{\cdots}{20} = \frac{40}{\cdots} = \frac{\cdots}{40}$

   (e) $\frac{3}{4} = \frac{6}{\cdots} = \frac{\cdots}{12} = \frac{12}{\cdots}$

9. Of 21 games Manchester United played, they won 15, drew 4 and lost 2. What fraction of these games did Manchester United win?

10. Copy this table of fractions.

$\frac{1}{1}$	$\frac{5}{10}$	$\frac{2}{5}$	$\frac{2}{2}$	$\frac{81}{100}$	$\frac{1}{10}$	$\frac{3}{10}$
$\frac{2}{4}$	$\frac{65}{100}$	$\frac{70}{100}$	$\frac{4}{4}$	$\frac{3}{4}$	$\frac{3}{10}$	$\frac{1}{2}$
$\frac{50}{100}$	$\frac{6}{10}$	$\frac{75}{100}$	$\frac{100}{100}$	$\frac{4}{5}$	$\frac{1}{4}$	$\frac{4}{10}$
$\frac{2}{1}$	$\frac{70}{100}$	$\frac{3}{5}$	$\frac{10}{10}$	$\frac{3}{5}$	$\frac{2}{4}$	$\frac{40}{100}$
$\frac{10}{100}$	$\frac{7}{10}$	$\frac{7}{10}$	$\frac{5}{5}$	$\frac{85}{100}$	$\frac{20}{100}$	$\frac{45}{100}$

$\left(\frac{1}{2}\right)$ $\left(\frac{3}{5}\right)$ $\left(\frac{3}{4}\right)$ $\left(1\right)$ $\left(\frac{8}{10}\right)$ $\left(\frac{25}{100}\right)$ $\left(\frac{2}{5}\right)$

Find the fractions in each column which are equivalent to the fraction in the circle at the bottom of that column.
Shade the boxes containing these equivalent fractions. The shading will make a pattern.

Review 1 Find the missing numbers.

   (a) $\frac{3}{5} = \frac{12}{\square}$ (b) $\frac{2}{3} = \frac{\square}{12}$ (c) $\frac{24}{30} = \frac{\square}{5}$ (d) $\frac{36}{45} = \frac{12}{\square}$

Review 2 Copy and complete. $\frac{3}{5} = \frac{6}{\cdots} = \frac{12}{\cdots} = \frac{\cdots}{25}$

Review 3 Write these fractions in their lowest terms.

   (a) $\frac{80}{100}$ (b) $\frac{18}{42}$ (c) $\frac{12}{50}$ (d) $\frac{5}{45}$

Review 4 In a survey of the heating in 45 houses it was found that 24 had gas furnaces, 15 had coal furnaces and 6 had electric heating.
What fraction of these houses had electric heating?

PUZZLES 2:3

? ?

1.   I am equivalent to $\frac{1}{2}$.

The sum of my numerator and denominator is 15.

What fraction am I?

2.   I am equivalent to $\frac{2}{5}$.

The product of my numerator and denominator is 40.

What fraction am I?

3.   I am equivalent to $\frac{2}{3}$.

My denominator is 10 more than my numerator.

What fraction am I?

4.   I am equivalent to $\frac{80}{100}$.

My denominator is a prime number.

What fraction am I?

? ?

INVESTIGATION 2:4

PATTERNS in EQUIVALENT FRACTIONS

$$\frac{1}{2} = \frac{2}{4} = \frac{3}{6} = \frac{4}{8} = \frac{5}{10} = \frac{6}{12} = \ldots$$

The numbers on the top form the pattern 1, 2, 3, 4, 5, 6, . . .
The numbers on the bottom form the pattern 2, 4, 6, 8, 10, 12, . . .

$$\frac{2}{3} = \frac{4}{6} = \frac{6}{9} = \frac{8}{12} = \frac{10}{15} = \ldots$$

What patterns are formed by these equivalent fractions?

Investigate the patterns formed by other equivalent fractions. As part of your investigation, you could investigate the patterns formed when the top number of each equivalent fraction is subtracted from the bottom number.

What if the top number and bottom number of each equivalent fraction are added?

What if they are multiplied?

Worked Example

> **This mixture contains**
>
> **150ml oil**
> **50ml vinegar**

What fraction of this mixture is vinegar?

Answer In total there are 150 + 50 = 200ml.

50ml out of 200ml is vinegar.

The fraction that is vinegar is $\frac{50}{200} = \frac{50 \div 50}{200 \div 50}$

$$= \frac{1}{4}$$

$\frac{1}{4}$ of the mixture is vinegar.

EXERCISE 2:5

1. A bowl of fruit had 9 apples, 3 oranges and 8 bananas.

   What fraction of the fruit were bananas?

2. In an office of 27 people, 9 are women.

   What fraction are men?

3. In a play there were 12 adults, 3 teenagers and 3 children.

   What fraction were children?

4. Leanne sprinted 500m, jogged 1500m and walked 3000m each day. On Tuesday she hurt her ankle after 1000m.

   What fraction of her exercise had she still to complete?

5. Basking sharks grow to be about 12m long. A young shark 8m long was found.

   What fraction did it still have to grow to be full length?

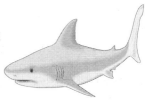

Review A healthy adult should sleep about 8 hours each day.

   What fraction of the day should be spent awake?

ORDERING DECIMALS

DISCUSSION EXERCISE 2:6

- Angela has £1·34; Derek has £1·43.
  Who has more, Angela or Derek?

  Angela lives 0·54km from school; Derek lives 0·57km from school.
  Who lives nearer to school?

- **Discuss** what you do to put the following names into alphabetical order.

  Smith   Samson   Tyler   Taylor   Smythe   Samuels   Tyland   Trainor

  Discuss what you do to put the following whole numbers in order, beginning
  with the smallest and finishing with the largest.

  2534   235   3425   3542   5432   4352   4235   2345   352   253

  Put these into order, from smallest to largest.

  £5·64   £4·65   £5·61   £4·56   £5·46   £5·16

  Write these lengths, from shortest to longest.

  0·285m   0·284m   0·254m   0·245m   0·248m   0·258m

  The following times were recorded by the runners in a sprint race.
  Place the runners from 1st to 7th.

  A. 12·32sec   B. 12·25sec   C. 10·98sec   D. 11·12sec

  E. 12·82sec   F. 11·59sec   G. 12·23sec

- **Discuss** how to put the decimals in each of the following lists into order, from the smallest to the largest.

  List A: 0·1   0·23   0·2   0·15   0·05   0·25

  List B: 2·781   4·871   2·871   1·874   2·178   2·718

  List C: 3·4   3·2   3·45   4·3   3·25   4·2

  List D: 0·6   0·54   0·62   0·602   0·543   0·459

  List E: 0·1   0·101   0·001   0·11   0·011

- Think of situations where you would want to put decimals in order, from the largest to the smallest. **Discuss.**

-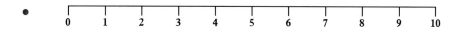

  Discuss where the following numbers would be on this number line.

  0·5   0·25   3·5   8·9   6·5   6·58   6·582

  Where would the following numbers be on a number line? **Discuss.**

  0·5   0·50   0·500

On a number line, the smaller a number is, the further to the left it is.

To put a list of decimal numbers in order it is a good idea to first write them all with the same number of figures after the decimal point.

Example   2·63   2·6   3·421   4·32   3·4   3·399   4·098

To put these numbers in order, from the smallest to largest, proceed as follows.

Rewrite the numbers as:
2·630   2·600   3·421   4·320   3·400   3·399   4·098

Now choose the numbers with the smallest number before the decimal point.
These are   2·630   2·600.

Put these in order. Since   600 < 630,   then   2·600 < 2·630.

The first two numbers are then   2·6   2·63

Now choose the numbers with a 3 before the decimal point.
These are   3·421   3·400   3·399.

Since   399 < 400 < 421,   then   3·399 < 3·400 < 3·421

The first five numbers are then   2·6   2·63   3·399   3·4   3·421

Which of 4·320 and 4·098 is the smaller?
Complete the list of seven numbers, written in order from smallest to largest.

Worked Example 6·2   6·39   6·45   6·321

These numbers are to be written on the number line given below. One of them is written at A, another at B, another at C and another at D.

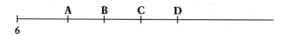

Which number must be written at C ?

Answer Firstly write the list of numbers in order, from smallest to largest.
The numbers can be rewritten as   6·200   6·390   6·450   6·321.

In order, these are   6·200   6·321   6·390   6·450.
That is, the order from smallest to largest is   6·2,   6·321,   6·39,   6·45.

The number at C must be 6·39 since this is the third number when they are written from smallest to largest.

EXERCISE 2:7

1. Which is the larger of each of these pairs of numbers?

   (a) 0·75   0·57   (b) 16·95   17·59   (c) 0·6134   0·6314

   (d) 8·07   8·1   (e) 0·059   0·5

2. Put these numbers in order, from the smallest to the largest.

   (a) 0·821   0·281   0·128   0·218   0·812   0·182

   (b) 0·7   0·69   0·702   0·689   0·73   0·68

   (c) 2·48   4·28   8·24   8·42   2·84   4·82

   (d) 13·6   14·05   17·792   14·83   17·8   13·099

3.

	Runner 1	Runner 2	Runner 3	Runner 4
City	10·31 sec	10·04 sec	10·46 sec	10·09 sec
Colts	9·98 sec	10·68 sec	10·10 sec	10·18 sec
Newton	10·06 sec	10·13 sec	10·24 sec	10·01 sec
TocH	10·53 sec	10·96 sec	10·42 sec	10·18 sec

This table shows the time taken by each runner in the relay teams, for a 400m relay, at an athletics competition.

(a) How many teams were in this 400m race?

(b) How many runners were in each team?

(c) Which runner, from which team, had the fastest time?

(d) Which runner had the slowest time?

(e) Which team won this relay?

(f) Which team came last?

4. Are these statements true or false?

(a) $0.8 > 0.7$ (b) $0.23 > 0.32$ (c) $0.105 < 0.099$

(d) $0.01 < 0.9$ (e) $2.95 > 2.99$

5.

Draw a number line, as shown above, for each of the following. Place the numbers given in each at A, B and C.

(a) 1·66   1·6   1·06   (b) 0·34   0·3   0·43

(c) 2·624 2·426 2·42   (d) 0·1   0·019 0·09

6.

A, B, C, D give the positions, on the number line, of the four numbers in each of the following lists. Which number from each list is at B?

(a) 0·123 0·321 0·312 0·213   (b) 3·247 3·47 3·24   3·2

(c) 0·5   0·501 0·51   0·511

Review 1 (a) Which is the smaller of 3·51 and 3·493?

(b) $0.13 > 0.103$. Is this statement true?

(c) Place the following numbers in order, from smallest to largest.

4·1   3·05   3·5   3·124   4·12   4·214   3·99

Review 2 3·4   3·41   3·401

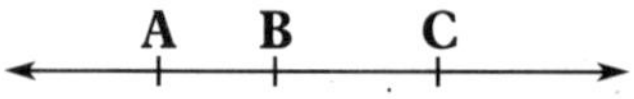

One of these numbers is at A, another at B and the other at C.

(a) Which is at A?   (b) Which is at C?

Review 3

	Vault	Bars	Beam	Floor
A. Chan	7·85	6·05	8·15	7·10
T. Pilling	6·20	8·10	7·65	6·75
V. de Groot	8·00	6·95	8·15	7·95
L. Jack	7·65	6·85	6·35	7·25
T. Kahn	6·95	7·00	6·80	7·50
B. Mann	7·40	6·80	8·20	6·75

This table gives the scores of the six girls from the Newton School team in a secondary schools competition.

(a)   Which girl had the best score for the beam exercise?

(b)   Which exercise (vault, bars, beam or floor) did this team score best in?

(c)   Which girl scored the least number of points for the team?

FRACTIONS and DECIMALS

To write a fraction as a decimal, divide the numerator (top) by the denominator (bottom).

Example   To write $\frac{5}{8}$ as a decimal, key $\boxed{5}$ $\boxed{\div}$ $\boxed{8}$ $\boxed{=}$ to get the answer 0·625.

DISCUSSION EXERCISE 2:8

● Use the calculator to write $\frac{1}{10}$, $\frac{2}{10}$, $\frac{3}{10}$, $\frac{4}{10}$ as decimals.

Discuss how to write fractions, with denominator 10, as decimals without using the calculator.
Make and test statements as part of your discussion.

What if the denominator was 100?

What if the denominator was 1000?

What if . . .

- $\frac{2}{5} = \frac{4}{10}$, $\frac{3}{5} = \frac{6}{10}$, $\frac{7}{25} = \frac{28}{100}$, $\frac{9}{25} = \frac{36}{100}$

Discuss how to write fractions, with denominator 5 or 25, as decimals.

What other fractions can be written as decimals using a similar method? **Discuss.**

DISCUSSION EXERCISE 2:9

We know $\frac{1}{10} = 0\cdot1$, $\frac{3}{10} = 0\cdot3$, $\frac{1}{100} = 0\cdot01$, $\frac{19}{100} = 0\cdot19$, $\frac{47}{1000} = 0\cdot047$

Writing this the other way around: $0\cdot1 = \frac{1}{10}$, $0\cdot3 = \frac{3}{10}$, $0\cdot01 = \frac{1}{100}$, $0\cdot19 = \frac{19}{100}$,

$$0\cdot047 = \frac{47}{1000}$$

Discuss how to write the following as fractions.

$0\cdot7$, $0\cdot9$, $0\cdot07$, $0\cdot29$, $0\cdot37$, $0\cdot003$, $0\cdot013$, $0\cdot113$

Worked Example Write $0\cdot5$ and $0\cdot015$ as the simplest possible fractions.

Answer $0\cdot5 = \frac{5}{10}$ $0\cdot015 = \frac{15}{1000}$

$ = \frac{1}{2}$ $ = \frac{3}{200}$

Worked Example Are the following statements true?

$$\text{(a)} \quad \frac{3}{20} < 0\cdot2 \qquad \text{(b)} \quad \frac{17}{25} < \frac{13}{20}$$

Answer We can compare the numbers in both of the statements by firstly writing them as decimals.

(a) $\frac{3}{20} = 0\cdot15$ Since $0\cdot15 < 0\cdot2$, then $\frac{3}{20} < 0\cdot2$.

(b) $\frac{17}{25} = 0\cdot68$, $\frac{13}{20} = 0\cdot65$ Since $0\cdot68 > 0\cdot65$, then $\frac{17}{25} > \frac{13}{20}$.

Statement **(a)** is true,   statement **(b)** is not true.

On a calculator, $\frac{1}{3}$ is given as the decimal 0·3333333.
If the calculator had room for more digits, more 3's would be given.

If we divide 1 by 3, we could continue forever.
The answer to 1 ÷ 3 could be given as 0·333 . . .
In fact, we use the notation 0·$\dot{3}$ for 0·333 . . .
The dot over the digit 3 means this digit is repeated.

We say 0·$\dot{3}$ is a **recurring decimal**.

Worked Example Write $\frac{3}{11}$ and $\frac{5}{18}$ as decimals.

Answer On a calculator, $\frac{3}{11}$ = 0·2727272.

The group of digits, 27, repeats. $\frac{3}{11}$ = 0·$\dot{2}\dot{7}$

On a calculator, $\frac{5}{18}$ = 0·2777777.

The digit 7 repeats. $\frac{5}{18}$ = 0·2$\dot{7}$

EXERCISE 2:10

1. Write these as decimals.

   (a) $\frac{7}{10}$ (b) $\frac{34}{100}$ (c) $\frac{4}{100}$ (d) $\frac{25}{1000}$ (e) $\frac{3}{4}$ (f) $\frac{1}{2}$

   (g) $\frac{9}{20}$ (h) $\frac{7}{25}$ (i) $\frac{5}{8}$ (j) $\frac{7}{8}$ (k) $\frac{13}{16}$

2. Write these as the simplest possible fraction.

   (a) 0·8   (b) 0·23   (c) 0·7   (d) 0·25   (e) 0·12   (f) 0·09

   (g) 0·48   (h) 0·003   (i) 0·017

3. Are these statements true or false?

(a) $\frac{5}{8} > 0{\cdot}58$ (b) $\frac{7}{20} < 0{\cdot}3$ (c) $\frac{3}{4} > \frac{7}{8}$

(d) $\frac{17}{100} < \frac{3}{20}$ (e) $\frac{9}{25} > \frac{2}{5}$ (f) $\frac{17}{20} < \frac{4}{5}$

4.

$\frac{1}{2}$	$\frac{3}{4}$	$\frac{5}{8}$	$\frac{9}{16}$	$\frac{3}{5}$

Write the fractions in the box in order, from smallest to largest.

5. Use your calculator to write the following fractions as recurring decimals.

(a) $\frac{1}{9}$ (b) $\frac{2}{3}$ (c) $\frac{5}{9}$ (d) $\frac{1}{6}$ (e) $\frac{5}{6}$ (f) $\frac{2}{11}$ (g) $\frac{7}{18}$

Review Copy this chart.

6	10	1	13	7	9	2	5	12	9	1	8	13	4	11	3
		C								C					

Match each number from **Box A** with a number from **Box B**.
Complete the chart.
For instance, **1** matches with **C** so **C** is filled in as shown.

Box A

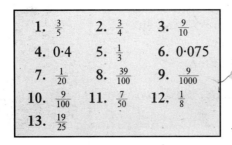

1. $\frac{3}{5}$ 2. $\frac{3}{4}$ 3. $\frac{9}{10}$

4. $0{\cdot}4$ 5. $\frac{1}{3}$ 6. $0{\cdot}075$

7. $\frac{1}{20}$ 8. $\frac{39}{100}$ 9. $\frac{9}{1000}$

10. $\frac{9}{100}$ 11. $\frac{7}{50}$ 12. $\frac{1}{8}$

13. $\frac{19}{25}$

Box B

A. $0{\cdot}009$ I. $0{\cdot}76$ R. $0{\cdot}125$

C. $0{\cdot}6$ L. $0{\cdot}75$ S. $0{\cdot}9$

D. $\frac{3}{40}$ M. $0{\cdot}05$ T. $0{\cdot}39$

E. $0{\cdot}09$ N. $0{\cdot}14$

F. $0{\cdot}\dot{3}$ O. $\frac{2}{5}$

APPROXIMATING: DECIMAL PLACES

Keying 11·9 ÷ 6 on the calculator gives 1·9833333 on the screen.
It isn't sensible to give an 8-digit answer to 11·9 ÷ 6.

For instance, chickens could be priced at £11·90 for 6.
To find the price of each chicken we would key 11·9 ÷ 6 on the calculator. We certainly wouldn't give the answer as £1·9833333.

To give sensible answers to calculations we often need to **approximate**.

In the case of the price of a chicken we would probably give the answer as £1·98, to the nearest penny. This is approximating to 2 decimal places.

DISCUSSION EXERCISE 2:11

- The 12 office staff at The Tannery won a prize of £34859 on the pools. This prize was to be divided equally between the 12 people. How should they share this prize? **Discuss.**

- Three families picked a total weight of 12·4kg of raspberries. These raspberries were to be shared equally between the three families. When they calculated 12·4 ÷ 3, their calculator gave an answer of 4·1333333.
  How should the families share the raspberries? **Discuss.**

- Robert was to rule an A4 piece of paper into 13 equally spaced columns. His calculation for the width of each column was 210mm ÷ 13. The calculator display for this calculation was 16·153846.
  How wide should Robert make each column? **Discuss.**

- Six cupboards are to be built along a 4 metre wall in a kitchen. The width of each cupboard was worked out on the calculator. The calculator display was 0·6666666.
  How wide should each cupboard be made? **Discuss.**

Rounded to 1 decimal place   3·6438 is 3·6.
Rounded to 1 decimal place   236·847 is 236·8.
Rounded to 2 decimal places   3·6438 is 3·64.
Rounded to 2 decimal places   236·847 is 236·85.

To **round** to a given number of **decimal places:**

1. Keep the number of figures asked for after the decimal point. For instance if asked to round to 3 decimal places, keep 3 figures after the decimal point.

2. Omit all the following figures. If the first figure omitted is 5 or greater, increase the last figure kept by 1.

Rounding to a given number of decimal places is also called **approximating** to this number of decimal places.

The words "decimal places" are often abbreviated to d.p.

Worked Example   Round 3·6472 to   (a)   2 d.p.

(b)   1 d.p.

Answer (a)   We are to round to 2 d.p. which means we want 2 figures after the decimal point. With just 2 figures after the decimal point, 3·6472 is 3·64.
The first figure omitted is 7 so we must increase the last figure kept (the 4) by 1.
We then get 3·6472 = 3·65 to 2 d.p.

(b)   We need 1 figure after the decimal point.
With just 1 figure after the decimal point, 3·6472 is 3·6.
The first figure omitted is 4 which is not large enough to alter the last figure we kept.
We then get 3·6472 = 3·6 to 1 d.p.

EXERCISE 2:12

1. Approximate these to 2 d.p.

(a)   2·8237   (b)   6·827   (c)   0·0348   (d)   1·292   (e)   1·835

(f)   2·896   (g)   12·995   (h)   0·0038   (i)   1·0037   (j)   22·881

(k)   0·859   (l)   0·895   (m)   0·995   (n)   325·099

2. Round these to the stated number of decimal places.

   (a) 3·4215 (2 d.p.)   (b) 24·01 (1 d.p.)   (c) 0·004 (2 d.p.)

   (d) 13·995 (2 d.p.)   (e) 64·58 (1 d.p.)   (f) 2·0997 (1 d.p.)

   (g) 125·704 (2 d.p.)   (h) 4·98 (1 d.p.)   (i) 14·003 (1 d.p.)

   (j) 1·638 (2 d.p.)   (k) 13·6492 (3 d.p.)   (l) 0·0507 (3 d.p.)

   (m) 29·9967 (1 d.p.)   (n) 29·9967 (2 d.p.)   (o) 29·9967 (3 d.p.)

3.

   The calculator display for the answer to a calculation was 346·79515.

   (a) Ann rounded the answer to 1 d.p. What was Ann's answer?

   (b) Karim rounded the answer to 2 d.p. What was Karim's answer?

   (c) Jake approximated the answer to 3 d.p. What did Jake get?

4. Do these calculations on the calculator. Give your answers to 1 d.p.

   (a) 8 ÷ 3   (b) 43 ÷ 9   (c) 7·5 ÷ 6   (d) 82·1 ÷ 4

   (e) 0·57 ÷ 12   (f) 2·68 ÷ 11   (g) 22·9 ÷ 3   (h) 85 ÷ 7

5. Copy this chart.

4·7	5·9	9	0·6	0·6		3·2	0·9	5·9	9	8·3	5·8	88·3	88·3	8·83
P														

   The calculation 5·3 ÷ 0·6 is to be done on the calculator and the answer rounded to 1 d.p. The correct answer is 8·8.

   Some students got the answers given in the chart.
   They got these incorrect answers by making the mistakes listed below.

   Match these mistakes with the incorrect answers. Complete the chart by writing the letter beside each mistake under the incorrect answer.

   For example, pressing – instead of ÷ gives answer of 4·7 rounded to 1 d.p. so **P** is written under **4·7** as shown.

   P. Pressed – instead of ÷   E. Rounded to the nearest whole number
   S. Forgot to press =   R. Pressed + instead of ÷
   U. Keyed 3·5 instead of 5·3   L. Keyed 53 instead of 5·3
   C. Pressed × instead of ÷   A. Keyed 6 instead of 0·6
   F. Read an 8 on the display as a 3 Y. Rounded to 2 d.p.

Review 1 Karen rounded these calculator displays to 2 decimal places. What answers should Karen get?

(a)
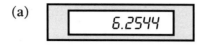
6.2544

(b)
32.9955

(c)
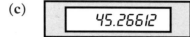
45.26612

(d)
0.3678

(e)
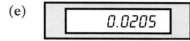
0.0205

(f)
10.0392

Review 2 Andrew rounded the calculator displays in **Review 1** to 3 d.p. What answers should Andrew get?

Review 3 Approximate the answers to these calculations to 1 decimal place.

    (a) 25 ÷ 6   (b) 31 ÷ 3   (c) 1·24 ÷ 9   (d) 0·7 ÷ 11

FINDING APPROXIMATE VALUES for SQUARE and CUBE ROOTS

The **square root** of a square number is a whole number. For instance $\sqrt{49} = 7$.
The **cube root** of a cube number is a whole number. For instance $\sqrt[3]{8} = 2$.

The square root of a number other than a square number and the cube root of a number other than a cube number is *not* a whole number. The answers we get for these are non-terminating and non-recurring decimals. We will need to round these answers.

Worked Example Find   (a) $\sqrt{6}$ (b) $\sqrt[3]{24}$

Answer   (a) **Key** 6 √ to get a calculator display of 2·4494897.

           Rounding the answer to 1 d.p. we get $\sqrt{6} = 2\cdot4$ to 1 d.p.

      (b) **Key** 24 SHIFT √ to get a calculator display of 2·8844991.

           Rounding the answer to 1 d.p. we get $\sqrt[3]{24} = 2\cdot9$ to 1 d.p.

DISCUSSION EXERCISE 2:13

Sharyn was using a calculator which didn't have a $\sqrt{\ }$ or $\sqrt[3]{\ }$ key.

She decided to use trial and improvement to find $\sqrt{19}$ to 3 decimal places. She began as follows.

19 lies between the two square numbers 16 and 25.
$\sqrt{19}$ lies between $\sqrt{16}$ and $\sqrt{25}$.
$\sqrt{19}$ lies between 4 and 5.

Try 4·5   4·5 × 4·5 = 20·25   too big
Try 4·3   4·3 × 4·3 = 18·49   too small
Try 4·4   4·4 × 4·4 = 19·36   too big
I now know that $\sqrt{19}$ lies between 4·3 and 4·4

Try 4·35   4·35 × 4·35 = 18·9225 too small
Try 4·36   4·36 × 4·36 = 19·0096 too big
I now know that $\sqrt{19}$ lies between 4·35 and 4·36

Discuss Sharyn's method. How could Sharyn continue? As part of your discussion continue Sharyn's working.

EXERCISE 2:14

1. Find these, giving the answers to 2 decimal places.

    (a) $\sqrt{5}$ (b) $\sqrt{20}$ (c) $\sqrt{7\cdot8}$ (d) $\sqrt{2}$ (e) $\sqrt{82\cdot6}$ (f) $\sqrt{172}$

    (g) $\sqrt{1\cdot2}$ (h) $\sqrt{0\cdot4}$ (i) $\sqrt{3\cdot92}$ (j) $\sqrt{0\cdot1}$

2. Round the answer to these to 1 d.p.

    (a) $\sqrt[3]{7}$ (b) $\sqrt[3]{11}$ (c) $\sqrt[3]{100}$ (d) $\sqrt[3]{6\cdot4}$ (e) $\sqrt[3]{8\cdot95}$ (f) $\sqrt[3]{0\cdot8}$

    (g) $\sqrt[3]{1\cdot34}$ (h) $\sqrt[3]{25\cdot6}$ (i) $\sqrt[3]{21\cdot43}$

3. Approximate the answer to these to 3 decimal places.

    (a) $\sqrt{27}$ (b) $\sqrt[3]{9}$ (c) $\sqrt{2\cdot8}$ (d) $\sqrt[3]{0\cdot6}$ (e) $\sqrt[3]{4\cdot9}$ (f) $\sqrt{12\cdot65}$

4. Round the answer to these to the given number of decimal places.

    (a) $\sqrt[3]{30}$ (to 2 d.p.)   (b) $\sqrt{68}$ (to 3 d.p.)   (c) $\sqrt[3]{4\cdot2}$ (to 1 d.p.)

(d) $\sqrt{9\cdot9}$ (to 2 d.p.) (e) $\sqrt[3]{105}$ (to 3 d.p.)

5. Use trial and improvement to find these, accurate to 3 d.p. Do not use the $\sqrt{}$ or $\sqrt[3]{}$ key.

(a) $\sqrt{8}$ (b) $\sqrt{24}$ (c) $\sqrt[3]{50}$ (d) $\sqrt[3]{81}$

Review 1 Find these, giving the answers to 1 decimal place.

(a) $\sqrt{29}$ (b) $\sqrt{74}$ (c) $\sqrt[3]{66}$ (d) $\sqrt[3]{8\cdot7}$ (e) $\sqrt[3]{0\cdot8}$

Review 2 Use trial and improvement to find these, accurate to 2 d.p. Do not use the $\sqrt[3]{}$ or $\sqrt{}$ key.

(a) $\sqrt{35}$ (b) $\sqrt[3]{16}$

FOR YOUR INTEREST

- Choose a workplace you know something about.
  List the occupations of the people who work there.

  Discuss the following statement in relation to each of these occupations.

  People in higher paid jobs use decimals more often than those in lower paid jobs.

  Write a summary of your discussion.

- Wages clerks, cashiers, hotel staff, builders, pilots, teachers, mechanics are some of the people who use decimals.

  Discuss the following statement in relation to one or more of these people.

  An understanding of the relationship between fractions and decimals is important.

  Write a summary of your discussion.

  Instead of a discussion, you could hold a mock interview.
  If you do this, you may like to make a tape recording of the mock interview.

DISCOVER, DISCUSS, DO

-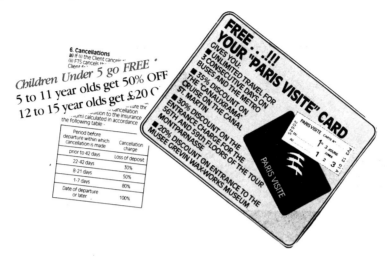

6. Cancellations
a) if (i) the Client cancels ···
(ii) FTS cancels ···
Client ···

Children Under 5 go FREE
5 to 11 year olds get 50% OFF
12 to 15 year olds get £20 C···

··· ···ture thi··· ···cancellation
···num) calculated in accordance
the following table:

Period before departure within which cancellation is made	Cancellation charge
prior to 42 days	Loss of deposit
22-42 days	30%
8-21 days	50%
1-7 days	80%
Date of departure or later	100%

FREE...!!!
YOUR "PARIS VISITE" CARD
GIVES YOU:
■ UNLIMITED TRAVEL FOR 3 CONSECUTIVE DAYS ON BUSES AND THE METRO
■ 35% DISCOUNT ON THE "CANAUXRAMA" CRUISE ON THE CANAL ST. MARTIN
■ 30% DISCOUNT ON THE ENTRANCE CHARGE FOR THE 56TH AND 59th FLOORS OF THE TOUR MONTPARNASSE
■ 20% DISCOUNT ON ENTRANCE TO THE MUSEE GREVIN WAX-WORKS MUSEUM

What do the percentages in these cuttings refer to? **Discuss.**

- Plan a holiday to a destination of your choice.
    Decide what transport to use.
    Decide what sort of accommodation you will use.
    Decide what to buy before you go on holiday.
    Make other necessary decisions.
Write up your holiday plan, referring to percentages wherever possible.

- **A Working Day in the Life of a . . .**

Complete the sentence given above with one of the following words: farmer, teacher, football player, singer, bus driver.

Discuss a day in the life of the person you chose. List the things he or she might see, or do, that involve percentages in some way.
Discuss percentage calculations that he or she may have to make.

- Where are the following words used? **Discuss** their meaning.

    commission   discount   VAT   depreciation   appreciation

WRITING PERCENTAGES as a FRACTION or DECIMAL

15% means 15 out of every hundred.

15% may be written as $\frac{15}{100}$.

Worked Example Write 15% as the simplest possible fraction.

Answer $15\% = \frac{15}{100}$

$\qquad = \frac{3}{20}$ (dividing top and bottom of the fraction by 5)

As a fraction, $15\% = \frac{15}{100}$.

Since $\frac{15}{100}$ may be written as 0·15, then 15% = 0·15.

Worked Example Write 12% and 7% as decimals.

Answer $\qquad 12\% = \frac{12}{100} \qquad\qquad\qquad 7\% = \frac{7}{100}$

$\qquad\qquad\quad = 0·12 \qquad\qquad\qquad\qquad = 0·07$

DISCUSSION EXERCISE 3:1

$\qquad 15\% = 0·15 \qquad 12\% = 0·12 \qquad 7\% = 0·07$

$12\tfrac{1}{2}\% = 12·5\% = 0·125$

"To write a percentage as a fraction or decimal we divide by 100". Is this statement true? **Discuss.**

- "It is possible to write a percentage as a decimal without first writing the percentage as a fraction".
  Discuss this statement.

- $0 \cdot 15 = 15\%$ $\qquad$ $0 \cdot 12 = 12\%$ $\qquad$ $0 \cdot 07 = 7\%$ $\qquad$ $0 \cdot 125 = 12 \cdot 5\%$

  How do we write decimals as percentages? **Discuss.**
  As part of your discussion, make and test statements.

- $\frac{1}{2} = 50\%$ $\qquad$ $\frac{3}{4} = 75\%$ $\qquad$ $\frac{4}{10} = 40\%$ $\qquad$ $\frac{9}{10} = 90\%$

  How do we write fractions as percentages? **Discuss.**
  As part of your discussion, make and test statements.

- Is it possible to have a percentage that is greater than 100%?
  Discuss.

Worked Example Write $\frac{4}{5}$, $2\frac{5}{8}$ and $\frac{1}{3}$ as percentages, giving the answers to the nearest percentage.

Answer $\quad \frac{4}{5} = \frac{4}{5} \times 100\%$
$\qquad \quad = 80\%$

$2\frac{5}{8} = 2 \cdot 625 \times 100\%$
$\qquad = 262 \cdot 5\%$
$\qquad = 263\%$ to the nearest percentage

$\frac{1}{3} = 0 \cdot \dot{3} \times 100\%$
$\quad = 33 \cdot 3\%$ to 1 d.p.
$\quad = 33\%$ to the nearest percentage

EXERCISE 3:2

1. Which of the words **divide** or **multiply** goes in the space in the following two statements?

   (a) To write a decimal or fraction as a percentage, _____ by 100%.

   (b) To write a percentage as a fraction or decimal, _____ by 100%.

2. Write as a percentage.

   (a) 0·29   (b) 0·03   (c) 0·8   (d) 1·8   (e) 2

   (f) $\frac{7}{10}$ (g) $\frac{3}{5}$ (h) $\frac{1}{4}$ (i) $2\frac{1}{2}$ (j) $1\frac{3}{4}$

   (k) 1   (l) 1·3   (m) 2·8

3. What percentage of these figures is shaded? (Give the answers to the nearest percentage.)

      (a)   (b)   (c)   (d)   (e)

4. Write these as a decimal.

   (a) 10%   (b) 75%   (c) 30%   (d) 150%   (e) 210%   (f) 6%

   (g) 4%   (h) 21%   (i) 1%   (j) 2·1%   (k) 0·02%

5. Write these as the simplest possible fraction.

   (a) 20%   (b) 75%   (c) 83%   (d) 5%   (e) 2%   (f) 3%

   (g) 8%   (h) 15%   (i) 1·5%   (j) 0·5%   (k) $12\frac{1}{2}$%

6. Copy and complete.

   (a) $\frac{1}{5} = \frac{...}{10} = 0·... = ...%$ (b) $\frac{3}{5} = \frac{...}{10} = 0·... = ...%$

   (c) $\frac{7}{20} = \frac{...}{100} = 0·... = ...%$ (d) $\frac{7}{25} = \frac{...}{100} = 0·... = ...%$

7. $\frac{2}{5}$ of the pages in a book have illustrations. What percentage of pages are illustrated?

8. 2% of the nurses at St. Helen Hospital have applied for leave at Christmas time.

   What fraction of nurses at this hospital is this?

9. Copy and complete this table. (Write fractions as simply as possible.)

fraction	$\frac{6}{25}$	$\frac{3}{5}$			$\frac{7}{8}$		$\frac{21}{1000}$	
percentage	24%			29%				65%
decimal	0·24		0·68			0·02		

Review 1 Copy and complete. $\frac{4}{5} = \frac{...}{10} = 0 \cdot \ldots = \ldots\%$

Review 2

2	12	3	4		7	5	2	8	12		11	5	4		6	10	9	1		10	5	4	1
																		Y					**Y**

Copy this chart.

Match each percentage in **Box A** with a decimal or fraction from **Box B**.
Then complete the chart.
For example, **1** matches with **Y**, so **Y** is filled in as shown.

Box A

1. 10%	5. 60%	9. 92%
2. 20%	6. 70%	10. 100%
3. 25%	7. 80%	11. 150%
4. 50%	8. 90%	12. 200%

Box B

A. $\frac{3}{5}$	I. $\frac{1}{4}$	T. $\frac{1}{5}$
C. 0·9	M. $\frac{4}{5}$	V. $\frac{7}{10}$
E. 1	R. 0·92	W. 1·5
H. 2	S. 0·5	Y. 0·1

Review 3 47% of Year 3 students are girls.

   What fraction of Year 3 students are girls?

Review 4 VAT is $17\frac{1}{2}\%$. What fraction is this?

ESTIMATING PERCENTAGES

10% can be written as $\frac{10}{100}$ which can be simplified to $\frac{1}{10}$. That is, 10% can be written as $\frac{1}{10}$. We use 10% = $\frac{1}{10}$ to quickly estimate percentages of 10%, 20%, 30%, 40%, 50%, 60%, 70%, 80% and 90%.

For instance, if we were finding 40% of £7·00 we would proceed as follows:
$$10\% \text{ of } £7·00 = \tfrac{1}{10} \text{ of } £7·00$$
$$= 70p.$$
Since 40% = 4 × 10%, then 40% of £7·00 = 4 × 70p
$$= £2·80$$

25% can be written as $\frac{25}{100}$ which can be simplified to $\frac{1}{4}$. We use 25% = $\frac{1}{4}$ to quickly estimate percentages of 25% and 75%.

Worked Example In a sale, all shoes are reduced by 20%. Estimate the saving on a pair which were originally priced at £29·95.

Answer The original price was about £30.

A 10% saving on £30 is $\frac{1}{10}$ of £30 = £3

A 20% saving on £30 is 2 × £3 = £6

The estimated saving is about £6.

EXERCISE 3:3

Estimate each of the 20 percentages given at the top of the next page. After you have estimated each answer, use the calculator to find the exact answer.

Begin with 20 points.

If your estimate was close, add 1 point.
If your estimate was not very close, subtract 1 point.

10% of	(a) £80	(b) £4	(c) £12·95	(d) £34·99
25% of	(a) £80	(b) £4	(c) £19·95	(d) £9·99
50% of	(a) £120	(b) £1	(c) £10·05	(d) £3·45
20% of	(a) £200	(b) £20	(c) £1·99	(d) £7·95
5% of	(a) £50	(b) £20	(c) £39·99	(d) £14·85

Score

40 points	Excellent
30–39 points	Good
20–29 points	Take care when shopping
less than 20 points	Take a calculator when shopping

A NUMBER as a PERCENTAGE of ANOTHER NUMBER

DISCUSSION EXERCISE 3:4

- What percentage of cars passing the school have no passengers?

  What percentage of students in Year 9 have part-time jobs?

  What percentage of books in the library are non-fiction?

  Each of the above involves finding one number as a percentage of another number.
  What numbers are involved in each of the above questions?
  Discuss.

- Think of more situations where you might want to find one number as a percentage
  of another number. **Discuss.**

To find a given number as a percentage of another number proceed as follows.

Step 1   Write the given number as a fraction of the other number.

Step 2   Rewrite this fraction as a percentage.

Worked Example   Paul's family had a total income of £35000.
This family paid a total of £1800 in council tax.
What percentage of their total income was this tax?

Answer   Fraction of income paid in council tax $= \dfrac{\text{council tax}}{\text{income}}$

$$= \dfrac{1800}{35000}$$

% of income $= \dfrac{1800}{35000} \times 100\%$

$= 5\%$ (to the nearest percentage)

Worked Example   There are seven species of tiger left in the world. One species, the Bali tiger, is extinct. What percentage of species are not extinct?

Answer   7 out of 8 species are not extinct.

Fraction not extinct $= \frac{7}{8}$

% not extinct $= \frac{7}{8} \times 100\%$

$= 87 \cdot 5\%$

EXERCISE 3:5

Round your answers sensibly in this exercise.

1. Of the 50 houses in Melville Street, 40 have garages.

    What percentage of houses in Melville Street have garages?

Chapter 3

2. At a meeting, 58 out of 85 people voted in favour of a motion.

   What percentage of these people voted in favour of the motion?

3. Sue was doing a survey on cars.
   Of 150 cars that went past her, 3 were
   sports cars.

   What percentage of the cars, that went past
   Sue, were sports cars?

4. The results of Nathan's survey on sport showed that 4 out of 50 students played no sport.

   What percentage of the students, that Nathan surveyed, played sport?

5. Annette kept a table of the amount she earned, and the amount she saved, for each of the first six months of last year. Her table is shown below.

	Earnings	Savings	% saved
Jan.	£50	£25	
Feb.	£80	£20	
March	£66	£66	
April	£104	£26	
May	£85	£34	
June	£60	£44	

   Copy this table and complete the last column.

6. In Nazir's class there are 14 girls and 18 boys.

   What percentage are boys?

7. 2341 out of a workforce of 11345 were unemployed.

   What percentage of this workforce was unemployed?

8. Out of a dance class of 28, 2 were absent.

   What percentage of the class was present?

9. Of 1450 videos at the Video Village, 84 were new releases.

   What percentage were not new releases?

10. In one litre of air there is about

    | 210m*l* | oxygen |
    | 780m*l* | nitrogen |
    | 10m*l* | argon |

    About what percentage of the air is oxygen?

11. Alexander Bell, who invented the telephone, lived from 1847 to 1922. He emigrated to Canada when he was 23.

    What percentage of his life did he spend in Canada?

Review 1 Pure gold is 24 carat gold.

   What percentage of pure gold is 18 carat gold?

Review 2 A tutor, at a Polytechnic, chose 5 classes to survey.
   This tutor was comparing the number of females with the number of males.

   Copy and complete the following table.

Class	Total present	Females present	% Females
Word Processing	140	112	
Computing	130	26	
Mathematics III	100	14	
Biology I	75	15	
Interior Design	15	10	

Review 3

Butterscotch

6 tablespoons sugar
2 tablespoons vinegar
2 tablespoons butter

1. Put all ingredients in a bowl.
   Microwave on high 5 mins. Stir.
2. Microwave on high 2 more mins.
   Stir twice during cooking.
3. Allow to cool and set.

What percentage of this recipe is sugar?

PUZZLE 3:6

Five students estimate the speed of a car as it passes.
Jamie's estimate is 20% out and Susie's estimate is 10% out.

The estimates of the five students are:

    56km/h   65km/h   70km/h   77km/h   80km/h

One of the five students correctly estimated the speed.

What was the speed of the car?

PRACTICAL EXERCISE 3:7

1. Carry out a survey to find one of the following percentages.

   percentage of female drivers

   percentage of cars with just one occupant

   percentage of cars with personalised number plates

   percentage of students taking a particular subject, perhaps French percentage of people who regularly eat Indian food

percentage of students who are from two-child families

percentage of students who don't have any brothers

percentage of houses that are detached

2. Each night for a month, keep a note of the times you spend on homework for each subject. At the end of the month, work out the percentage of the total homework time spent on each subject.

Draw up a wall chart to illustrate.

3. For the next week, every time you realise you have stopped concentrating in class, make an estimate of the time your attention has not been on the classwork. Note this estimate down and note the name of the subject.

At the end of the week, use this information along with the number of minutes per week spent on each subject to work out the % of time your concentration lapsed in each subject.

Illustrate on a poster.

4. From the Situations Vacant section of one day's newspaper find the % of jobs vacant that: are part-time
give wages or salary
are in the farming sector
are in the finance sector
are in factories
are labouring jobs for adults
are for people with University degrees
are suitable for school leavers

Choose the way in which you will present your research.

5. Investigate various ways of financing a motorbike or a car.
Include such things as: hire purchase
personal loan from a bank
cash advance on a credit card

Also include charges such as: interest charges
insurance
office or administration charges

FOR YOUR INTEREST

Discuss one of the following statements.

In real life, percentages occur much more often than fractions.

Percentages are more important than decimals.

Farmers use percentages more often than travel agents.

In newspaper articles, percentages have more impact than decimals.

Make a summary of your discussion.

You could present this summary on a poster.
You could use cuttings from the newspaper on your poster.

DISCOVER, DISCUSS, DO

Anti-freeze	1 part
Water	3 parts

  What other things do we mix in parts? **Discuss.**

- Mario's head circumference is 55cm.
  He is 165cm tall.
  Think of different ways of comparing Mario's head circumference with his height.
  Find the head circumference and height of the students in your group. Compare these. **Discuss** your findings.

- What is meant by a "gear ratio"? **Discuss.**

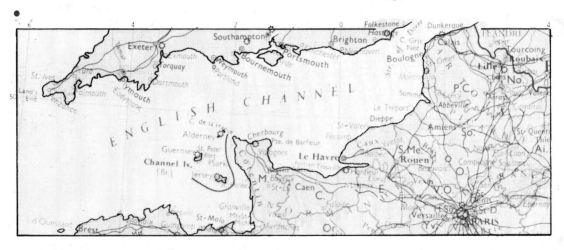

  How far is it from Le Havre to Paris?
  Is it possible to work this out from the map given above? What other information would you need?
  Discuss.

- Without taking measurements, try and sketch a plan of your house or part of your school buildings.
  Was it difficult to do this?

WRITING RATIOS

The ratio of two quantities x and y is written as x : y.
x : y is read as "the ratio of x to y".

The order is important. x : y is different from y : x.

A ratio compares quantities of the same kind.

Worked Example   On a bus there are 17 adults and 5 children.

Find the ratio of   (a)   adults to children

(b)   children to adults.

Answer (a)   In our ratio we must have the number of adults first, then the number
of children.
The ratio of adults to children is 17 : 5.

(b)   In our ratio we must have the number of children first, then the
number of adults. The ratio of children to adults is 5 : 17.

Worked Example   The length of a bus is five times its width.
Find the ratio of its length to its width.

Answer The ratio of length to width is 5 : 1 since for every 5 units of length we
have 1 unit of width.

Worked Example   A bus fare for an adult is £1·05 and for a child 49p. What is the
ratio of a child's fare to an adult's fare?

Answer We are asked for the ratio of a child's fare to an adult's so we must have the
child's fare first in the ratio. Also, the units must be the same. We will
write both fares in pence (we could have written them both in £).
Ratio of child's fare to adult's fare is 49 : 105.

EXERCISE 4:1

1. The height of a thistle is 31 centimetres.
   The height of a sedge-grass plant is 18 centimetres.
   What is the ratio of the height of the thistle to the height of the sedge-grass?

2. The capacities of two rucksacks are 32 litres and 35 litres.
   Find the ratio of the capacity of the smaller rucksack to the larger rucksack.

3. The floor area of Bea's bedroom is 16m². The floor area of Aaron's bedroom is 15m².
   Find the ratio of the floor area of Aaron's bedroom to Bea's bedroom.

4.

Horse	Height
Pegasus	14
Daffodil	15
Count Jolly	16
Shamus	12
Hillbilly	17

This table gives the height (in hands) of five horses.

Find the ratio of the height of   (a) Pegasus to Hillbilly

                                (b) Count Jolly to Daffodil

                                (c) Shamus to Hillbilly

                                (d) Hillbilly to Daffodil.

5. Meghan's ruler is twice the length of Abe's.
   What is the ratio of the length of Meghan's ruler to Abe's ruler?

6. Darren spent four times as long on his project as Rona.
   Find the ratio of the time Rona spent on her project to the time Darren spent.

7. The cost of a ride on a Big Wheel at the
   Brighton seaside fair is shown here.
   Find the ratio of the cost for an adult to the cost
   for a child.

RIDES

Adult £2·49

Child 79p

8. In a flock of 280 sheep, 3 are black and the rest white.
   Find the ratio of black sheep to white sheep.

9. Winstone, who weighs 40kg, goes on a diet and loses 7kg.
   Find the ratio of Winstone's weight after dieting to his weight before dieting.

10. Sarah and Kate bought a raffle ticket which cost £2. Sarah paid 89p and Kate
    paid the rest.
    What was the ratio of the amount Kate paid to the amount Sarah paid?

Review 1 A cordial is made into a drink by mixing one part of the cordial with
         three parts of water.
         Find the ratio of cordial to water in this drink.

Review 2 A blend of tea consists of two parts China tea to three parts Ceylon tea.
         What is the ratio of Ceylon tea to China tea in this blend?

Review 3

CRISPS

Small 38p

Family £1·05

What is the ratio of the price of a small pack
of crisps to a family pack?

Review 4 On one of the stands at Wimbledon there were 521 spectators. Of these,
         237 were female.
         Find the ratio of male spectators to female spectators.

USING RATIOS

Ratios are used in the **drawing of plans**.
The plan will be the same shape as the original, only smaller.

The ratio used may be 1 : 2 which means that the original will be twice as large as the plan. In other words, the plan will be $\frac{1}{2}$ the size of the original.

The ratio used may be 1 : 5 which means that the original will be five times as large as the plan. The plan would be $\frac{1}{5}$ the size of the original.

Many other ratios could be used.

Worked Example Alexis drew this plan of a t-shirt she had just bought.
To draw this plan she used the ratio 1 : 20.
On her t-shirt, what were the lengths of NO and SR?

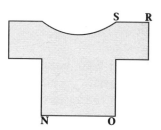

Answer Since the ratio used for the plan is 1 : 20, the t-shirt is 20 times as large as the plan.
On the plan, NO = 2cm.
On the t-shirt, NO = 20 × 2cm   i.e. NO = 40cm.

On the plan, SR = 0·9cm.
On the t-shirt, SR = 20 × 0·9cm   i.e. SR = 18cm.

EXERCISE 4:2

1.

fig 1   *fig 2*

The ratio used for these drawings is 1 : 10.

(a) Measure, in cm, the length of the horizontal line in *fig 1*.
Find the actual length of this horizontal line.

(b) Measure, in cm, the length of the horizontal line in *fig 2*.
Find the actual length of this horizontal line.

2. Ian read about a puzzle.
The puzzle consisted of 20 triangles, each with the measurements shown.
Ian decided to make the puzzle pieces. He thought the pieces were too big, so he made them smaller. He used the ratio 1 : 4.

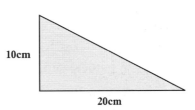

(a) How long did Ian make his puzzle pieces?

(b) How high did he make them?

3.

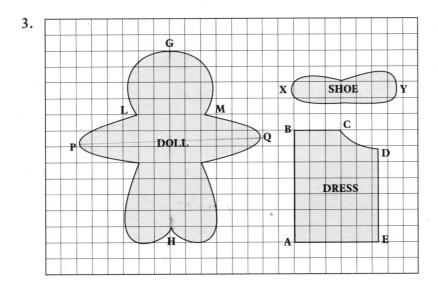

This pattern, for a felt doll, was in a magazine.
The actual pattern pieces are 5 times this size.

(a) Copy and complete: The ratio used in this drawing of the pattern pieces is 1 : . . .

(b) Take measurements, in cm, from this plan and work out the actual length of the following:
   GH, PQ, LM, XY, AB

4. A forestry researcher planted two plots of trees, Plot A and Plot B. After 5 years, the ratio of the height of trees in Plot A to the height of trees in Plot B was 1 : 2. If the height of the trees in Plot B was 6·2m, how high were the trees in Plot A?

5. Latif was using the following information to decide which of the two teams in his club had won the most games. What answer should Latif get?

Ratio of games won by team A to games won by Team B	
Round 1	2 : 1
Round 2	1 : 3
Round 3	2 : 1

Number of games won by Team A	
Round 1	4
Round 2	3
Round 3	2

Review 1

Gingerbread People
100g (or 4oz) margarine
100g (or 4oz) brown sugar
300g (or 12oz) flour
100g (or 4oz) syrup
2tsp   ginger
1tsp   bicarbonate of soda
enough currants to decorate

Miranda doubled this recipe to make enough Gingerbread People for her little brother's birthday party.

(a) What is the ratio of sugar to flour in the recipe given above?

(b) What ratio of sugar to flour did Miranda use?

(c) How much ginger did Miranda use?

Review 2 Arna worked part time and earned £3350. Her brother Ernst earned five times as much.

(a) What is the ratio of Arna's income to Ernst's income?

(b) How much did Ernst earn?

PRACTICAL EXERCISE 4:3

1. Make the 20 puzzle pieces described in **question 2** of the previous exercise. Choose the ratio that you will use.
Invent a puzzle using these 20 puzzle pieces.

2. Make a full size pattern for the felt doll described in **question 3** of the previous exercise. You may like to make the doll.
   You could make a padded paper doll instead of a felt doll. If you do, colour and decorate the doll.

3. Choose two of your favourite recipes.
   Adapt these recipes to feed the whole class. Think carefully about a sensible ratio to use.
   Write your adapted recipes on a poster for the classroom wall.

4.  Take measurements from this road sign.
   Make a larger one.
   Choose the ratio that you will use.

5. Take the measurements of something in your classroom. It could be a piece of equipment or a poster on the wall or an article of clothing etc.
   Draw an accurate plan of this.
   Choose a sensible ratio for your plan.

EQUIVALENT RATIOS

DISCUSSION EXERCISE 4:4

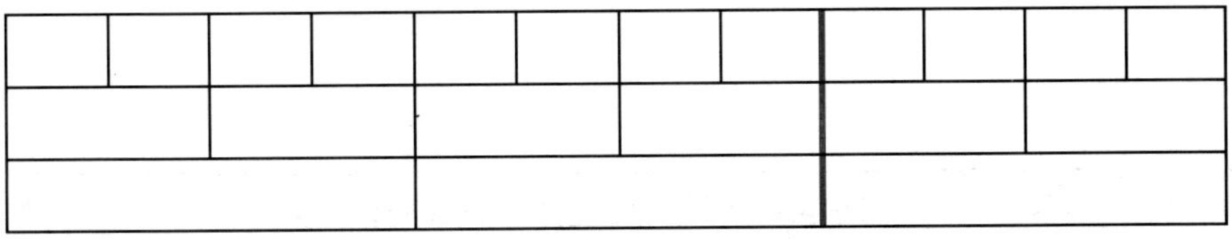

This diagram shows that the ratio 8 : 4 equals the ratio 4 : 2. How does this diagram show this?
What other equal ratios are shown in this diagram? **Discuss.**

Discuss how to show the ratio 4 : 6 on this line.
What other ratio is equal to 4 : 6? Is there more than one? **Discuss.**

- **Discuss** how to shade a circle so that the ratio of the shaded part to the unshaded part is 10 : 2.

  What other ratios could you show by shading parts of a circle? **Discuss.**

Example

The ratio of the number of dots in *fig 1* to the number of dots in *fig 2* is 12 : 4.

We can also say there are three times as many dots in *fig 1* as there are in *fig 2*. We can write this as the ratio 3 : 1.

The ratios 12 : 4 and 3 : 1 are equal.

Notice that if we divide both sides of the ratio 12 : 4 by 4 we get $\frac{12}{4} : \frac{4}{4}$ or 3 : 1.

Equivalent ratios are equal. For instance 8 : 2 and 4 : 1 are equivalent ratios.

We can divide both sides of a ratio by the same number.
We can also multiply both sides of a ratio by the same number.

A ratio is in its **simplest form** if the numbers in the ratio are the smallest possible whole numbers.

Worked Example Write these ratios in their simplest form.

      (a) 1mm : 5m   (b) 45p : £2   (c) £3·50 : £2

Answer (a) 1mm : 5m = 1mm : 5000mm   (b) 45p : £2 = 45p : 200p
                    = 1 : 5000   = 45 : 200
                                                = 9 : 40

      (c) £3·50 : £2 = 3·5 : 2
                    = 7 : 4

DISCUSSION EXERCISE 4:5

- Linus made scale models of the furniture in the sitting room of his home. He used the scale 5 : 100.
  His sister also made scale models of the same furniture. She made her models one-twentieth ($\frac{1}{20}$) size.

  Did Linus and his sister make their models the same size? **Discuss.**

- "If two numbers A and B are in the ratio of 3 : 5, then A is $\frac{3}{5}$ of B". **Discuss** this statement.

- "Ratios behave like fractions." **Discuss** this statement.

Worked Example The ratio of boys to girls in a school is 3 : 4.
How many boys are there if there are 600 girls?

Answer Number of boys = $\frac{3}{4}$ the number of girls
= $\frac{3}{4}$ × 600
= 450

Note We could find the number of boys by using equivalent ratios. This is shown below.

Let x be the number of boys in the school.

$$3 : 4 \quad = \quad x : 600$$
boys girls   boys girls

Since we multiply 4 by 150 to get 600 then we must multiply 3 by 150 to get x.

That is, x = 450.

EXERCISE 4:6

1. Write these ratios in their simplest form.

   (a) 10 : 40   (b) 18 : 42   (c) 18 : 10   (d) 1·5 : 4

   (e) 2mm : 5mm   (f) 2mm : 5m   (g) 15min : 1 hour   (h) £3 : £4·50

2. A concrete mix consisted of 1 part cement, 2 parts sand and 2 parts aggregate.
   In this concrete mix, find the ratio of   (a)   cement to sand
                                             (b)   aggregate to sand.

3. The ratio of jeans to shirts in Hari's wardrobe is 2 : 5.
   If Hari has 10 shirts, how many pairs of jeans does he have?

4. The ratio of competitors to spectators at the school athletic sports was 2 : 15.
   How many competitors were there if there were 600 spectators?

5. The ratio of cordial to water in a fruit drink is 3 : 8.
   How much cordial is used with 2 litres of water?

6. Anita worked out that the ratio of females to males on the 8:30 bus was 4 : 3.
   There were 48 females on this bus.
   How many males were there?

7. A passport photo was enlarged in the ratio of 5 : 9.
   The enlarged photo was 63mm long.
   How long was the passport photo?

Review 1 Write these ratios in their simplest form.

   (a) 6 : 15   (b) £3 : 40p   (c) 35min : 2 hours   (d) 8·2mm : 4cm

Review 2 Write the ratio of the length of the horizontal
         line to the length of the vertical line in its
         simplest form.

Review 3 The ratio of anti-freeze to water, in a mix used in very cold weather, is **2 : 3.**

How much anti-freeze should be used with 6 litres of water?

INVESTIGATION 4:7

RATIO in SQUARES and RECTANGLES

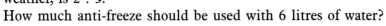

For each of these squares find the ratio   *length of side : length of diagonal.*
Investigate this ratio for other squares.

Which of these rectangles is most pleasing to your eye?

Draw many other rectangles. Choose the ones you like best.
For these rectangles find the ratio   *length : width.*

Investigate the Golden Rectangle and the Golden Ratio. Good sources of information would be the art room, the school library or the local library.

Find examples of the Golden Ratio in the interior of your home, on the exterior of your home, in the town's architecture, in the playground of the local primary school, in design, in fashion and in nature.

Produce a project, with each member of the group concentrating on one aspect of the Golden Ratio.

READING SCALE DRAWINGS

A scale of 1mm to 5m means 1mm on the scale drawing represents 5m on the actual object.
A scale of 1 : 5000 means 1 unit on the scale drawing represents 5000 units on the actual object i.e. 1mm represents 5000mm, 1cm represents 5000cm, etc.

The scales 1mm to 5m and 1 : 5000 are the same.
Since 5m = 5000mm, 1mm to 5m may be written as 1mm to 5000mm which is the same as writing 1 : 5000.

Worked Example Bill's mother wanted a conservatory built exactly the same as her friend's conservatory. She took measurements from her friend's conservatory and drew a working drawing for the builder to use. For her drawing she used the scale 1 : 50. On the drawing the length of the conservatory was 78mm.
How long did the builder build the conservatory?

Answer 1 unit on the drawing represents 50 units on the conservatory.
1mm on the drawing represents 50mm on the conservatory.
78mm on the drawing represents 78 × 50mm = 3900mm
= 3·9m
That is, the builder built the conservatory 3·9m long.

Worked Example This is the scale drawing Latif made of his family's car.
Find the length of this car.

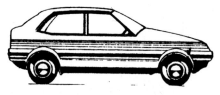

Scale: **1mm to 6cm**

Answer Measuring the length on the drawing we get 56mm.
1mm on the drawing represents 6cm on the car.
56mm on the drawing represents 56 × 6cm = 336cm
= 3·36m
The length of the car is 336cm or 3·36m.

EXERCISE 4:8

1.

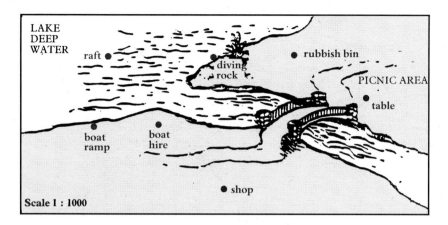

This map shows a picnic area near the Turner's home.

(a) Copy and complete. Map distance from shop to boat hire = ⋯ mm

(b) Copy and complete. Actual distance from shop to boat hire = ⋯ × 1000mm

            = ⋯ m

(c) Find the actual distance from the table to the rubbish bin.

(d) Verity swam from the diving rock to the raft. How far did she swim?

(e) Annabel and Anthony hired a canoe and paddled from the boat ramp to the raft and back again. How far did they paddle altogether?

2. Jafar made an accurate floor plan of his house.
He used the scale 1cm to 4m.
On his plan the games room measured 2cm × 1·6cm.
What were the actual dimensions of this room?

3. At the scene of an accident the police made a scale drawing showing all the relevant details. They used the scale 1 : 250.
On the drawing one of the skid marks was 84mm long. How long were these actual skid marks in (a) mm
                (b) m?

4. A scale of 1 : 10000 was used to draw a plan of the proposed extension to the Eastern Motorway. On the plan this extension was 750cm long.
What was the actual length of this proposed extension?

5. The scale of a map is 1 : 250000.
   What actual distance (in km) do these measurements, taken from the map, represent?

   (a) 5cm   (b) 5mm   (c) 150mm

6. Joe is drawing a map. He is using the scale 1 : 1000000. How long (in mm) will these distances be on his map?

   (a) 1km   (b) 5km   (c) 50km   (d) 500m

7.

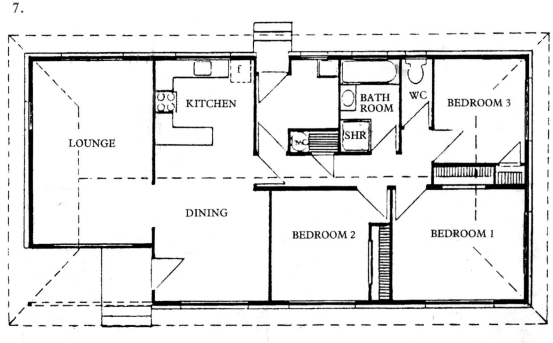

Scale 1 : 100

This is a scale drawing of a new bungalow on the Fairview Housing Estate.

(a) What are the inside dimensions of the lounge?

(b) What are the inside dimensions of bedroom 1?

(c) How long is the window in bedroom 3?

(d) The outside dotted line is the edge of the roof. What are the dimensions of the roof?

(e) How deep is the wardrobe in bedroom 2?

(f) How long is the bath?

8. This shows the cutting layout for a shirt.
The pattern pieces are as follows:
1 – front   2 – back
3 – front band
8 – collar   9 – sleeve

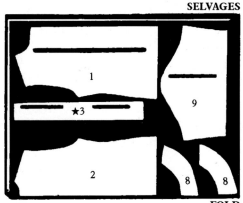

SELVAGES

FOLD

Scale: 1mm to 2cm

(a) What is the width of the collar at the fold line?

(b) What is the length of the back at the fold line?

(c) What are the dimensions of the front band?

(d) What is the width of the sleeve at its widest point?

(e) What is the length of the front at the selvage line?

9.

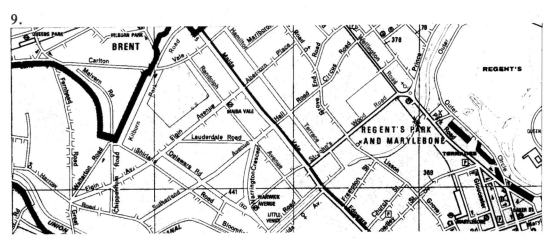

Scale 1 : 25000

(a) How long is Hamilton Terrace? (Give the answer to the nearest 100 metres.)

(b) How long is St-John's Wood Road? (Give the answer to the nearest 100 metres.)

(c) Ann goes for a walk. She begins at the corner of Harrow Road and Sutherland Avenue. She walks along Sutherland Avenue, turns left into Randolph Avenue, then right down Abercorn Place, then right down Hamilton Terrace, then left down St-John's Wood Road. She finishes her walk at the corner of St-John's Wood Road and Wellington Road. Find how far Ann walked, to the nearest kilometre.

Review 1 The scale 1mm to 2m is used on a scale drawing of the school grounds.

(a) On this scale drawing, the distance between the gymnasium and the tennis courts is 15mm. How far is it from the gymnasium to the tennis courts?

(b) The distance from the main gate to the main entrance is 64m. How far is this on the scale drawing?

Review 2

Scale 1 : 4000

This is a map of the No. 5 hole at the Summerhill Golf Course. Wiesje and Frank were playing this hole. Wiesje's wood shot, from the tee, landed on the fairway at A while Frank's landed in the rough at B.

(a) On this map find the distance (in mm) from the tee to A and B.

(b) What distance (in m) did Wiesje's ball travel?

(c) How far did Frank's ball travel?

PRACTICAL EXERCISE 4:9

1. Use a map of your town or district to find distances between landmarks. You could write some questions and give these to the rest of your group or your neighbour to answer.

2. Use a road map of some part of Great Britain to find the distance, "as the crow flies", between towns and cities.

3. Find a scale drawing and work out actual measurements. You could use a scale drawing of a boat, an aeroplane, a park or of something else.

MAKING SCALE DRAWINGS

Worked Example A farmer wanted to make a scale drawing of the fields on his farm. He made this sketch. From this sketch, he made the scale drawing. He used a scale of 1 : 2000. Work out the lengths for the scale drawing. Make the scale drawing.

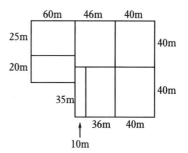

Answer 1 : 2000 is the same as 1mm to 2000mm which is the same as 1mm to 2m.

40m is represented by 20mm.	46m is represented by 23mm.
60m is represented by 30mm.	25m is represented by 12·5mm.
20m is represented by 10mm.	35m is represented by 17·5mm.
10m is represented by 5mm.	36m is represented by 18mm.

The scale drawing is shown below.

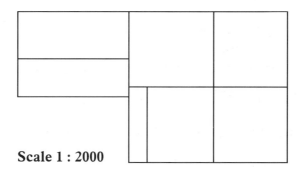

Scale 1 : 2000

To make a scale drawing you should take the following steps:

Step 1 Make a rough sketch.

Step 2 Take measurements.
Write these on the sketch.

Step 3 Decide on the scale.

Step 4 Work out what each measurement will be on the scale drawing.

Step 5 Make the scale drawing.

PRACTICAL EXERCISE 4:10

1. Make a scale drawing of a classroom or of a section of your school.

2. Make a scale drawing of the floor plan of your house.

3. Make a scale drawing of a room in your house. Make separate scale drawings of the furniture in this room.

   Arrange the scale drawings of the furniture on the scale drawing of the room. Rearrange the furniture. Make sure doorways aren't blocked. Make sure there is sufficient room between the pieces of furniture so that it is easy to move around the room.

4. Make a scale drawing of the grounds of your school. Make scale drawings of each building of your school. Place these on the scale drawing of the grounds.

5. Make a scale drawing of some part of your community. You could choose a park or the streets around your school or your High Street or something else.

6.

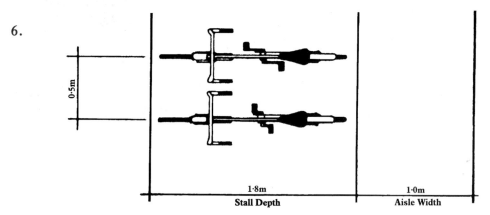

0·5m		
	1·8m	1·0m
	Stall Depth	Aisle Width

   This diagram shows the recommended dimensions used in the construction of cycle stands.

   Use these dimensions to design a new layout for the cycle stands at your school.

7. Make a scale drawing of some article of clothing. You may choose an article that you already own or design one that you would like to own.

8. Make a scale drawing of some aspect of life you have studied in another subject. It might be a farm, a town, a type of house or an article of clothing. These could be from another country or another period of history that you have studied. You will need to make a sketch first and estimate measurements.

SHARING in a GIVEN RATIO

DISCUSSION EXERCISE 4:11

- What is the ratio of shaded to unshaded squares?

  What fraction of the squares is shaded?

  What fraction of the squares is unshaded?

- How would you divide these sweets equally between two people?
  How would you divide them equally between three people?

  Now suppose the sweets are to be divided between two people, but this time one person is to get twice as many as the other.
  How could you divide them in this way?

What if they were to be divided between two people so that one person gets three times as many as the other?

What if they were to be divided between two people in the ratio of 1 : 4 ? Does one person get $\frac{1}{4}$ of them and the other $\frac{3}{4}$? Does one person get $\frac{1}{5}$ of them and the other $\frac{4}{5}$? **Discuss.**

What if the ratio was 2 : 3 ?

What if . . .

Now suppose the sweets are to be divided between three people in the ratio 1 : 1 : 2. What fraction of the sweets does each person get?

What if the ratio was 1 : 2 : 2 ?

What if the ratio was 2 : 3 : 1 ?

What if the ratio was 2 : 1 : 3 ?

What if the ratio was 5 : 2 : 3 ?

What if . . .

Worked Example The apples in a container are to be divided between two families in the ratio of 2 : 5.

How many apples does each family get if there are 280 apples in the container?

Answer 280 apples are to be divided in the ratio 2 : 5.

For every 2 apples that one family gets, the other family gets 5.

That is, one family gets 2 out of every 7 or $\frac{2}{7}$ and the other family gets 5 out of every 7 or $\frac{5}{7}$.

$$\frac{2}{7} \text{ of } 280 = \frac{2}{7} \times 280 \qquad\qquad \frac{5}{7} \text{ of } 280 = \frac{5}{7} \times 280$$
$$= 80 \qquad\qquad\qquad\qquad\qquad = 200$$

One family gets 80 apples, the other gets 200 apples.

Note: The answer to this sort of problem can be easily checked. How?

Worked Example A concrete mix consists of cement, sand and aggregate in the ratio of 1 : 2 : 5.

How much cement is needed to make 2 cubic metres of concrete?

Answer For every 1 part of cement, there are 2 parts of sand and 5 parts of aggregate.

$\frac{1}{8}$ of the concrete is cement.

$$\text{In 2 cubic metres, amount of cement} = \frac{1}{8} \times 2$$
$$= 0 \cdot 25 \text{ cubic metres.}$$

EXERCISE 4:12

1. Halima and Brian shared the driving, on a 450km journey, in the ratio 5 : 4.

    (a) What fraction of the driving did Halima do?

    (b) What fraction of the driving did Brian do?

    (c) How far did Halima drive?

    (d) How far did Brian drive?

Chapter 4

2. The ratio of girls to boys in Stephanie's Technology class is 3 : 2.

    (a) What fraction of this class is boys?

    (b) There are 30 students in Stephanie's Technology class. How many of these are boys?

3. A 1400mm length of wood is cut into two parts in the ratio of 3 : 4.

   How long is the shorter piece?

4. The ratio of Ceylon tea to China tea in a tea blend is 5 : 3.

   How much Ceylon tea is in 560g of this blend?

5. Felicity and Gareth bought a £1 raffle ticket.
   Felicity paid 70p and Gareth paid 30p.
   This raffle ticket won a prize of £50.

   How should Felicity and Gareth share this prize?

6. Joanne and Daphne job share in the ratio of 1 : 2.
   The salary for the job they share is £12000.

   What is Daphne's salary?

7. Two friends bought a house for £150000. Deirdre paid £50000. Siobhan paid the rest. They later sold this house for £180000.

   How should the friends share this?

8. Kate was mixing concrete.
   The mix she used was 1 part cement to 2 parts sand to 4 parts aggregate.

    (a) Write the mix as a ratio.

    (b) How much sand would Kate need to make 3·5 cubic metres of concrete?

9. The three angles of a triangle are in the ratio 2 : 3 : 4.

   What is the size of the smallest angle of this triangle?

Review 1 A 35cm length of liquorice is cut into two parts in the ratio of 2 : 3.

What is the length of the longest piece?

Review 2 This year a farmer planted 40 acres in crops.
He planted wheat, barley and oats in the ratio 5 : 1 : 2.

How many acres did this farmer plant in oats?

INVESTIGATION 4:13

TRIANGLE PATHS

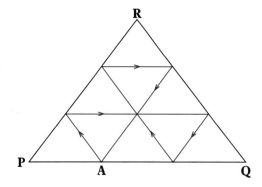

In this triangle, A divides the side PQ in the ratio 1 : 2.

From A, a line is drawn parallel to the side RQ.
This is the first part of the path.

The rest of the path is found by turning each time a side is reached, and then moving parallel to another side.

The path which began at A in this triangle, finishes at A.

What if the triangle had been a different shape? **Investigate.**

What if A divided the side in the ratio 1 : 3? **Investigate.**

"For the path shown in the triangle above, each side has been divided in the ratio 1 : 2." Is this statement true?

Make and test similar statements about other triangles and other beginning points A.

FOR YOUR INTEREST

- Discuss fully one of the following statements.

  Map and model makers use ratios more than anyone else.

  A knowledge of ratio is essential to an architect.

  If you understand fractions you don't need to know about ratios.

  Make a summary of your discussion.

- Discuss the following statement in relation to one of these industries: health, building, farming, advertising, decorating.

  Everyone involved in this industry needs an understanding of ratio.

  Make a summary of your discussion.

  You may wish to present your summary as a poster, a mock interview or an illustrated talk.

Number Review

1. Write these as the simplest ratio.

   (a) 5 : 15   (b) 28 : 16   (c) £3 : 20p   (d) £1·20 : £1

2.
   | ˙0·02   ˙0·082   ˙0·28   0·802   ˙0·208   ˙0·08   ˙0·2   0·82   ˙0·002 |

   Put these numbers in order, from the smallest to the largest.

3. A plan of a house is drawn using the scale 1 : 100.

   (a) The width of the house on the plan is 96mm. How wide is the actual house?

   (b) The sitting room is 3·4m long. How long is the sitting room on the plan?

4.
   | 39.9696 |

   This is the calculator display for the answer to a problem.
   Philippa rounded the answer to 2 decimal places.
   Shani rounded it to 1 decimal place.
   Anna rounded it to 3 decimal places.

   What answers should Philippa, Shani and Anna get?

5. Copy and complete. $\frac{3}{4} = \frac{\cdots}{20} = \frac{\cdots}{100} = 0\cdot\ldots = \ldots\%$

6. What percentage of each figure is shaded?

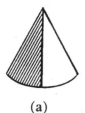   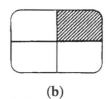   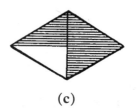   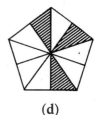

   (a)   (b)   (c)   (d)

7. There were 168 runners in a marathon. Of these, 47 were women. Find the ratio of women to men in this marathon.

8. Maryanne is making a scale drawing of the school grounds. She is using the scale 1cm represents 10m. This is the same as:

   A. 1 : 10   **B.** 1 : 100   **C.** 1 : 1000   **D.** 1 : 10000

9. Write these fractions in their lowest terms.

   (a) $\frac{18}{40}$ (b) $\frac{15}{45}$ (c) $\frac{10}{25}$ (d) $\frac{28}{70}$ (e) $\frac{24}{64}$

10. A jar of beans has a mixture of red, white and green beans.
    The total of red and white beans is 395.
    The total of white and green beans is 330.
    There are 60 more white beans than green, and 65 fewer green beans than red.
    How many beans, of each colour, are there in this jar?

11. The following fractions are to be written as decimals. Which of them will be recurring decimals?

    $$\frac{5}{6} \qquad \frac{5}{8} \qquad \frac{5}{15} \qquad \frac{5}{11}$$

12. Adapt the following recipe to make 30 pieces.

    Chocolate Fudge (24 pieces)

    Ingredients   200g sugar
                      40g cocoa
                      100m*l* milk or cream or water
                      20g butter
                      1tsp vanilla essence

    Method   Heat all the ingredients (except the vanilla) in a saucepan, stirring until boiling.
                 Boil until a soft ball is formed when a few drops are placed in cold water.
                 Add vanilla, then cool until lukewarm.
                 Beat until creamy.
                 Pour into a buttered dish. Mark into 24 pieces. Leave until set.

13. Find the value of x in each of these.

    (a) $\frac{4}{10} = \frac{x}{5}$ (b) $\frac{3}{x} = \frac{15}{25}$ (c) $\frac{x}{32} = \frac{3}{4}$ (d) $\frac{x}{8} = \frac{9}{24}$

14. A box of homemade sweets contained chocolate fudge and coconut ice in the ratio of 2 : 3.
    What fraction of the sweets were chocolate fudge?

15. Use your calculator to find these. Give the answers to 3 decimal places.

    (a) $\sqrt{71}$ (b) $\sqrt[3]{71}$ (c) $\sqrt{6\cdot9}$ (d) $\sqrt[3]{0\cdot94}$

16. Of 165 members of a youth group, 45 have their driving licence.

    (a) What fraction have their driving licence?

    (b) What percentage have their driving licence? Round your answer to 1 d.p.

17. In the week before Christmas, 32 cats were received by the Clanhill RSPCA.
The ratio of dogs to cats received in that week was 1 : 4.
How many dogs were received?

18. Which of these statements are true?

    A. $\frac{5}{6} > 0\cdot6$ B. $54\% = 0\cdot054$ C. $0\cdot\dot{6} = \frac{2}{3}$ D. $0\cdot81 > \frac{4}{5}$

19. The scale of a map is 1 : 500000.
What actual distance (in km) do these measurements, taken from the map, represent?

    (a) 1mm   (b) 25mm   (c) 4·5mm   (d) 4cm

20. Lucinda made a profit of £15 on an investment of £120.
What percentage profit did Lucinda make?

21.

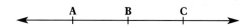

On this number line, one of the numbers 2·04, 2·041, 2·014 is at A, another at B and the other at C.
Which number is at each of A, B and C?

22. James multiplies his house number and half his house number together. His answer is 288.

Use trial and improvement, or some other method, to find James' house number.

Is there more than one possible answer?

23. Shannan and Barbara job share in the ratio of 5 : 3.
The salary for this job is £9000.

(a) What is Shannan's salary?

(b) How many hours does Barbara work if this is a 40 hour per week job?

24. Copy and complete this table. Write the fractions as the simplest possible fraction.
The first column is done for you.

Percentage	85%	68%					$12\frac{1}{2}\%$
Decimal	0·85		0·44		0·08		
Fraction	$\frac{17}{20}$			$\frac{3}{25}$		$\frac{7}{50}$	

25. What is the ratio of the price of apples to the price of cherries?

Cherries £2·50 per kg
Apples 95p per kg

26.

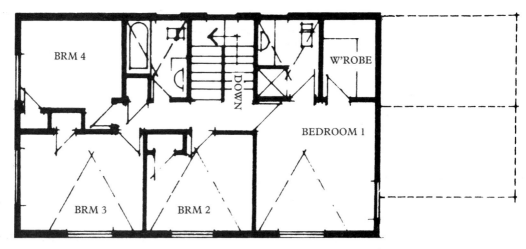

Scale: 1cm to 1·5m

This plan is of the top floor of a house.

(a) How long is the outside wall that runs alongside Bedrooms 3 and 4?

(b) How wide is the inside of Bedroom 1?

(c) What are the inside dimensions of Bedroom 3?

(d) The dotted lines indicate the ceiling of the sitting room which is at ground level. What are the dimensions of this sitting room?

27. A stainless steel container is made from iron, chromium and nickel in the ratio of 7 : 2 : 1.

How much iron is there in one of these containers which weighs 1500g?

28. **(a)** I am equivalent to $\frac{4}{5}$.
   The sum of my denominator and numerator is 81.
   What fraction am I?

   (b) I am equivalent to $\frac{16}{48}$.
   My denominator is 10 more than my numerator.
   What fraction am I?

29.

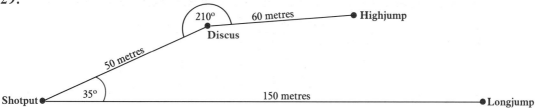

Make an accurate scale drawing of this sketch.
Choose the scale you will use.

On your scale drawing measure the distance between the Highjump and Longjump.

Work out the actual distance between the Highjump and Longjump giving the answer to the nearest 10 metres.

30. The $\sqrt{}$ key on Wael's calculator wasn't working. He began, as follows, to find the value of $\sqrt{34}$ accurate to 2 d.p.

Since 34 is between the square numbers 25 and 36 then $\sqrt{34}$ is between 5 and 6.

Try 5.5   5.5 x 5.5 = 30.25   too small

Try 5.7   5.7 x 5.7 = 32.49   too small

Try 5.8   5.8 x 5.8 = 33.64   too small

Try 5.9   5.9 x 5.9 = 34.81   too big

Continue to find $\sqrt{34}$ accurate to 2 d.p.

31. There is three times as much water area as land area on the Earth's surface.

What percentage of the Earth's surface is land area?

ALGEBRA

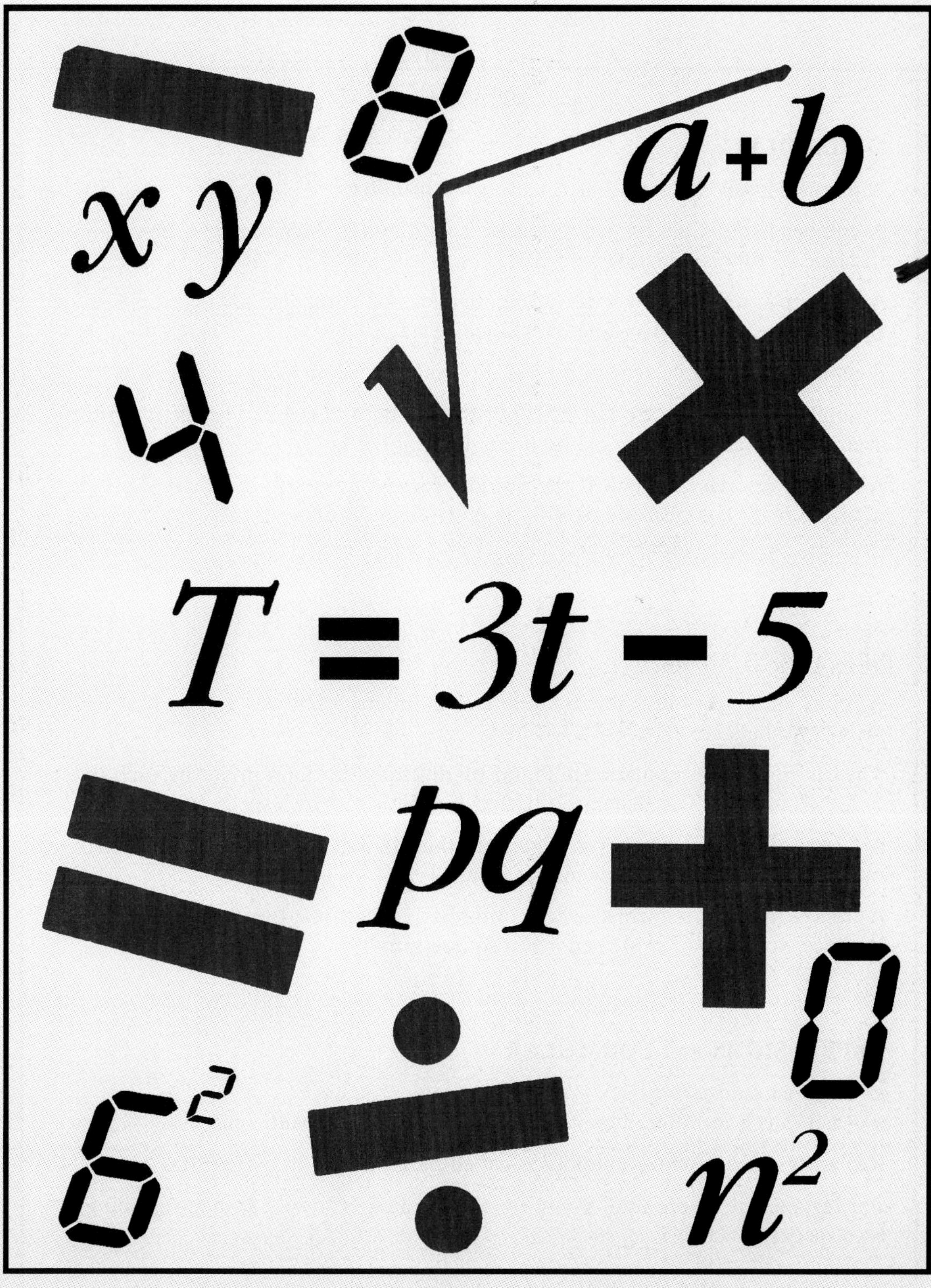

xy

8

$a+b$

4

$\sqrt{}$

$\times$

$T = 3t - 5$

$=$

pq

$+$

0

6^2

$\div$

n^2

Algebra from Previous Levels

DIVISIBILITY

A number is **divisible by** 2 if it is an even number.

A number is **divisible by** 3 if the sum of its digits is divisible by 3. For instance 259104 is divisible by 3 since $2 + 5 + 9 + 1 + 0 + 4 = 21$ is.

A number is **divisible by** 4 if the number formed from the last two digits is. For instance, 7532 is divisible by 4 since 32 is.

A number is **divisible by** 5 if its last digit is either 5 or 0.

A number is **divisible by** 6 if it is divisible by both 2 and 3. That is, if it is an even number and the sum of the digits is divisible by 3.

A number is **divisible by** 8 if the number formed from the last three digits is divisible by 8. For instance, 259104 is divisible by 8 since 104 is.

A number is **divisible by** 9 if the sum of its digits is divisible by 9.

SPECIAL NUMBERS

A **prime number** is divisible by only two numbers, itself and 1. The first few prime numbers are 2, 3, 5, 7, 11, 13.

The **multiples** of a number are found by multiplying the number by each of 1, 2, 3, 4, 5, 6, . . . For instance, the first few multiples of 5 are 5, 10, 15, 20.

A **factor** of a given number is a number that divides exactly into the given number. For instance, the factors of 20 are 1, 2, 4, 5, 10, 20.

A **square number** is formed when a number is multiplied by itself. For instance, since $2 \times 2 = 4$ then 4 is a square number.

EXPRESSIONS and FORMULAE

$x + 3$ is an expression.
$a = x + 3$ is a formula. The value of **a** depends on the value of x.

Replacing a letter with a number is called **substituting in a formula**.

For instance, if we are told $x = 6$ in the formula $a = x + 3$, then replacing x by 6 we get $a = 6 + 3$
$\qquad = 9.$

continued . . .

. . . from previous page

SIMPLIFYING EXPRESSIONS

ab means a × b   ba is the same as ab
2a means 2 × a
a² means a × a

5a + 2a can be simplified to 7a
5a + 3b − a + 2b can be simplified to 4a + 5b

When we remove the brackets from 5 (2a − 3) we get 10a − 15.

COORDINATES

The **x-axis** is the horizontal axis.
The **y-axis** is the vertical axis.
The **coordinates** of a point are a pair of numbers
such as (5, 3). The first number is the x-coordinate
and the second number is the y-coordinate. For
the point P (5, 3), the x-coordinate is 5 and the
y-coordinate is 3.

REVISION EXERCISE

1.

| 1830 | 3380 | 8310 | 8330 | 8031 | 1380 | 8103 | 3308 | 3810 | 3801 |

Which of these numbers is divisible by 3, 4, and 5?

2. Dale is making a fruit drink for his party. He needs to allow 2
glasses of drink for each person plus 5 glasses more. How many
glasses should Dale make for

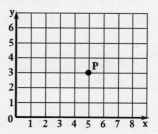

(a) 8 people   (b) 15 people   (c) 25 people?

3. Copy this grid of numbers.

Cross out the numbers that are squares.
Cross out the numbers that are cubes.
Cross out the prime numbers.
Cross out the numbers that are factors of 6.
Which numbers are left?

50	32	20	28	24	40
35	1	7	29	16	34
10	19	36	3	27	12
22	4	31	9	11	30
15	6	25	2	8	21
39	18	33	26	38	14

4.

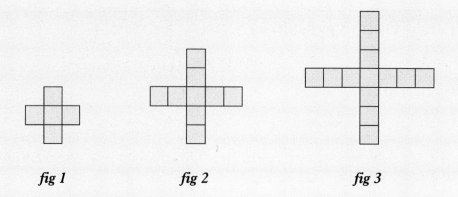

fig 1   fig 2   fig 3

"Crosses" are made from squares as shown.
fig 1 has "arms" of length 1. *fig 2* has "arms" of length 2. *fig 3* has "arms" of length 3.

How many squares will there be in the cross which has arms of length 7?

5. $t = 30n$ is a formula for the time t, in seconds, given to answer n multi-choice maths. questions.

(a) How much time, in seconds, is given for 10 questions?

(b) How much time, in minutes, is given for 30 questions?

6. I am a factor of 48.
I am not a multiple of 4.
I am not a prime number.
I am not a factor of 50.
   What number am I?

7. "Sound and Vision" sell high quality video tapes for £1·49 each.

(a) How much do n of these cost?

(b) Write a formula for the cost V, in pounds, of n of these tapes.

8. If I double a number then add 1, the answer is 49.
What is the number?

9. Copy this chart.

D		D
(5, 4)	(7, 1)	(5, 4)

(1, 2)	(7, 7)	(2, 1)

(2, 5)	(4, 5)	(5, 2)

(7, 5)	(5, 7)	(5, 7)

(7, 7)	(1, 7)

(5, 2)	(1, 1)	(4, 5)	(5, 1)	(4, 5)

(1, 4)	(7, 1)	(2, 5)	(1, 1)	(5, 2)

Complete your chart by finding the letter that represents each coordinate. D is filled in for you.

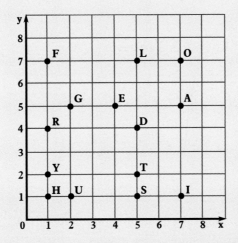

10. "Mary-Anne" Easter eggs cost £19 per kg. What is the cost of   (a)   2 kg

(b)   1·5 kg

(c)   x kg?

11.
```
10  FOR N = 3 TO 10
20  PRINT N – 2
30  NEXT N
40  END
```

Write down the output from this program.

12. Simplify these.

(a) $3 \times a$ (b) $n \times n$ (c) $7a + 3a$ (d) $n + n + n$

(e) $5x – 4x$ (f) $3a \times a$ (g) $4n – 3a + n + 2a$

13. Smokey weighs x kg.
   Bluey is 3kg heavier than Smokey.
   Toffee is twice as heavy as Smokey.
   Sassy is 3kg lighter than Toffee.

   Write expressions for the weight of
   each of these pet sheep.

14. $23 \times 9 = 207$
        $34 \times 9 = 306$
        $45 \times 9 = 405$
        $56 \times 9 = 504$
   Write down the next line in this pattern.

15.

(a) How many dots are there in the next "picture" in this pattern? How many red dots are there?

(b) A formula for finding the number of red dots in any of the pictures is "subtract 1 from the number of dots on the bottom row then multiply the answer by 3".
   Linda used this formula to find the number of red dots in the picture that has 10 dots on the bottom.
   What answer should Linda get?

16. Draw up a set of axes.
   Label the x-axis from 0 to 9. Label the y-axis from 0 to 4.

   Plot each point in the lists. Join the points in order, as you plot them.

   (a) $(1, 3), (3, 3)$ (b) $(6, 3), (5, 3), (4, 2), (5, 1), (6, 1)$

   (c) $(7, 2), (8, 2)$ (d) $(8, 3), (7, 3), (7, 1), (8, 1)$

   (e) $(2, 3), (2, 1)$ (f) $(1, 1), (3, 1)$

   What do you get?

17. (a) Use your calculator to find the answer to these.

$$202 \times 37 =$$
$$2002 \times 37 =$$
$$20002 \times 37 =$$
$$200002 \times 37 =$$

(b) Use the number pattern from (a) to write down the answer to $2000000002 \times 37 =$

18. $S = 150 + 75n$ is the formula that gives Victoria's weekly wage. Victoria earns a basic salary of £150 and £75 for every set of encyclopaedias she sells.

How much does Victoria earn in a week in which she sells

(a) no encyclopaedias   (b) 3 sets of encyclopaedias?

19. Choose the correct answer.

(a) $2(n - 8)$ A. $n - 16$ B. $n - 8$ C. $2n - 8$ D. $2n - 16$

(b) $3(5n + 1)$ A. $15n + 1$ B. $15n + 3$ C. $8n + 3$ D. $5n + 3$

(c) $2(3n - 1) + 3(n + 2)$ A. $7n + 4$ B. $9n + 5$ C. $9n + 4$ D. $9n - 5$

(d) $6n + 4(2 - 3n)$ A. $8 - 6n$ B. $2n$ C. $6n - 4$ D. $3n + 8$

20. Wheels A and B each have one black tooth. When the wheels start turning the black teeth are together.

How many turns does A make before the black teeth are together again if

(a) A has 6 teeth and B has 8

(b) A has 6 teeth and B has 9?

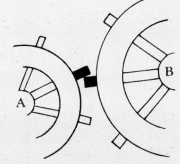

21. Which number does not belong in the list? Explain your answer.

(a) 3 21 27 31 33 48 57   (b) 3 7 11 19 22 27 35 39

(c) 4 8 36 49 81 100   (d) 1 3 7 13 17 29 31 37

22. Hamish's group were making up maths. quizzes. Hamish, who is 14, made up this quiz.

My house number has 3 digits.
The sum of these digits is 5 more than my age.
If you double my age then subtract 20 you get the last digit.
If you add 4 to my age then divide the answer by 3 you get the first digit.

What is Hamish's house number?

DISCOVER, DISCUSS, DO

Gillian decides to wash her hair every 3rd day during January, beginning on January 2nd. She writes down the list of dates on which she will wash her hair. 2, 5, 8, 11, 14, 17, 20, 23, 26, 29.

Adele has just bought her first car. The mileage reading is 34530. Adele decides to check the oil level, every 50 miles, for the next 200 miles. She writes a list of the mileage readings for when she will do this. Her list is   34580, 34630, 34680, 34730.

What list of numbers might a weight lifter use? **Discuss.**

In what other everyday situations might you find a number pattern? **Discuss.**

- 3, 6, 9, 12, 15, . . .   90, 80, 70, 60, . . .

  7, 11, 15, 19, 23, . . .   1, 4, 9, 16, 25, . . .

Think of everyday situations where you might find these number patterns? **Discuss.**

SEQUENCES

A **sequence** is a list of numbers. There is usually a relationship between the numbers.

Examples 1, 4, 9, 16, 25, . . . is a sequence of square numbers.
3, 6, 9, 12, . . . is a sequence of the multiples of 3.

DISCUSSION EXERCISE 6:1

5	6	4	5	3	4	2
4	6	8	10	11	12	13
2	11	14	15	48	24	18
6	3	18	20	54	16	5
10	6	15	25	18	9	24
14	12	10	8	6	4	2
18	24	16	12	2	1	1

There are many sequences in this number square. How many can you find?

Discuss with your neighbour or group or class.

WRITING SEQUENCES from INSTRUCTIONS

The first number in a sequence is called the **first term**, the second number is called the **second term**, the third number is called the **third term** and so on.

Example For the sequence 1, 4, 9, 16, 25, . . . the first term is 1, the second term is 4 and so on.

The instructions may give the first term (or the first few terms) and the relationship between the terms.

Worked Example   Write down the first 6 terms of the sequence in which the first term is 2 and every term, after the first, is 4 more than the previous term.

Answer   Begin with 2 for the first term. Add 4 to 2 to get 6 for the second term.
Add 4 to 6 to get 10 for the third term etc.
The first 6 terms of the sequence are 2, 6, 10, 14, 18, 22.

Worked Example   A sequence has first term equal to 2 and second term equal to 4. Every term, after the second term, is found by adding the two previous terms. Write down the first 5 terms of this sequence.

Answer   First term is 2. Second term is 4.
Third term is 4 + 2 = 6.
Fourth term is 6 + 4 = 10.
Fifth term is 10 + 6 = 16.
The first 5 terms are 2, 4, 6, 10, 16.

EXERCISE 6:2

1. Write down the first 5 terms of these sequences.

    (a)   First term equal to 2. Every term, after the first, is 3 more than the previous term.

    (b)   First term 5. Every term, after the first, is twice the previous term.

2. Write down the first 7 terms of these sequences.

    (a)   First term 1. Second term 3.
    Every term, after the second, is found by adding the two previous terms.

    (b)   First term 1. Second term 2. Third term 2.
    Every term, after the third, is found by adding the three previous terms.

3. Donna was going to spend 5 hours making candles to sell at her family's market stall. She set herself the following targets.
    In the first hour she hoped to make one; in the second hour she hoped to make two. In each hour after this she hoped to make as many as she had in the two previous hours.
    How many candles did Donna hope to make in the 5 hours?

4. A computer salesperson was set a sales target of 2 computers in the first month. For every month after this, the target was 3 more than in the previous month.

 The salesperson met the targets for the first 6 months. How many computers did the salesperson sell in this time?

5. Lucy began an exercise programme. For the first week she was to exercise for 5 minutes each day. For each week after this she was to double the time spent exercising.

 How many minutes altogether did Lucy exercise for in the 4th week?

6. Write down the sequences given by working through these flow charts.

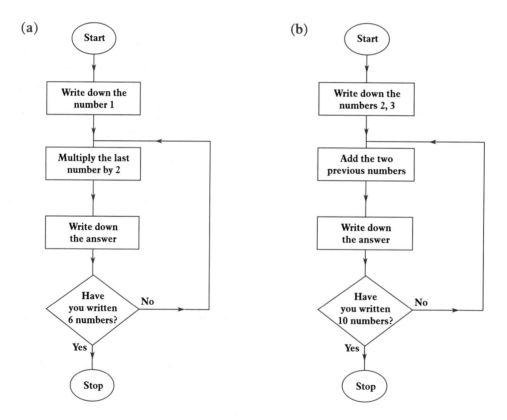

(a)

Start

Write down the number 1

Multiply the last number by 2

Write down the answer

Have you written 6 numbers? — No

Yes

Stop

(b)

Start

Write down the numbers 2, 3

Add the two previous numbers

Write down the answer

Have you written 10 numbers? — No

Yes

Stop

Review Write down the first 6 terms of these sequences.

 (a) First term 2. Every term is 2 more than the previous term.

 (b) First term 1. Second term 4.
    Every term, after the second, is found by adding the two previous terms.

 (c) First term 3. Every term is twice the previous term.

INVESTIGATION 6:3

CALCULATOR GENERATED SEQUENCES

Key $\boxed{3}$, then repeatedly key $\boxed{+}\boxed{2}\boxed{=}$
Write down the sequence of numbers generated.

Key $\boxed{3}$, then repeatedly key $\boxed{\times}\boxed{2}\boxed{=}$
Write down the sequence of numbers generated.

Write down the sequence of numbers generated by
the following keying sequences.

$\boxed{3}$ then repeatedly $\boxed{+}\boxed{1}\boxed{\times}\boxed{2}$

$\boxed{3}$ then repeatedly $\boxed{\times}\boxed{1}\boxed{+}\boxed{2}$

$\boxed{3}$ then repeatedly $\boxed{\times}\boxed{2}\boxed{+}\boxed{1}$

Investigate other calculator generated sequences by keying other numbers and
operations.

FINDING RULES for GENERATING SEQUENCES

By finding the pattern in a sequence, we can continue the sequence or find missing terms.

Worked Example How many dots are there in the next diagram of this sequence?

•   • •   • • •

• •   • • •   • • • •

Answer Each diagram has 2 more dots than the previous diagram.

The next diagram is   • • • •

There are 9 dots in this diagram.   • • • • •

The terms of a sequence are often found by adding the same number to each previous term. They are also often found by multiplying each previous term by the same number.

Worked Example Find a rule that generates these sequences. Write down the next term.

$\qquad$ (a) $3, 7, 11, \ldots$ $\qquad$ (b) $1, 3, 9, 27, \ldots$

Answer $\quad$ (a) $\quad$ Each term of this sequence could be found by adding 4 to the previous term. The rule for generating this sequence is "add 4". The next term is 15.

$\qquad$ (b) $\quad$ Each term of this sequence could be found by multiplying the previous term by 3. The rule for generating this sequence is "multiply by 3". The next term is 81.

Sequences are often based on these special numbers: odd numbers, even numbers, multiples, squares, cubes.

Worked Example Find the missing term in these sequences.

$\qquad$ (a) $2, 4, \square, 8, 10$ $\qquad$ (b) $3, \square, 9, 12$ $\qquad$ (c) $\square, 4, 9, 16$

Answer $\quad$ (a) $\quad$ This is a sequence of even numbers.
$\qquad\qquad$ The missing term is 6.

$\qquad$ (b) $\quad$ This is a sequence of the multiples of 3.
$\qquad\qquad$ The missing term is 6.

$\qquad$ (c) $\quad$ This is a sequence of square numbers.
$\qquad\qquad$ The missing term is 1.

EXERCISE 6:4

1. How many dots are there in the next diagram of each of these sequences?

   (a)

   (b)

2. Find a rule that generates these sequences. Test your rule, then write down the next two terms.

   (a) 6, 8, 10, 12, . . .   (b) 0, 3, 6, 9, . . .   (c) 10, 1, 0·1, 0·01, . . .

   (d) 36, 32, 28, . . .   (e) 1, 6, 11, . . .   (f) 2, 2, 2, 2, . . .

   (g) 2, 6, 18, . . .   (h) 16, 8, 4, 2, . . .

3. Find the missing term in these sequences.

   (a) 1, □, 9, 13   (b) 1, □, 9, 16   (c) 1, □, 9, 27

4.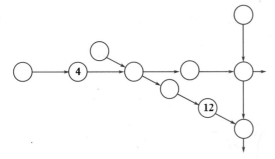

   Copy this diagram.

   Place numbers in the circles so that sequences of multiples are formed.

5. Draw the missing diagrams in these sequences.

   (a) 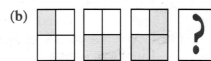   (b)

6. A spider was crawling up the wall. Every minute it crawled 4cm further than in the previous minute. It crawled 5cm in the first minute.

   (a) Write a sequence to show the spider's progress.

   (b) How far did the spider crawl in the fifth minute?

7. Ann cycled a total of 85km over a period of 5 days. Each day she cycled 5km more than the day before.

   (a) Use a trial and improvement method to find a sequence for this.

   (b) How many kilometres did Ann cycle on the first day?

Review 1

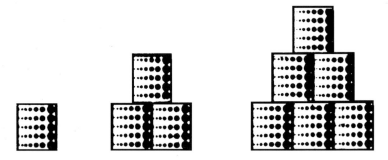

How many tins are there in the next diagram of this sequence?

Review 2 Find a rule that generates these sequences. Test the rule, then write down the next two terms of each sequence.

   (a) 2, 5, 8, 11, . . .   (b) 2, 4, 8, 16, . . .   (c) 20, 2, 0·2, 0·02, . . .

Review 3 Victoria decided to practise her goal shooting. Each practice, she shot 5 more goals than in her previous practice. On her first practice she shot 12 goals.

   (a) Write down a sequence to show the number of goals Victoria shot during each practice.

   (b) How many goals did she shoot on the sixth practice?

INVESTIGATION 6:5

NEW SEQUENCES FROM OLD

Consider the sequence 1, 4, 7, 10, 13, . . .
Many sequences can be generated from this sequence.

One is 1, 5, 12, 22, 35, . . .
This new sequence is generated by adding the terms of 1, 4, 7, 10, 13, . . .
Discuss.

2, 10, 24, 44, 70, . . . How is this generated from 1, 5, 12, 22, 35, . . .? **Discuss.**

8, 14, 20, 26, . . . How is this generated from 2, 10, 24, 44, 70, . . .? **Discuss.**

What other sequences could you generate from 1, 4, 7, 10, 13, . . .? **Discuss.**

What if you began with another sequence such as 2, 4, 6, 8, . . .
or 2, 4, 8, 16, . . .
or 1, 4, 9, 16, . . .
or 1, 1, 2, 3, 5, 8, . . .

Investigate other sequences that can be generated from a sequence of your choice.

Sometimes sequences can be continued in different ways.

Example 3, 8, 13, . . .

The next term of this sequence could be found by adding 5 to each previous term to get:
3, 8, 13, 18, 23, . . .

The sequence could have been continued as follows:
3, 8, 13, 18, 113, 118, 1113, . . .

DISCUSSION EXERCISE 6:6

- **Discuss** other ways of continuing the sequence 3, 8, 13, ...

- **Discuss** ways of continuing these sequences (a) 1, 2, 3, ...

    (b) 1, 2, 4, ...

INVESTIGATION 6:7

PASCAL'S TRIANGLE

$$
\begin{array}{ccccccccc}
 & & & & 1 & & & & \\
 & & & 1 & & 1 & & & \\
 & & 1 & & 2 & & 1 & & \\
 & 1 & & 3 & & 3 & & 1 & \\
1 & & 4 & & 6 & & 4 & & 1
\end{array}
$$

In Pascal's triangle the numbers down the left and right-hand sides are always 1. That is, each row begins and ends with 1. All other numbers are the sum of the two numbers immediately above on the previous row.

Investigate the number patterns and sequences in Pascal's triangle. Before you begin your investigation write down at least 10 rows of Pascal's triangle.

As part of your investigation you could consider looking at some of the following:

        sums of rows
        sums of diagonals
        small triangles within Pascal's triangle
        the position of the square numbers
        the six numbers that form a "ring" around a number

You might like to consider the colour patterns obtained when all the multiples of a prime number are coloured. If you colour the multiples of 2, write down at least 32 rows of Pascal's triangle; if you colour multiples of 3, write down at least 27 rows; if you colour multiples of 5, have at least 25 rows; if you colour multiples of 7, have at least 21 rows.

FIBONACCI SEQUENCE and related sequences

Some special sequences are formed by adding together previous terms. These are the **Fibonacci** and related sequences.

Example   The Fibonacci sequence begins with 1, 1. Each term, from the third term on, is found by adding together the two previous terms.

The first three terms are 1, 1, 2. The first four terms are 1, 1, 2, 3. The first five terms are 1, 1, 2, 3, 5. What is the next term of this sequence?

EXERCISE 6:8

1.   1, 3, 4, 7, 11, 18, 29, . . .
    This is the **Lucas** sequence.

    (a) How is the **Lucas** sequence formed?

    (b) What is the next term in this sequence?

2.   1, 1, 2, 4, 8, 15, 29, . . .
    This is the **Tetranacci** sequence.

Write down the next term of this sequence.

3.

Amount of change	10p	20p	30p	40p	50p	60p	70p	80p	90p	£1
Number of ways	1	2	3							

The top line of this table shows the amount of change to be given.
This change is to be given with just 10p and 20p coins.
The order in which the 10p and 20p coins are given is important.
For instance, 30p change can be given as 10p, 10p, 10p or 10p, 20p or 20p, 10p.
The first three entries on the bottom line of the table show the number of different ways change of 10p, 20p and 30p can be given.

Copy the table and complete the bottom line.

4.

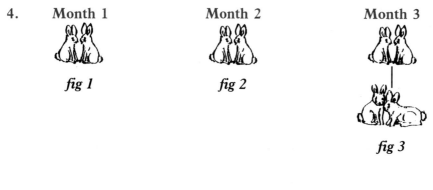

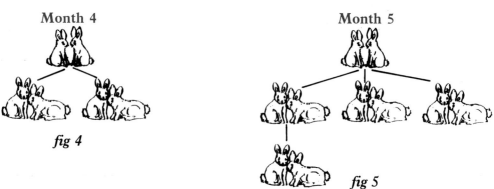

This picture shows generations of rabbits.

Assume that each pair of rabbits gives birth to another pair of rabbits every month.
Assume that rabbits are two months old when they first give birth.

fig 1 shows the first pair of rabbits at the beginning of month 1.

fig 2 shows the first pair of rabbits at the beginning of month 2.

fig 3 shows the first pair of rabbits and their offspring at the beginning of month 3.

fig 4 shows the rabbit population at the beginning of month 4. It shows the first pair of rabbits, with their offspring from months 3 and 4.

fig 5 shows the rabbit population at the beginning of month 5. The first pair of rabbits have their offspring from months 3, 4, and 5. The offspring from month 3 are now old enough to produce offspring of their own; the offspring of this pair is also shown.

Draw diagrams to show the number of pairs of rabbits at the beginning of the next three months.

Review 1   1, 1, 2, 4, 7, 13, 24, 44, . . .
This is the **Tribonacci** sequence.

(a) How is the Tribonacci sequence formed?

(b) What are the next two terms of this sequence?

Review 2 A cow has her first calf at the beginning of her third year. She continues to calve each year for the next 6 years.
Assume that this cow has only female calves.
Assume that her offspring also begin calving at the beginning of their third year and have only female calves.

Draw a sequence of pictures to show the number of cows in this family at the end of each of the first 6 years.

INVESTIGATION 6:9

STAIRCASE

fig 1   *fig 2*   *fig 3*   *fig 4*

Investigate the number of steps taken in climbing a staircase. The stairs may be taken either one at a time as shown in *fig 1* or two at a time as shown in *fig 2* or some combination of these as shown in *fig 3* and *fig 4.*

Begin your investigation with a small staircase and gradually make it larger.

WRITING SEQUENCES from PROGRAMS

Worked Example   10   FOR NUMBER = 1 TO 6
                     20   PRINT NUMBER * NUMBER
                     30   NEXT NUMBER
                     40   END

Write down the sequence that this program generates.

Answer 10   FOR NUMBER = 1 TO 6   means we take the value of NUMBER to be first 1, then 2, then 3, then 4, then 5, then 6.

20   PRINT NUMBER * NUMBER   means that for each value of NUMBER, the number is multiplied by itself and the result printed.

30   NEXT NUMBER   means that as soon as a calculation has been done and printed out, the next value of NUMBER is taken, the calculation done and printed. This happens until we reach our last value of NUMBER i.e. until NUMBER = 6.

40   END   means that when the last value of NUMBER has been taken and the calculation done and printed, the program finishes.

The following table gives each value of NUMBER and NUMBER * NUMBER.

NUMBER	1	2	3	4	5	6
NUMBER * NUMBER	1	4	9	16	25	36

The sequence generated is 1, 4, 9, 16, 25, 36.

EXERCISE 6:10

Write down the sequences generated by these programs.

1. 10   FOR NUMBER = 1 TO 5
    20   PRINT 2 * NUMBER
    30   NEXT NUMBER
    40   END

2.   10   FOR NUMBER = 1 TO 10
    20   PRINT NUMBER + 2
    30   NEXT NUMBER
    40   END

3. 10   FOR NUMBER = 3 TO 8
   20   PRINT NUMBER * NUMBER
   30   NEXT NUMBER
   40   END

4. 10   FOR NUMBER = 10 TO 20
   20   PRINT NUMBER − 3
   30   NEXT NUMBER
   40   END

5. 10   FOR NUMBER = 1 TO 5
   20   PRINT NUMBER ∧ 3
   30   NEXT NUMBER
   40   END

6. 10   FOR NUMBER = 1 TO 4
   20   PRINT 2 * NUMBER + 1
   30   NEXT NUMBER
   40   END

Review   10   FOR NUMBER = 2 TO 8
           20   PRINT 3 * NUMBER
           30   NEXT NUMBER
           40   END

WRITING PROGRAMS for SEQUENCES

Worked Example   4, 8, 12, . . .
           Write a program to print the first 100 terms of this sequence.

Answer   4 is 1×4
        8 is 2×4
      12 is 3×4

The sequence of 100 terms is formed by multiplying each of the numbers 1, 2, 3, . . . 100 by 4.
A suitable program would be:

   10   FOR NUMBER = 1 TO 100
   20   PRINT 4 * NUMBER
   30   NEXT NUMBER
   40   END

Worked Example 8, 12, 16, 20, . . .

Write a program to print the first 20 terms of this sequence.

Answer 8 is 2 × 4
12 is 3 × 4
16 is 4 × 4

The sequence of 20 terms is formed by multiplying each of the numbers 2, 3, 4, . . . 21 by 4.

A suitable program would be:

10   FOR NUMBER = 2 TO 21
20   PRINT 4 * NUMBER
30   NEXT NUMBER
40   END

EXERCISE 6:11

Write programs to print the following sequences.

1. The first 50 terms of 3, 6, 9, 12, . . .

2. The first 500 terms of 2, 4, 6, 8, . . .

3. The first 100 terms of 4, 6, 8, 10, . . .

4. The first 200 terms of 15, 20, 25, 30, . . .

Review The first 100 terms of 6, 8, 10, 12, . . .

INVESTIGATION 6:12

GENERATING SEQUENCES on the COMPUTER

What sequences are generated by the following programs? **Investigate.**

```
10  FOR NUMBER = 1 TO 5        10  FOR NUMBER = 1 TO 5
20  PRINT 3 * NUMBER – 2       20  PRINT 3 * NUMBER + 2
30  NEXT NUMBER                30  NEXT NUMBER
40  END                        40  END
```

Investigate to find suitable programs to print a number of terms of the following sequences.

1, 5, 9, 13, . . .   3, 7, 11, 15, . . .   2, 7, 12, 17, . . .

Investigate using a spreadsheet to generate sequences.

	A	B	C	D	
1	1	(A1 * 3)	(A1 * A1)	(A1 + 3)	
2	2	(A2 * 3)	(A2 * A2)	(A2 + 3)	
3	3	(A3 * 3)	(A3 * A3)	(A3 + 3)	

PUZZLE 6:13

Which three numbers could complete this number square?

Discuss with your neighbour or group or class.

2	4			
2	3	4	3	2
3	1	3	1	2
3	4	4	3	2
4	3	2	1	1

FOR YOUR INTEREST

LUCKY NUMBERS

Find all the Lucky Numbers between 1 and 100 as follows.

Step 1   Write down all the numbers from 1 to 100.

1	2	3	4	5	6	7	8	9	10
11	12	13	14	15	16	17	18	19	20
21	22	23	24	25	26	27	28	29	30
31	32	33	34	35	36	37	38	39	40
41	42	43	44	45	46	47	48	49	50
51	52	53	54	55	56	57	58	59	60
61	62	63	64	65	66	67	68	69	70
71	72	73	74	75	76	77	78	79	80
81	82	83	84	85	86	87	88	89	90
91	92	93	94	95	96	97	98	99	100

continued . . .

. . . from previous page

***Step* 2** Circle the first number.

The first row will then be ① 2　3　4　5　6　7　8　9　10.

The first number not circled is **2**.
Counting from 1, cross out every **2nd** number.
The first four rows will then be

   ① 2̸　3　4̸　5　6̸　7　8̸　9　1̸0̸

   11　1̸2̸　13　1̸4̸　15　1̸6̸　17　1̸8̸　19　2̸0̸

   21　2̸2̸　23　2̸4̸　25　2̸6̸　27　2̸8̸　29　3̸0̸

   31　3̸2̸　33　3̸4̸　35　3̸6̸　37　3̸8̸　39　4̸0̸

***Step* 3** The first number not circled or crossed out is **3**.
Circle this number.
Counting from 1, cross out every **3rd** number not crossed out.
The first four rows will then be

   ① 2̸　③　4̸　5̸　6̸　7　8̸　9　1̸0̸

   1̸1̸　1̸2̸　13　14　15　1̸6̸　1̸7̸　1̸8̸　19　2̸0̸

   21　2̸2̸　2̸3̸　2̸4̸　25　2̸6̸　27　2̸8̸　2̸9̸　3̸0̸

   31　3̸2̸　33　3̸4̸　3̸5̸　3̸6̸　37　3̸8̸　39　4̸0̸

***Step* 4** The first number not circled or crossed out is **7**.
Circle this number.
Counting from 1, cross out every **7th** number not crossed out.
The first four rows will then be

   ① 2̸　③　4̸　5̸　6̸　⑦　8̸　9　1̸0̸

   1̸1̸　1̸2̸　13　14　15　1̸6̸　1̸7̸　1̸8̸　1̸9̸　2̸0̸

   21　2̸2̸　2̸3̸　2̸4̸　25　2̸6̸　27　2̸8̸　2̸9̸　3̸0̸

   31　3̸2̸　33　3̸4̸　3̸5̸　3̸6̸　37　3̸8̸　3̸9̸　4̸0̸

***Steps* 5, 6, 7, . . .** Continue like this until all the numbers are either circled or crossed out.

The circled numbers are Lucky Numbers.
Investigate Lucky Numbers.
You could look for patterns.
You could investigate the sums or differences of Lucky Numbers.
You could find all the Lucky Numbers which are smaller than 1000.

DISCOVER, DISCUSS, DO

- Marty and Adam are making pickles.
  Marty made 2 litres more than Adam.
  Altogether, they made 18 litres.
  How much did Marty make? **Discuss.**

  What if Marty made twice as much as Adam?

  What if Marty made four litres less than Adam?

  What if Marty made three litres less than twice what Adam made?

- Ali and Jake needed £15·00 to pay for a meal. Ali paid £7 more than Jake. How much did Jake pay? **Discuss.**

  What if Ali paid £3 more than Jake?

  What if Ali paid half as much as Jake?

  What if Ali paid £3 more than three times as much as Jake?

- Elizabeth and Cameron live 24km apart. They ran to meet each other. Cameron ran 4km further than Elizabeth. How far did Elizabeth run? **Discuss.**

  What if Elizabeth ran 2km less than Cameron?

  What if Elizabeth ran three times as far as Cameron?

  What if Elizabeth ran 12km more than twice as far as Cameron?

FORMULAE and EQUATIONS

	List 1		List 2

List 1	**List 2**
$S = N + 1$	$2x = 8$
$L = a + 4$	$n + 2 = 11$
$H = 2h$	$3h - 1 = 17$
$P = 2(l + b)$	$\dfrac{c}{2} = 4$

In **List 1** we have **formulae**. We can find many different values for S or L or H or P. For instance, the value of S depends on the value of N. If $N = 1$ then $S = 2$, if $N = 3$ then $S = 4$, if $N = 9$ then $S = 10$ etc.

In **List 2** we have **equations**. Only one value can be found for x or n or h or c. In each of these equations there is only one thing we do not know. In the first equation this is x, in the second it is n, in the third it is h, in the fourth it is c.

DISCUSSION EXERCISE 7:1

- It is quite easy to find the number that n represents in equations such as those shown in the box.

  For $n + 4 = 9$ we can say to ourselves "4 added to what number gives 9" to get an answer of 5 for n.

  For $3n = 6$ we can say to ourselves "3 multiplied by what number gives 6" to get an answer of 2 for n.

$n + 4 = 9$
$3n = 6$

  It is a little more difficult to find the number that n represents in equations such as $2n - 3 = 7$ and even more difficult in an equation such as $5n + 2 = 6$.
  Discuss ways of finding the value of n if $2n - 3 = 7$ or if $5n + 2 = 6$.

- Yesterday, Sarah loaned me some books. Today she loaned me 4 more. Altogether she loaned me 11 books. I could write an equation for the number of books Sarah loaned me yesterday. It could be $n + 4 = 11$.

What other situations can you think of for which you could write an equation?
Discuss with your neighbour or group or class.

WRITING EQUATIONS

Worked Example Take a number, multiply it by 2. The answer is 8.
Write this as an equation.

Answer Let the number be x.
x multiplied by 2 is 2x.
We are told the answer is 8 so we have 2x = 8.

Worked Example Gregg bought a number of disco tickets.
He paid £2 for each of them. The total
cost was £8.
Write an equation for this.

Answer Let the number of disco tickets that Gregg bought
be x.
The cost of x tickets at £2 each is £2x.
We are told the total cost was £8, so £2x = £8 or
2x = 8.

Worked Example When 2 is added to a number the answer is 11.
Write an equation for this.

Answer Let the number be n.
2 added to n is n + 2.
We are told the answer is 11 so we have n + 2 = 11.

Worked Example Louise took a number of pencils from her pencil case.
Only 2 pencils remained in her case.
Before she took the pencils out there were 11 pencils in her pencil
case.
Write an equation for this.

Answer Let n be the number of pencils Louise took out.
Altogether she must have n + 2 pencils.
We are told she has 11 altogether so n + 2 = 11.

Worked Example There were 3 queues, with the same number of people in each, at the supermarket checkouts. When 1 person left one of these queues there were 17 people left.
Write an equation for this.

Answer Let there be h people in each of the queues.
In the 3 queues there must have been 3h people.
When 1 person left the queues the number left would be 3h – 1.
We are told there were 17 people left so 3h – 1 = 17.

Worked Example Winstone's group was divided into two to make equation wheels. Four students worked on each of the equation wheels.
Write an equation for this.

Answer Let the number of students in Winstone's group be c.
When the group is divided into two there will be $\frac{c}{2}$ students in each smaller group.
We are told there are 4 students in these smaller groups so $\frac{c}{2} = 4$.

DISCUSSION EXERCISE 7:2

- This is the list of equations that was on **page 121**.

$$2x = 8$$
$$n + 2 = 11$$
$$3h - 1 = 17$$
$$\frac{c}{2} = 4$$

Compare the equations from this list with the previous Worked Examples.
Discuss with your neighbour or group.

-

$$3a = 21$$
$$a - 3 = 2$$
$$2h + 3 = 7$$
$$\frac{x}{4} = 9$$

Invent problems for each of these equations.
Discuss.

EXERCISE 7:3

Write equations for each of the following. In each, let the unknown be n.

1. When a number is multiplied by 3 the answer is 15.

2. Two less than a number is 7.

3. When a number is divided by 5 the answer is 2.

4. Three more than a number is 15.

5. Three more than twice a number is 15.

6. Twice the length of a hedge is 14 metres.
   (n is the length of the hedge.)

7. When Fred divided his height by 4 the answer was 42cm. (n is Fred's height.)

8. When Allanah doubles her lucky number and then adds 4, she gets an answer of 30. (n is Allanah's lucky number.)

9. When a class of 29 students is divided into 5 groups, one of the groups has one fewer students than the other groups. (n is the number of students in each of the equal sized groups.)

10. When Ann divided a box of 28 chocolates between her three friends there was just one chocolate left for her.
    (n is the number of chocolates Ann gave to each of her friends.)

Review 1   Five less than twice a number is 11.

Review 2   Andrew told Ann that if he multiplied his house number by 3 and then subtracted 5, the answer was 19. (n is Andrew's house number.)

SOLVING EQUATIONS: Trial and Improvement

Solving an equation means we find the value of the unknown.

There are many methods of solving equations.
One method is by using **trial and improvement.**

Worked Example Use trial and improvement to find the value of n if $2n + 3 = 18$.

Answer Try n = 10.   Then $2n + 3 = 2 \times 10 + 3$
$= 23$ which is too large.
Try n = 5.   Then $2n + 3 = 2 \times 5 + 3$
$= 13$ which is too small.
Try n = 7.   Then $2n + 3 = 2 \times 7 + 3$
$= 17$ which is too small.
Try n = 8.   Then $2n + 3 = 2 \times 8 + 3$
$= 19$ which is too large.
Try n = 7·5.   Then $2n + 3 = 2 \times 7·5 + 3$
$= 18$ which is correct.
The solution of $2n + 3 = 18$ is n = 7·5.

EXERCISE 7:4

Use trial and improvement to solve these equations.

1. (a) $2n + 5 = 11$　(b) $3a - 5 = 16$　(c) $5x - 1 = 29$
   (d) $4a + 3 = 13$　(e) $2x - 5 = 4$　(f) $4n + 1 = 7$
   (g) $17 - 2a = 11$　(h) $5 + 4x = 19$　(i) $19 - 3a = 13$
   (j) $11 + 6a = 14$　(k) $1 + 2n = 12$

2. (a) $\frac{n}{5} = 9$　(b) $\frac{x}{3} = 8$　(c) $\frac{2x}{3} = 6$　(d) $\frac{2a}{3} = 1$　(e) $\frac{5a}{2} = 3$
   (f) $\frac{2a}{7} = 3$　(g) $\frac{4n}{5} = 3$

3. (a) $\frac{n+3}{2} = 5$　(b) $\frac{n-5}{3} = 2$　(c) $\frac{2a-1}{3} = 5$
   (d) $\frac{3a+1}{5} = 5$　(e) $\frac{19-x}{2} = 7$　(f) $\frac{4x-4}{5} = 2$
   (g) $\frac{2a+8}{7} = 3$　(h) $\frac{25-6n}{2} = 5$

Review (a) $4a - 15 = 11$　(b) $4 + 3n = 31$　(c) $\frac{5a}{4} = 3$
   (d) $\frac{7-n}{3} = 1$　(e) $\frac{4x-1}{3} = 7$

125

SOLVING EQUATIONS: Flowchart method

In the **flowchart method** we use the facts that multiplication and division are inverse operations as are addition and subtraction. This means that to "undo" a multiplication we divide, to "undo" a division we multiply, to "undo" an addition we subtract and to "undo" a subtraction we add.

Worked Example   Use the flowchart method to find the value of n if $2n + 3 = 18$.

Answer   Begin with n $\longrightarrow$ $\boxed{\times 2}$ $\longrightarrow$ 2n $\longrightarrow$ $\boxed{+3}$ $\longrightarrow$ 2n + 3

7·5 $\longleftarrow$ $\boxed{\div 2}$ $\longleftarrow$ 15 $\longleftarrow$ $\boxed{-3}$ $\longleftarrow$ Begin with 18

The solution of $2n + 3 = 18$ is n = 7·5.

Note   We write the first line from left to right, beginning with x. We list each operation that is performed and the results of these operations. We finish when we have the complete left-hand side of the equation.

We write the second line from right to left, beginning with the right-hand side of the equation. Each operation that is listed is the inverse of the operation directly above, on the first line. As we progress from right to left we perform each of these operations and list the results. We finish when we have performed all the operations. The number we have at the finish is the solution of the equation.

EXERCISE 7:5

1. Brady used the flow chart method to solve the equations
    $x + 5 = 8$, $2x = 9$, $4n - 1 = 9$, $4 + 3n = 19$, $\frac{4n}{3} = 11$ and $\frac{x}{2} + 3 = 7$.

    The first line of each flow chart is shown. Copy this and write down the second line. Give the solution of each equation.

    (a) $x + 5 = 8$
         Begin with x $\longrightarrow$ $\boxed{+5}$ $\longrightarrow$ x + 5

    (b) $2x = 9$
         Begin with x $\longrightarrow$ $\boxed{\times 2}$ $\longrightarrow$ 2x

    (c) $4n - 1 = 9$
         Begin with n $\longrightarrow$ $\boxed{\times 4}$ $\longrightarrow$ 4n $\longrightarrow$ $\boxed{-1}$ $\longrightarrow$ 4n - 1

(d) $4 + 3n = 19$

Begin with n $\longrightarrow$ $\boxed{\times 3}$ $\longrightarrow$ $3n$ $\longrightarrow$ $\boxed{+4}$ $\longrightarrow$ $4 + 3n$

(e) $\frac{4n}{3} = 11$

Begin with n $\longrightarrow$ $\boxed{\times 4}$ $\longrightarrow$ $4n$ $\longrightarrow$ $\boxed{\div 3}$ $\longrightarrow$ $\frac{4n}{3}$

(f) $\frac{x}{2} + 3 = 7$

Begin with x $\longrightarrow$ $\boxed{\div 2}$ $\longrightarrow$ $\frac{x}{2}$ $\longrightarrow$ $\boxed{+3}$ $\longrightarrow$ $\frac{x}{2} + 3$

2. Use flow charts to solve these equations.

(a) $n + 2 = 9$ (b) $3 + a = 7$ (c) $2x = 17$

(d) $5n = 11$ (e) $\frac{x}{4} = 3$ (f) $\frac{n}{2} = 5$

(g) $3x - 2 = 13$ (h) $3 + 2a = 6$ (i) $4n - 3 = 19$

(j) $1 + 5n = 3$ (k) $\frac{2x}{3} = 3$ (l) $\frac{5n}{4} = 3$

(m) $23 - 6a = 8$ (n) $5n - 4 = 7$ (o) $3a + 2 = 14$

(p) $\frac{n}{2} - 3 = 2$ (q) $\frac{2n}{5} + 1 = 4$ (r) $1 + 4n = 3$

(s) $17 - 2a = 2$ (t) $3a - 7 = 38$

Review Copy this chart.

| 9 | 14 | 4 | 5 | 10 | 7 | 13 | 3 |

| 7 | **D** | 2 | 6 |
| | 1 | | |

| 14 | 2 | 4 | 12 | 10 | 11 | 8 | 7 |

Match the equations in Box A with their solutions in Box B. Complete the chart. For instance, since the solution to $n - 5 = 8$ is 13   then 1. matches with **D**. **D** is filled in for you.

Read your completed chart, from right to left.

Box A

1. $n - 5 = 8$	8. $4n = 2$
2. $3 + n = 21$	9. $2a - 9 = 11$
3. $5n = 15$	10. $7a - 4 = 10$
4. $\frac{n}{4} = 2$	11. $\frac{2a}{3} = 5$
5. $3x + 1 = 19$	12. $1 + 2n = 10$
6. $7 + n = 11$	13. $3 + 4x = 9$
7. $\frac{x}{6} + 1 = 3$	14. $\frac{a}{3} - 2 = 3$

Box B

A. 2	K. 6
B. 3	N. 15
C. 4	O. 18
D. 13	Q. 0·5
E. 12	R. 1·5
G. 10	T. 4·5
I. 8	U. 7·5

PRACTICAL EXERCISE 7:6

1. Make a poster of equations where the numbers and the symbols you use are pictures.

For instance,   =   could be

8   could be

2. Make and use an equation wheel as follows:

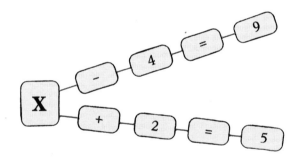

Equipment: Cardboard and string.

Making the Equation Wheel: Draw a large **x** on a piece of cardboard. Using smaller pieces of cardboard, make 8 or 12 spokes of equations (2 spokes are shown). Use string to assemble the spokes.
Pin the equation wheel to the classroom wall.

Using the Equation Wheel: Each group could make an equation wheel. Then a competition could be held to solve all the equations on all the wheels.
The winner or winning group is the first to correctly solve all the equations.

Variation: The numbers can be made interchangeable by writing them on velcro. The equation wheels can then be used for many different competitions.

The x could be replaced with 2x or 3x etc.

CHECKING SOLUTIONS

Always check your solution by substituting it back into the equation.

Worked Example Jocelyn's solution for the equation 5x – 13 = 3 was 3·2. Andrew's solution was 4. Who got the correct solution?

Answer Check Andrew's solution: If x = 4, then 5x – 13 = 5 × 4 – 13
$$= 7$$
Andrew's solution is not correct.

Check Jocelyn's solution: If x = 3·2, then 5x – 13 = 5 × 3·2 – 13
$$= 3$$
Jocelyn's solution is correct.

EXERCISE 7:7

1. Who got the correct solution?

   (a) For 4a + 3 = 15, Tina got a = 3 and Michael got a = 4·5.

   (b) For $\frac{n}{2}$ = 8, Victoria got n = 4 and Ann got n = 16.

   (c) For 3 (x – 5) = 9, James got x = 3 and Kojo got x = 8.

   (d) For 7a – 2a = 14, William got a = 2 and Sara got a = 2·8.

   (e) For 3x – 5 = 15, Jon got x = 5 and Holly got x = 3.

2. Use a method of your choice to solve these equations.
   Check your answer.

   (a) 2n = 17   (b) a – 3 = 16   (c) 2x + 7 = 9   (d) 4n – 1 = 5

   (e) 3a – 7 = 11   (f) 5n + 3 = 5   (g) $\frac{n}{4}$ = 3   (h) $\frac{2x}{5}$ = 3

   (i) 5n – 3 = 6   (j) $\frac{3x}{4}$ = 15

Review Solve these equations.

Find the solutions on the diagram.

Trace the diagram and shade those sections which contain the solutions.

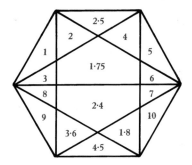

(a) $2a = 5$ (b) $x - 4 = 2$ (c) $\frac{n}{4} = 2$

(d) $3x = 9$ (e) $5n - 5 = 7$ (f) $\frac{4n}{3} = 6$

(g) $\frac{2a}{7} = 2$ (h) $4x + 3 = 10$

SOLVING EQUATIONS: Balance method

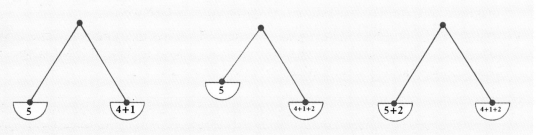

An equation remains true if the same number is added to (or subtracted from) both sides or if both sides are multiplied (or divided) by the same number.

Worked Example Use the balance method to solve $x + 2 = 14$.

Answer

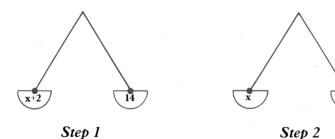

Step 1   **Step 2**

Step 1 The equation $x + 2 = 14$ is shown balanced.

Step 2 2 is taken from the left-hand pan of the balance to leave x.

2 must also be taken from the right-hand pan to keep the pans balanced.

The solution of $x + 2 = 14$ is $x = 12$.

130

DISCUSSION EXERCISE 7:8

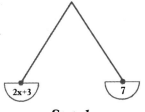 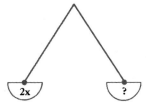 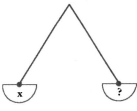

Step 1   *Step 2*   *Step 3*

Copy the above diagrams.
Discuss what goes in the right-hand pan in *Step 2* and *Step 3*.

Draw diagrams to solve the equations $2x = 10$, $\frac{x}{2} = 5$, $4x - 1 = 7$. **Discuss** with your group or class or neighbour.

• **The answer is 5.** Make up some equations which have the solution $n = 5$. Draw diagrams to show that the solution is indeed $n = 5$. **Discuss.**

• **Think of any number.** Make up an equation which has this number as the solution. Ask the rest of your group or your neighbour to solve this equation. **Discuss.** Repeat this several times for other numbers.

EXERCISE 7:9

Use the balance method to solve these equations.

1. (a) $n + 6 = 8$
   (b) $x - 5 = 4$
   (c) $a - 3 = 1$
   (d) $\frac{n}{3} = 5$
   (e) $\frac{a}{6} = 1$
   (f) $\frac{x}{2} = 5$
   (g) $3 + n = 4$
   (h) $1 + n = 3$

2. (a) $2a + 1 = 7$
   (b) $3a - 2 = 10$
   (c) $3n + 4 = 19$
   (d) $3 + 4a = 5$
   (e) $1 + 2a = 13$
   (f) $2 + 5a = 3$

3. (a) $\frac{2x}{3} = 4$
   (b) $\frac{3x}{2} = 9$
   (c) $\frac{4a}{3} = 1$
   (d) $\frac{5n}{2} = 2$
   (e) $\frac{4a}{5} = 2$
   (f) $\frac{2n}{5} = 3$

4. (a) $\frac{x}{2} + 1 = 5$
   (b) $\frac{n}{3} - 1 = 3$
   (c) $\frac{a}{5} + 3 = 5$
   (d) $2 + \frac{n}{2} = 3$
   (e) $3 + \frac{n}{4} = 5$

5. (a) $x + 2 = 9$
   (b) $\frac{x}{2} = 9$
   (c) $2x = 9$
   (d) $2x - 5 = 1$
   (e) $2 + 5x = 4$
   (f) $1 + \frac{x}{5} = 2$

Review (a) $3 + n = 5$ **(b)** $6n = 3$ **(c)** $2n - 1 = 6$

(d) $\frac{x}{3} = 2$ **(e)** $1 + 2x = 7$ **(f)** $\frac{x}{4} - 3 = 1$

(g) $\frac{2a}{7} = 5$ **(h)** $2a + 3 = 8$ **(i)** $3 + 5a = 5$

(j) $5n - 7 = 1$

EXERCISE 7:10

Use a method of your choice to solve the equations in this exercise.

1.
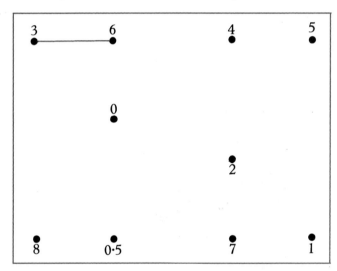

Trace the diagram given above.

Solve the equations given below.
Find the answers on the diagram.
Join the answer of **(a)** to the answer to **(b)**; join the answer of **(b)** to the answer of **(c)** and so on, finally joining the answer of **(j)** to the answer of **(k)**.
For instance, the answer of **(a)** is 3 and the answer of **(b)** is 6. On the diagram 3 is shown joined to 6.

(a) $2n = 6$ **(b)** $n + 1 = 7$ **(c)** $n - 1 = 1$ **(d)** $4n = 16$

(e) $2n - 1 = 9$ **(f)** $4n + 3 = 7$ **(g)** $2n - 3 = 11$ **(h)** $n + 3 = 3$

(i) $4n = 2$ **(j)** $\frac{n}{2} = 4$ **(k)** $n + 1 = 4$

What is the completed shape?

2. (a) $\frac{n}{5} = 4$ (b) $\frac{5n}{4} = 1$ (c) $5n - 4 = 1$

(d) $1 + 5n = 4$ (e) $\frac{n}{4} - 5 = 1$ (f) $\frac{n}{4} + 1 = 5$

(g) $2a - 3 = 5$ (h) $2a + 3 = 5$ (i) $2 + 3a = 5$

(j) $\frac{2a}{3} = 5$ (k) $\frac{5a}{2} = 3$ (l) $\frac{a}{3} + 2 = 5$

(m) $5x = 9$ (n) $4 + 5x = 9$ (o) $\frac{5x}{4} = 9$

(p) $\frac{4x}{9} + 2 = 5$ (q) $2 + \frac{5x}{9} = 5$ (r) $5x - 9 = 4$

(s) $4x - 5 = 9$

Review Copy the crossnumber.
Complete it by solving the equations given below.

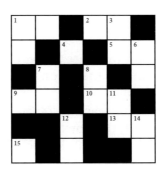

Across

1. $n - 7 = 4$
2. $\frac{n}{7} = 3$
5. $n - 20 = 12$
9. $n - 10 = 3$
10. $\frac{n}{3} = 14$
13. $2n - 1 = 41$
15. $\frac{n}{3} + 4 = 5$

Down

1. $\frac{3n}{4} + 1 = 10$
3. $n + 3 = 16$
4. $3n = 12$
6. $\frac{2n}{3} = 16$
7. $2 + n = 15$
8. $n - 1 = 13$
11. $2n = 44$
12. $1 + 2n = 21$
14. $2n - 3 = 19$

FURTHER EQUATIONS

Worked Example Solve $2a + a = 15$.

Answer
$$2a + a = 15$$
$$3a = 15$$

Now trial and improvement, the flowchart method or the balance method can be used to get $a = 5$. The complete solution using a shortened version of the balance method is:

$$2a + a = 15$$
$$3a = 15$$
$$a = 5 \quad \text{(dividing both sides by 3)}$$

Worked Example Solve $2(n - 3) = 7$.

Answer $2(n - 3) = 7$
$$2n - 6 = 7$$

Now trial and improvement, the flowchart method or the balance method can be used to get $n = 6.5$. The complete solution using a shortened version of the balance method is:

$$2(n - 3) = 7$$
$$2n - 6 = 7 \quad \text{(removing the brackets)}$$
$$2n = 13 \quad \text{(adding 6 to both sides)}$$
$$n = 6.5 \quad \text{(dividing both sides by 2)}$$

Worked Example Solve $7x - 3 = 2x + 9$.

Answer Notice that in this equation there are x's on both sides. We usually begin by getting all the x's on just one side.

$$7x - 3 = 2x + 9$$
$$5x - 3 = 9 \quad \text{(subtracting 2x from both sides)}$$

Now trial and improvement, the flowchart method or the balance method can be used to get $x = 2.4$. The complete solution using a shortened version of the balance method is:

$$7x - 3 = 2x + 9$$
$$5x - 3 = 9 \quad \text{(subtracting 2x from both sides)}$$
$$5x = 12 \quad \text{(adding 3 to both sides)}$$
$$x = 2.4 \quad \text{(dividing both sides by 5)}$$

Worked Example Solve $2(3x - 5) - x = 4$.

Answer $2(3x - 5) - x = 4$
$$6x - 10 - x = 4$$
$$5x - 10 = 4$$

Now trial and improvement, the flowchart method or the balance method can be used to get $x = 2.8$. The complete solution using the balance method is:

$$2(3x - 5) - x = 4$$
$$6x - 10 - x = 4$$
$$5x - 10 = 4$$
$$5x = 14 \quad \text{(adding 10 to both sides)}$$
$$x = 2.8 \quad \text{(dividing both sides by 5)}$$

Worked Example Solve the equation $\frac{8+3x}{2} = 7$.

Answer Trial and improvement, the flowchart method or the balance method can be used to get x = 2. Using the balance method, the solution is:

$$\frac{8+3x}{2} = 7$$

$$8 + 3x = 14 \qquad \text{(multiplying both sides by 2)}$$

$$3x = 6 \qquad \text{(subtracting 8 from both sides)}$$

$$x = 2 \qquad \text{(dividing both sides by 3)}$$

DISCUSSION EXERCISE 7:11

$$2a + a = 15 \qquad 2(n-3) = 7 \qquad 7x - 3 = 2x + 9 \qquad 2(3x-5) - x = 4 \qquad \frac{8+3x}{2} = 7$$

These equations were solved in the Worked Examples using the balance method. Do you think it would have been better to have used trial and improvement or the flowchart method? **Discuss.**
As part of your discussion, solve these using one, or both, of these other methods.

EXERCISE 7:12

1.

			C														C			
11	3	6	2	1	3	4	2	8	7	11	9	11	9	7	5	2	10	2	4	1	7	5	2

Copy the code-breaker.

Use a method of your choice to solve the equations in **Box A**. Match the equations with their solutions from **Box B** and fill in the code-breaker. For instance, 1. matches with **C** so **C** is filled in as shown.

Box A

1. $3(n-1) = 9$	2. $3n = 5 + n$
3. $5n - 3n = 18$	4. $3n + 1 = 2n + 7$
5. $2(2n+1) = 5$	6. $5n - 4 = 3 + 4n$
7. $5n - n = 7$	8. $8n - 4 = 5 - n$
9. $3n = 8 - 2n$	10. $4(n-3) + n = 13$
11. $1 + 2n = 5$	

Box B

A. 9	R. 6
C. 4	S. 0·75
E. 2·5	T. 2
H. 1·6	W. 1
I. 1·75	X. 5
K. 7	

135

2. Use a method of your choice to solve the following equations.

(a) $7a - 3a = 12$

(b) $5a = a + 2$

(c) $4p - 7 = 5 + p$

(d) $7x + 2 = 5 - 3x$

(e) $2(x - 4) = 3$

(f) $5(2a - 3) = 21$

(g) $2(3 + 2a) = 9$

(h) $2(4 + 5p) = 19$

(i) $3n + 2 = n + 5$

(j) $3n - 1 = 6 - n$

(k) $5(x - 4) = x$

(l) $2(2x - 3) = 3x$

(m) $5n + 2 = n + 7$

3. Solve these equations.

(a) $2(5 + x) - 13 = 4$

(b) $4 + 5(2x - 1) = 9$

(c) $3(2x + 1) + 4x = 9$

(d) $3x + 2(3 + x) = 8$

(e) $5 + 2(1 + 2x) = 8$

(f) $5(2x - 3) - 4 = 0$

(g) $5x + 3(4 - x) = 17$

(h) $4(3 + 2x) = 13 - 2x$

(i) $3(2 + 3x) = 7(1 + x)$

(j) $2(3x - 5) = 4(5 - x) + 6$

4. Find the value of n.

(a) $\frac{n - 5}{3} = 4$

(b) $\frac{2n + 1}{2} = 3$

(c) $\frac{3 + 2n}{3} = 2$

(d) $\frac{3n - 1}{5} = 10$

(e) $\frac{4 + 2n}{5} = 1$

(f) $\frac{4n - 5}{2} = 5$

(g) $\frac{5 + 2n}{5} = 1$

5. Using the method of your choice, find the value of x.

(a) $2x + 3 = 8$

(b) $2(x + 3) = 8$

(c) $\frac{2x}{3} = 6$

(d) $3x - 1 = 2 - x$

(e) $5x - x = 1$

(f) $\frac{x}{4} + 2 = 5$

(g) $\frac{x + 3}{4} = 1$

(h) $4x = 7 - x$

(i) $2(5x - 2) - 3 = 4$

(j) $5(1 + 2x) = 13$

(k) $5x - 3 = 3x$

(l) $\frac{2 + 5x}{3} = 4$

(m) $\frac{4x}{3} = 7$

(n) $3x - 1 = 1 - x$

(o) $6x = 3 + 5x$

(p) $3(x - 5) + 1 = 4$

(q) $\frac{6x - 1}{2} = 2x$

(r) $2(4x - 2) = 3(5 + 2x)$

(s) $\frac{2(5x + 1)}{5} = 5$

(t) $3(2x - 1) = x$

Review Solve these equations.

(a) $6n - 2 = 3 - 4n$

(b) $4(5x - 3) = 2$

(c) $3(1 + 2x) - x = 7$

(d) $5a = 3a + 1$

(e) $\frac{3+n}{2} = 9$

(f) $6n - 3 = 4 + n$

(g) $\frac{3+2x}{5} = 3$

(h) $2 + 5(3 + 2n) = 19$

(i) $\frac{5x-1}{4} = 3$

(j) $5 + 2(2x - 7) = 0$

(k) $3(4x - 1) = 5(3 + 2x)$

INVESTIGATION 7:13

SOLVING EQUATIONS

Consider the equation $2x = 8$.

This equation may be solved as follows:

Step 1 Let x be equal to any number, say $x = 5$.

Step 2 Multiply the value you gave to x by 2, the number on the left-hand side of the equation. The result is $5 \times 2 = 10$.

Step 3 Divide the number on the right-hand side of the equation by the result of **step 2**. We get $8 \div 10 = 0·8$.

Step 4 Multiply the result of **step 3** by the original guess in step 1. The result is $0·8 \times 5 = 4$.

The result of all of the above steps is 4. $x = 4$ is the solution of the equation $2x = 8$! That is, this seems to be a way to solve $2x = 8$. Was putting $x = 5$ in step 1 just lucky?

What if x = 10 in step 1?

What if x = 2 in step 1?

What if . . .

Can you use a method similar to that shown above to solve $3x = 12$? **Investigate.**

What if we began with the equation $\frac{x}{4} = 5$?

What if we began with the equation $2x + 3 = 8$?

What if . . .

PROBLEM SOLVING

DISCUSSION EXERCISE 7:14

- I am thinking of a number.
  I add 4.
  I double the result.
  The answer is 22.

  Write an equation for n, the number I am thinking of.

  Solve this equation to find the number.

- Take it in turns to make up similar "I am thinking of a number" problems.

  Have the rest of the group **discuss** how to write an equation for each problem.

  Discuss how to solve each equation.

Solving an equation is a useful technique for problem solving. This technique can be used if the information given in the problem can be written as an equation.

Worked Example When 14-year-old Garth asked 13-year-old Brian what his house number was, Brian replied "Three subtracted from double my house number gives the sum of our ages". What is Brian's house number?

Answer Let Brian's house number be n.
Three subtracted from double n is $2n - 3$.
The sum of Garth's and Brian's ages is 27.
The equation is $2n - 3 = 27$.
This equation may now be solved by a method of your choice to get $n = 15$.

Check Double 15 is 30.
3 subtracted from 30 is 27.
The sum of 14 and 13 is 27.

The previous Worked Example shows the steps that should be taken to solve a problem using equations. These are:

Step 1   Choose a variable such as n or a or x for the unknown quantity.

Step 2   Rewrite the statements in mathematical symbols.

Step 3   Combine these statements into an equation.

Step 4   Solve the equation.

Step 5   Check the answer with the information in the problem.

In the previous Worked Example,

Step 1 was: Let Brian's house number be n.

Step 2 was: Three subtracted from double n is $2n - 3$.
The sum of Garth's and Brian's ages is 27.

Step 3 was: The equation is $2n - 3 = 27$.

Step 4 was: Solve $2n - 3 = 27$ to get $n = 15$.

Step 5 was: Check the answer.

EXERCISE 7:15

1. **Choose the correct equation for each of the following.**

   (a) Emma had driven x kilometres. After another 5km she would have driven a total of 17km.

   A. $x + 17 = 5$ B. $x - 5 = 17$ C. $x + 5 = 17$ D. $x - 17 = 5$

   (b) Emma drove x km yesterday. After driving a further 52km today, she had driven a total of 95km.

   A. $x + 95 = 52$ B. $x - 52 = 95$ C. $x - 95 = 52$ D. $x + 52 = 95$

   (c) Emma drove 156km yesterday. Today she drove x km which was twice as far as yesterday.

   A. $\frac{x}{2} = 156$ B. $2x = 156$ C. $x + 2 = 156$ D. $x - 2 = 156$

(d) Emma drove x km yesterday. Today she drove 156km which was half the distance she drove yesterday.

    A. $\frac{x}{2} = 156$ **B.** $2x = 156$ **C.** $x + 2 = 156$ **D.** $x - 2 = 156$

(e) Emma drove 257km yesterday. She drove x km today which was 28km more than yesterday.

    A. $x + 257 = 28$ **B.** $x - 28 = 257$ **C.** $257 - x = 28$ **D.** $x + 28 = 257$

(f) Emma drove x km today. Yesterday she drove 89km which was 7km less than today.

    A. $x + 7 = 89$ **B.** $89 - x = 7$ **C.** $x - 7 = 89$ **D.** $x + 89 = 7$

2. Write equations for each of the following. Solve the equations.

(a) Twice a number plus three equals 15.

(b) The result of subtracting 5 from three times a number is 19.

(c) Adding 7 to a number is the same as subtracting 4 from double the number.

(d) The result of adding 8 to three times a number is the same as adding 12 to twice the number.

(e) Twice the result of adding 3 to a number is the same as adding 2 to three times the number.

3. Write and solve an equation to find the answer to these.

(a) Hassan and his friend have £10 between them. When Hassan gives his friend £2, they have the same amount of money. How much money did Hassan's friend have originally?

(b) A maths. class has 6 more girls than boys. Find the number of girls in this class if there are 28 students altogether.

(c) In a yacht race, the second leg is twice as long as the first. The total distance for both legs is 204km.
How long is the first leg?

(d) Ana scored 17 fewer marks for her History exam. than for her Maths. exam. If Ana got a total of 151 marks for both exams, what did she get for her Maths. exam?

(e) Two lorries arrived to deliver shingle. One lorry held three times as much shingle as the other. Together they held 16m^3.
How much shingle did the smaller lorry carry?

(f) "You are only 3 lengths short of swimming twice as far as you did last training session Diana" said her trainer. "You have swum 72 lengths in the two sessions. Well done". How far did Diana swim in her first training session?

Review 1 Subtracting 6 from five times a number is the same as adding 6 to the number. Write and solve an equation to find the number.

Review 2 Jayne had a 16cm length of liquorice. She shared this with a friend. The piece she gave her friend was 2cm less than twice the length she kept for herself. Write and solve an equation to find the length of the piece Jayne kept for herself.

PUZZLE 7:16

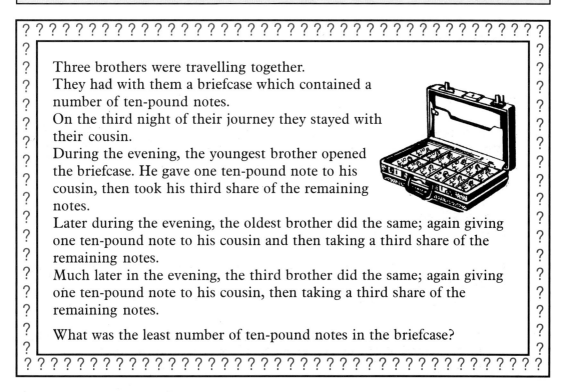

? ?

Three brothers were travelling together.
They had with them a briefcase which contained a number of ten-pound notes.
On the third night of their journey they stayed with their cousin.
During the evening, the youngest brother opened the briefcase. He gave one ten-pound note to his cousin, then took his third share of the remaining notes.
Later during the evening, the oldest brother did the same; again giving one ten-pound note to his cousin and then taking a third share of the remaining notes.
Much later in the evening, the third brother did the same; again giving one ten-pound note to his cousin, then taking a third share of the remaining notes.

What was the least number of ten-pound notes in the briefcase?

? ?

POLYNOMIAL EQUATIONS: Finding one solution.

We can find the value of x in equations involving x^2 or x^3 by using trial and improvement.

Worked Example $x^3 + 1 = 7$. Find the value of x, giving the answer accurate to 1 d.p.

Answer Try $x = 1$. Then $x^3 + 1 = 1^3 + 1$
$= 2$ which is too small.

Try $x = 3$. Then $x^3 + 1 = 3^3 + 1$
$= 28$ which is much too large.

Try $x = 2$. Then $x^3 + 1 = 2^3 + 1$
$= 9$ which is too large.

Try $x = 1.5$. Then $x^3 + 1 = 1.5^3 + 1$
$= 4.375$ which is too small.

Try $x = 1.8$. Then $x^3 + 1 = 1.8^3 + 1$
$= 6.832$ which is a little too small.

Try $x = 1.9$. Then $x^3 + 1 = 1.9^3 + 1$
$= 7.859$ which is a little too large.

We now know that x lies between 1·8 and 1·9.
We also know that x is closer to 1·8 than to 1·9 since 6·832 is closer to 7 than is 7·859.
Then, $x = 1.8$ to 1 d.p.

EXERCISE 7:17

Use trial and improvement to find the value of x in these equations. Give your answer accurate to 1 d.p.

1. $x^2 - 2 = 10$ 2. $x^2 + 2 = 24$ 3. $x^3 = 20$

4. $x^3 + 3 = 8$ 5. $4x^2 + 3 = 11$ 6. $2x^3 = 20$

7. $3x^2 - 1 = 7$ 8. $6x^3 + 2 = 25$

Review $x^3 - 4 = 15$

DISCUSSION EXERCISE 7:18

The equations in **Exercise 7:17** could have been solved by using a method other than trial and improvement. **Discuss.** *Hint:* Rewrite $x^2 - 2 = 10$ as $x^2 = 12$.

POLYNOMIAL EQUATIONS: finding all the solutions

Worked Example Use "trial and improvement" to find two solutions for the equation $2x^2 + x - 7 = 0$. (Answers to 1 d.p.)

Answer Try $x = 1$.   If $x = 1$, $2x^2 + x - 7 = -4$ which is too small.

Try $x = 2$.   If $x = 2$, $2x^2 + x - 7 = 3$ which is too large.

Try $x = 1\cdot5$.   If $x = 1\cdot5$, $2x^2 + x - 7 = -1$ which is too small.

Try $x = 1\cdot7$.   If $x = 1\cdot7$, $2x^2 + x - 7 = 0\cdot48$ which is too large.

Try $x = 1\cdot6$.   If $x = 1\cdot6$, $2x^2 + x - 7 = -0\cdot28$ which is too small.

We now know that one solution is between $1\cdot6$ and $1\cdot7$ and is closer to $1\cdot6$ than to $1\cdot7$ since $-0\cdot28$ is closer to 0 than is $0\cdot48$. We can say that, to 1 d.p., one solution is $1\cdot6$.

We have found one solution for $2x^2 + x - 7 = 0$. We will now find another.

   If $x = 2$, $2x^2 + x - 7 = 3$ which is too large.

Try $x = 3$.   If $x = 3$, $2x^2 + x - 7 = 14$ which is too large.

Try $x = 4$.   If $x = 4$, $2x^2 + x - 7 = 29$ which is even larger.

Try $x = 5$.   If $x = 5$, $2x^2 + x - 7 = 48$ which is larger still.

It seems that we are getting further and further away from 0. We will now try values of x that are less than 1.

   If $x = 1$, $2x^2 + x - 7 = -4$ which is too small.

Try $x = 0$.   If $x = 0$, $2x^2 + x - 7 = -7$ which is too small.

Try $x = -1$.   If $x = -1$, $2x^2 + x - 7 = -6$ which is too small.

Try $x = -2$.   If $x = -2$, $2x^2 + x - 7 = -1$ which is too small.

Try $x = -3$.   If $x = -3$, $2x^2 + x - 7 = 8$ which is too large.

Try $x = -2\cdot2$.   If $x = -2\cdot2$, $2x^2 + x - 7 = 0\cdot48$ which is too large.

Try $x = -2\cdot1$.   If $x = -2\cdot1$, $2x^2 + x - 7 = -0\cdot28$ which is too small.

We now know that one solution is between $-2\cdot1$ and $-2\cdot2$ and is closer to $-2\cdot1$ since $-0\cdot28$ is closer to 0 than is $0\cdot48$. We can say that, to 1 d.p., one solution is $-2\cdot1$.

Hence, to 1 d.p., the two solutions of $2x^2 + x - 7 = 0$ are $1\cdot6$ and $-2\cdot1$.

DISCUSSION EXERCISE 7:19

Halima was finding solutions for the equation $6x^2 + 7x - 24 = 0$. She set out her initial working as follows.

x	-4	-3	-2	-1	0	1	2	3
$6x^2 + 7x - 24$	44	9	-14	-25	-24	-11	14	51

From this working, Halima decided that one solution was between -3 and -2 and another was between 1 and 2. How did Halima come to this conclusion? Was she right? **Discuss.** As part of your discussion, use trial and improvement to find two solutions for the equation $6x^2 + 7x - 24 = 0$.

EXERCISE 7:20

1. Use "trial and improvement" to find solutions for the following equations. Where the solutions are not whole numbers give them to 1 d.p.

   (a) $x^2 = 10$ (two solutions)

   (b) $x^2 + 2x = 10$ (two solutions)

   (c) $2x^2 - 14x + 15 = 0$ (two solutions)

   (d) $x^2 - 3x - 4 = 0$ (two solutions)

   (e) $x^2 - 3x = 0$ (two solutions)

   (f) $4x^2 + 12x = -9$ (one solution)

   (g) $x^3 = 6$ (one solution)

   (h) $x^3 - 8x = 2$ (three solutions)

   (i) $x^3 + x^2 - 6x = 0$ (three solutions)

2. Three sections of a school are being extended to give each a floor area of 300m². The floor plans are shown below (the dimensions are in metres). The shaded areas are the extensions.

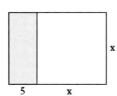 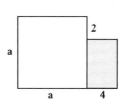 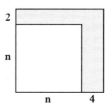

   (a) Which of these polynomial equations could be used to find **x**?

   A. $x^2 = 5x$ B. $x^2 + 5x = 300$ C. $x^2 + 5x + 300 = 0$

   (b) Which of these polynomial equations could be used to find **a**?

   A. $a^2 + 8 = 300$ B. $a^2 + 4a - 8 = 300$ C. $a^2 + 8a = 300$

   (c) Which of these polynomial equations could be used to find **n**?

   A. $n^2 + 6n + 8 = 300$ B. $n^2 + 6n = 300$ C. $n^2 + 8 = 300$

3. Solve polynomial equations to find the length of the original floor areas in question 2. That is, find x, a and n. (Give your answers to the nearest mm.)

Review Find two solutions for the equation $2x^2 - 7x + 4 = 0$.
Give the answers to 1 d.p.

PRACTICAL EXERCISE 7:21

Once Halima had used her calculator to find that one solution of the equation $6x^2 + 7x - 24 = 0$ was between -3 and -2 she then used a computer to find this solution to 2 d.p. She did this by using a spreadsheet. Calculations of $6x^2 + 7x - 24$ were made at 0.01 intervals between $x = -3$ and -2.

Use a spreadsheet in this way to find the solutions of $6x^2 + 7x - 24 = 0$ to 2 d.p.

INVESTIGATION 7:22

NUMBER of SOLUTIONS

In this investigation, you may like to use initial working similar to that in Discussion Exercise 7:19. You may like to use a spreadsheet.

Find two solutions for the equation $x^2 - 4 = 0$.

Can you find any solutions for the equation $x^2 + 4 = 0$?

Can you find more than one solution for the equation $x^2 - 9x + 3 = 0$?

Can you find more than two solutions for any equation in which the highest power of x is x^2? **Investigate.** As part of your investigation consider many equations such as $x^2 + 3x - 1 = 0$, $2x^2 - 5x + 3 = 0$, $3x^2 + 7 = 0$, $x^2 - 5x = 0$.

What is the solution to $x + 3 = 0$? How many solutions does this equation have?

What if the equation was $3x - 4 = 0$ or $5x + 1.5 = 0$?
Investigate to find the number of solutions for an equation in which the highest power of x is x.

Make and test statements about the maximum number of solutions for equations such as $x^3 + 8 = 0$, $x^3 - x^2 - 2x = 0$, $x^3 - 5x^2 + 2x + 8 = 0$; that is, equations in which the highest power of x is x^3.

You may wish to extend your investigation to equations in which the highest power of x is x^4 or x^5 or x^6 etc.

PRACTICAL EXERCISE 7:23

A spreadsheet is a useful tool to carry out calculations using "trial and improvement". It is also often used when one variable (e.g. interest rate) in a formula changes and the other variables remain the same; that is, a spreadsheet is a useful tool to answer "what if" questions.

Work as a group to produce a well researched and well presented project on the practical uses of the spreadsheet. You may like to base your project on a particular use of the spreadsheet; for instance, budgeting. You may like to consider all the uses of the spreadsheet within one industry.

Each group should initially discuss and make decisions on the following:
    what aspect of the spreadsheet the project is to be about
    how information is to be gathered
    how the project is to be presented
    what tasks are to be done by each student in the group
    what date each task is to be completed by

FOR YOUR INTEREST

- Greg and Anita played a game with counters. They both began with the same number.
  Each time one of them lost a round they had to give half of their counters to the other.
  Anita lost the first round but won the second. She then had 25 counters.
  How many counters did Anita begin with?

- The second time Greg and Anita played this game, Anita lost the first two rounds and won the third. She then had 16 counters more than Greg.
  How many counters did Anita begin with this time?

- Invent a game which uses counters.
  Make one of the rules the same rule that Greg and Anita had.

DISCOVER, DISCUSS, DO

Aaron and Anita are visiting England for two weeks in June. Before they arrived in England they had decided to do the following:

  spend a day sightseeing in London
  watch a football game
  visit museums
  spend a day at the beach
  go on an InterCity train
  visit a school for a day
  spend a weekend rambling
  go to the theatre
  fly home on the Concorde

Where, in each of their planned activities, will Aaron and Anita come across coordinates?

What other activities, which involve using coordinates, could they do?

Discuss.

READING and PLOTTING COORDINATES

The number line can be extended from the positive numbers

to the positive and negative numbers

In a similar way, the coordinate system can be extended.

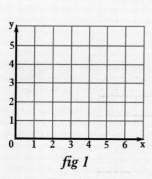

fig 1

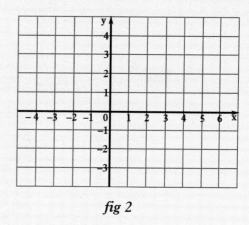

fig 2

In the coordinate system shown in *fig 1*, both the x and y-axes are number lines with just the positive numbers.

In the coordinate system shown in *fig 2*, both the x and y-axes are number lines with positive and negative numbers.

We use the coordinate system shown in *fig 2* in the same way we used that shown in *fig 1*.

Worked Example Plot the point A (3, –2).

Answer Begin at the origin i.e. where
the axes meet.
Move 3 in the x-direction,
then –2 in the y-direction.

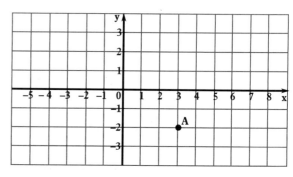

GAME 8:1

FOUR in a LINE — a game for 2 players.

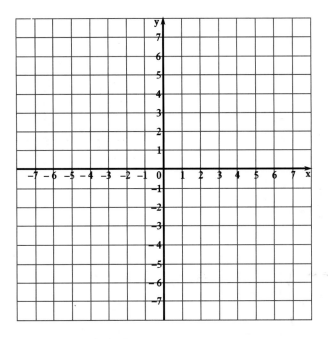

Equipment: a graph drawn up as shown

a blue pen for one player

a red pen for the other player

The Play: The players take it in turn to name and plot a point.

The winner is the first player to be able to draw a line joining 4 of his or her points.

None of the opponent's points may lie on this line.

Rules: If a player plots a point other than the point they have named, the opponent may plot 2 points at the next turn.

EXERCISE 8:2

1.

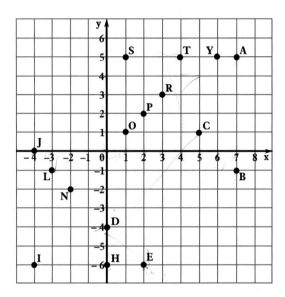

(a) Copy and complete the code-breaker given below.

J			
(−4, 0)	(1, 1)	(−4, −6)	(−2, −2)

(4, 5)	(0, −6)	(2, −6)

(−3, −1)	(2, −6)	(4, 5)	(4, 5)	(2, −6)	(3, 3)	(1, 5)

(7, 5)	(−3, −1)	(2, 2)	(0, −6)	(7, 5)	(7, −1)	(2, −6)	(4, 5)	(−4, −6)

(5, 1)	(7, 5)	(−3, −1)	(−3, −1)	(6, 5)

(b) Do as requested in (a). What do you get?

2.

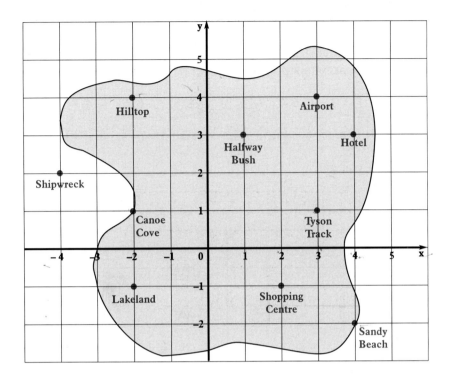

This map shows some of the features on an island that is a popular holiday resort.

(a) Write down the coordinates of   Halfway Bush   Canoe Cove
                                    Tyson Track   Shopping Centre

(b) Anne's favourite place on the island has coordinates (4, –2).
What is Anne's favourite place?

(c) Dave spends his leisure time at the place with coordinates (3, 4). Where does Dave spend his leisure time?

3. Draw a set of axes on which the x-axis goes from – 4 to 5 and the y-axis goes from –5 to 7.

On this graph, plot the following points:

A (2, 4)   B (2, – 4)   C (4, –2)   D (–3, – 4)   E (–3, 4)   F (4, 6)

With lines, join A to B, B to C, B to D, D to E, E to A, A to F, F to C, E to F.
Finally join C to D with a dotted line.

What is your completed shape?

4. Draw a set of axes.
   Have the x-axis going from –7 to 7 and the y-axis from –5 to 10.

   Plot the following points in the order in which they are given. As you plot each point, join it to the previous point.

   (–1, –4) (–2, –3) (–3, 1) (– 6, 0) (– 4, 2) (– 4, 4) (– 6, 6) (– 4, 8) (– 4, 10) (0, 2)

   (3, –1) (3, 8) (5, 10) (7, 8) (5, 7) (4, –3) (2, –5) (– 4, –5) (–1, – 4)

   What picture did you get?

·Review

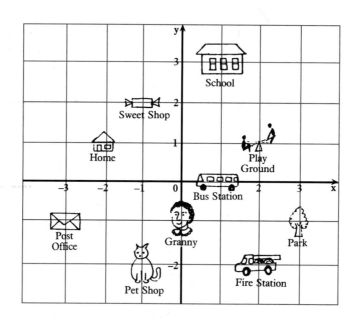

The places shown on this graph are the places that 5-year-old Jake is familiar with.

(a) Write down the coordinates of the school and the post office.

(b) One Sunday morning, while his parents were still asleep, Jake decided to go out. From his home he followed the route given by these coordinates (–1, 2), (1, 0), (2, 1), (2, –2), (–1, –2), (0, –1). Write down the names of all the places he visited, in the order in which he visited them.

(c) Copy the graph. Beginning at his home, join each point on Jake's route with a straight line. Join the last point on his route (0, –1) to his home.

(d) The diagram for (c) should tell you which place Jake likes best. Which place is this?

GAME 8:3

COLOURS — a game for 2 players.

Equipment   4 graphs (2 for each player) with both x and y values from –5 to 5.

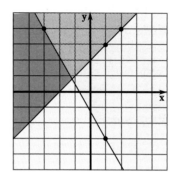

Preparation for Play   Each player divides one of their graphs into 4 sections by drawing two lines across it and colouring the 4 regions formed in different colours. Each of the two lines must pass through at least 2 points where the graph-squares meet. The coloured graph must not be seen by the opponent.

The Play   The aim is for a player to reproduce the opponent's coloured graph. Players take it in turn to name a point by stating its coordinates. The opponent must state which of their coloured regions this point is in, or whether it is on one of the two lines. The winner is the first player to accurately reproduce the other player's coloured graph.

PUZZLE 8:4

Plot the following points to form the outline of an ancient puzzle.

A (2, –2)   B (–1, 1)   C (– 4, –2)   D (– 4, 4)   E (2, 4)   F (–1, 7)

To solve the puzzle without retracing your steps, draw lines from point to point in the following order:
A to B to E to A to C to B to D to F to E to D to C

What was this puzzle?

Can you find other ways to solve this puzzle?

PRACTICAL EXERCISE 8:5

1. On a set of axes, draw a picture.

   Write down the coordinates of each point that would need to be plotted to get this picture. Write instructions for the order in which the points must be joined.

   Swap with your neighbour. Draw your neighbour's picture.

2. Write a code-breaker question similar to **question 1** of **Exercise 8:2.**

   Give your code-breaker to the other students in your group.

3. Invent a game that uses coordinates.

   You might like to base your game on **Game 8:3** or on some commercial game or you may like to invent quite a different type of game.

   Write clear playing instructions. Give your game to other groups to play.

USING COORDINATES

Example   *fig 1* gives one half of a shape which is symmetrical about the x-axis.

   fig 2 shows the completed shape.

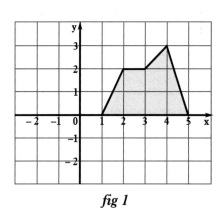

fig 1

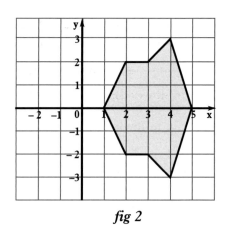

fig 2

If we were asked to locate the vertices of the other half of the symmetrical shape we would give these as: (1, 0), (2, −2), (3, −2), (4, −3), (5, 0).

If we were asked to give the coordinates of the vertices of the complete shape we would write these as: (1, 0), (2, 2), (3, 2), (4, 3), (5, 0), (4, −3), (3, −2), (2, −2).

154

EXERCISE 8:6

1. (a) Draw the shape with the following vertices:

   (–1, 2), (5, 2), (6, 0), (2, –1), (–2, 0)

   (b) How many axes of symmetry does this shape have?

2.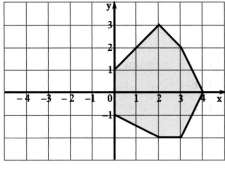

   fig 1

   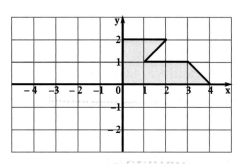

   fig 2

   (a) Copy and complete *fig 1* so it is symmetrical about the y-axis. Write down the coordinates of the vertices of the complete shape.

   (b) *fig 2* shows one quarter of a symmetrical shape. Both the x-axis and the y-axis are axes of symmetry of the completed shape.

   Copy *fig 2* and complete the shape.

   Write down the coordinates of the vertices of the completed shape.

3. Draw up a set of axes.
   Have the x-values from –10 to 10.
   Have the y-values from – 6 to 10.

   On this set of axes, draw the triangles with the given vertices:

   Triangle 1: A (–9, – 6), B (– 4, 8), C (6, 4)
   Triangle 2: D (– 6, 4), E (6, –2), F (–10, –5)
   Triangle 3: P (–8, 3), Q (8, 0), R (– 4, – 6)

   Which two of these triangles are congruent?

4. Write down the coordinates of the centre of rotational symmetry of each shape.

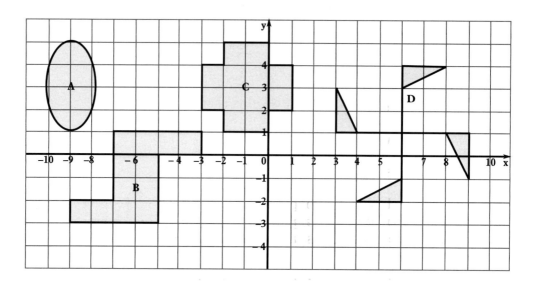

5. This diagram shows part of a shape.
   Copy the diagram.
   Complete the shape so that it has rotational
   symmetry of order 2 and the centre of rotational
   symmetry is the point (2, –1).
   Write down the coordinates of the vertices of the
   complete shape.

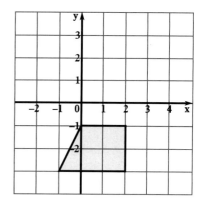

Review (a) A (–1, 1), B (1, –1), C (–3, –1). Draw the triangle ABC.

(b) How many axes of symmetry does the triangle ABC have?

(c) Triangle ABC is part of a symmetrical shape.
   Complete the shape if it has rotational symmetry of order 4 and the
   centre of rotational symmetry is the point A (–1, 1).
   Write down the coordinates of the vertices of the completed shape.

(d) P (2, 3), Q (6, 3), R (4, 1). Draw the triangle PQR.
   Are the triangles ABC and PQR congruent?

FOR YOUR INTEREST

Discuss one or more of the following statements.

A map could be read just as easily without a coordinate system.

Coordinates are used mostly in games.

If you want to travel abroad you must understand coordinate systems.

You could write a summary of your discussion.

You could join with another group and debate one of the statements. If you do this, one group should present arguments *for* the statement and the other group should present arguments *against* the statement.

DISCOVER, DISCUSS, DO

What do you already know about coordinates and plotting points on a graph? **Discuss.**

On a loose piece of paper draw up a set of axes, with both the x and y-axes numbered from – 6 to 6.

Mark these points: A (6, 6) B (6, – 6) C (– 6, – 6) D (– 6, 6) E (– 6, 0)
F (0, 6) G (–3, 3) H (3, 3) I (–3, –3)

Join A to B, B to C, C to D, E to F, A to C, B to G, G to H, D to A, E to I. Cut out the shapes you have drawn.

What is the connection between these shapes and the picture, shown below, of someone running? **Discuss.**

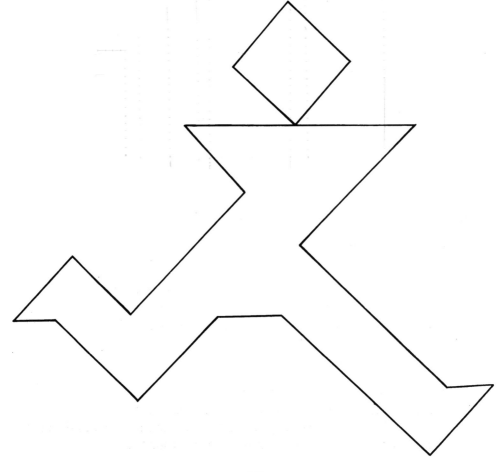

INTERPRETING GRAPHS

Worked Example This graph changes marks out of 40 to percentages.

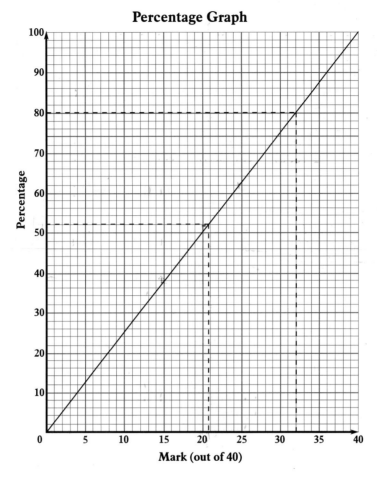

(a) Kyle got 32 out of 40. What percentage is this?

(b) Todd got 52%. What mark out of 40 did Todd get?

Answer (a) Find 32 out of 40. This is at 32 on the horizontal axis.
Draw a dotted line from this 32 up to the graph.
From where you reach the graph, draw a dotted line out to the other axis.
The percentage can then be read. It is 80%.

(b) Find 52%.
This is at 52 on the vertical axis.
Draw a dotted line from this 52 out to the graph.
From where you reach the graph, draw a dotted line down to the other axis.
The mark out of 40 can then be read. It is about 21.

EXERCISE 9:1

1. **Temperature Graph**

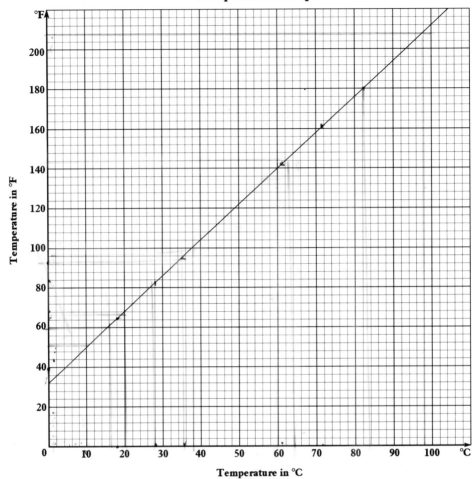

(a) How many °C does each small division on the horizontal axis represent?

(b) How many °F does each small division on the vertical axis represent?

(c) Change these to °F: 20°C, 60°C, 35°C, 82°C, 28°C.

(d) Change these to °C: 50°F, 65°F, 142°F, 161°F.

(e) Amanda is running a temperature. Her mother measured it as 100°F. Her nurse measured it in °C. What did the nurse get for Amanda's temperature?

(f) The hottest day recorded last century was 58°C. This was in Mexico. What temperature is this in °F?

(g) The normal temperature for the human body is about 98·4°F. Approximately what is this in °C?

2.

Currency Graph

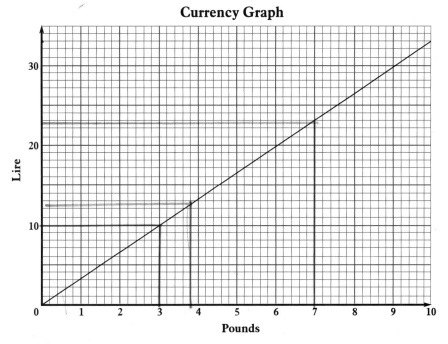

This graph shows the relationship between pounds and Turkish lire at a time when £1 would buy 3·3 lire.

(a) About how many lire would you get for each of £3, £7 and £10?

(b) How many pence does each small division on the horizontal axis represent?

(c) To the nearest 10p, how much British currency would you get for each of 13 lire, 21 lire and 2 lire?

3.

Speed Graph

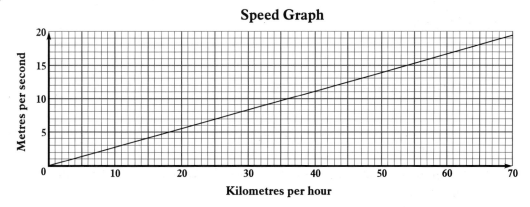

(a) The speed limit in a town is 50 km/h. A cyclist is travelling at a speed of 15 m/sec.
Is this cyclist exceeding the speed limit?

(b) This table shows the top speeds (in metres per second) of some animals.
Find their top speeds in kilometres per hour. Give the answers to the nearest km/h.

racehorse	18
antelope	15·5
deer	12·5

4.

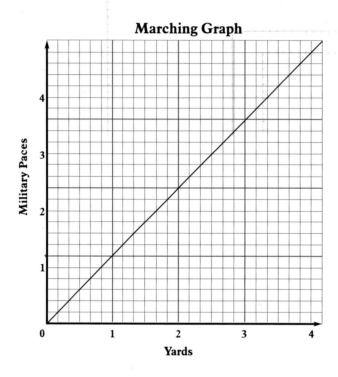

Marching Graph

This graph gives the relationship between yards and military paces.
Each small division on both the horizontal and vertical axes represents the same number of inches.

(a) How many inches does each small division on the horizontal axis represent?

(b) How many military paces are there in 2 yards 18 inches?

(c) How long is 5 military paces?

(d) How many inches are there in 1 military pace?

(e) On parade, a soldier takes 180 paces. How many yards is this?

Review

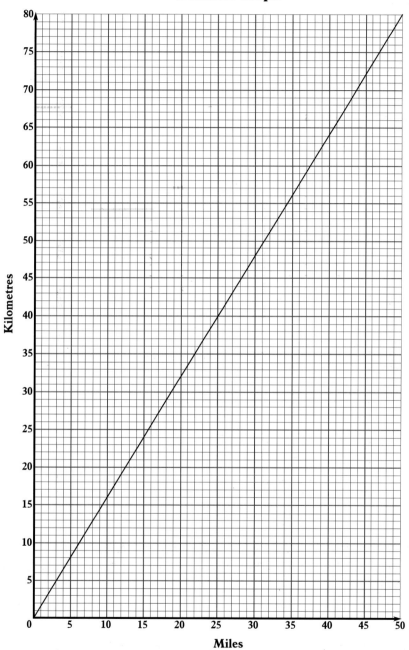

Distance Graph

(a) On a cycling holiday, Demsie travels 45 miles.
About how many kilometres is this?

(b) Brighton is 42km from Bea's farm. About how many miles is this?

DRADING GRAPHS of RELATIONSHIPS

DISCUSSION EXERCISE 9:2

k = 1·6m is an approximate relationship between miles (m) and kilometres (k). Wael was graphing this relationship for m between 0 and 50. He decided to find the coordinates of 3 points on the graph then draw the line through these points. Wael chose the points where m = 0, m = 25 and m = 50. His working to find the values of k was:

k = 1.6m   If m = 0, k = 1.6 × 0   If m = 25, k = 1.6 × 25   If m = 50, k = 1.6 × 50
                       = 0   = 40   = 80

3 points on the graph are (0, 0), (25, 40), (50, 80)

Wael could have plotted just 2 points and then drawn the line through these. Why do you think he plotted 3 points? **Discuss.**

Wael could have chosen to plot the points where m = 15, m = 20 and m = 60. Why do you think it was better to choose the points where m = 0, m = 25 and m = 50? **Discuss.**

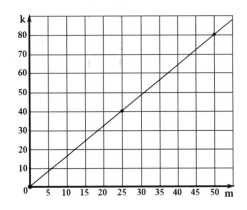

Example   To draw the graph of y = x + 1 for x between –5 and 5 we can begin by finding the coordinates of the points where x = –5, x = 0 and x = 5. These can be summarised in a table of values.

y = x + 1

x	–5	0	5
y	–4	1	6

We then plot (–5, –4), (0, 1), (5, 6) and draw the line that goes through these points.

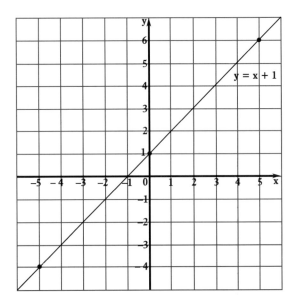

EXERCISE 9:3

1. (a) (–1,),   (2,),   (4,) Copy and complete these coordinates for the relationship y = x – 1.

   (b) Copy the set of axes.

   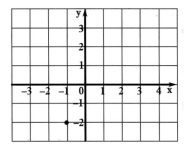

   Plot the three points found in (a). (The first one is plotted for you.) Draw the line that goes through all three points.

   (c) Write down the coordinates of two other points on the line. Substitute the x and y values of each into y = x – 1 to check that they satisfy this relationship.

2. (a)

x	1	2	3
y			

   Copy and complete this table of values for y = 2x – 1.

   (b) Copy and complete these coordinates of three points on the graph of y = 2x – 1.   (1,), (2,), (3,)

   (c) Draw the graph of y = 2x – 1.

   (d) Is the point (0·5, 0) on the graph?

   (e) Explain why you can tell from the graph that x = 1·5, y = 1 do not satisfy the relation y = 2x – 1.

3. Draw the graphs of the following.

   (a) y = x – 2   (b) y = 3x   (c) y = –x   (d) y = 3x – 2

   (e) y = – x + 3   (f) y = – x – 1

4. Lucy rowed a dinghy at a steady rate of 2km per hour for 3 hours. Lucy drew this graph of her progress.

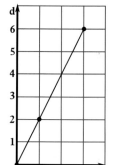

   (a) What does **t** stand for?

   (b) What does **d** stand for?

   (c) What three points did Lucy plot?

   (d) Why did she plot three points?

5. C = 6n gives the cost C, in pounds, of n kilograms of fish.

   (a) Copy and complete this table.

n	1	2	5
C, in pounds	6		

   (b) Draw a graph for the relationship C = 6n for n between 0 and 5.

   (c) Use your graph to write down the cost of 2·5kg of this fish.

   (d) Andrew bought some of this fish. He paid £9·60 for it. Use your graph to find how much Andrew bought.

6. One of Allie's tests was out of 20. She drew the graph of P = 5m to change her friends' marks, m, to percentages, P.

   (a) Draw this graph for m between 0 and 20.

   (b) Use your graph to find the percentage marks of these students. Tina 15, Menna 16, Lyndal 9, Liza 18.

7. The relationship d = 2·5p gives the number of New Zealand dollars, d, that can be bought with p pounds.

   (a) Draw a graph of this relationship for p between 0 and 10.

   (b) Use your graph to find the number of dollars that can be bought for £6.

   (c) Dan bought 22 dollars. Use your graph to find how many pounds Dan paid.

   (d) Angela bought £60 worth of dollars. Use your answer for (b) to find how many dollars Angela got.

8. g = 0·22*l* gives an approximate relationship between litres, *l*, and gallons, g.

   (a) Copy and complete this table.

l	0	10	20
g			

   (b) Draw a graph for the relationship g = 0·22*l* for *l* between 0 and 20.

   (c) Use your graph to find the approximate number of gallons in 16 litres.

   (d) A factory manufactures tanks. They label these tanks with both the metric size and the imperial size. These labels give the capacity to the nearest 10 litres and the nearest 10 gallons.

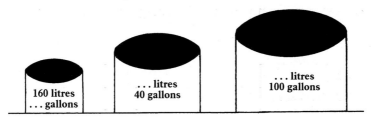

   160 litres
   ... gallons

   ... litres
   40 gallons

   ... litres
   100 gallons

   Copy and complete the labels.

9. The stopping distance, for cars travelling in wet weather on a particular road, was found to be very closely related to their speed.

   | d = 4 + 0·5s | gives the stopping distance d, in metres, for a car travelling at a speed s, in km/h.

   (a) Copy and complete this table for d = 4 + 0·5s.

s	10	50	100
d		29	

   (b) Copy and complete these coordinates (10,), (50, 29), (100,).

   (c) Draw the graph that relates the stopping distance to the speed.

   (d) Use your graph to find the distance a car, travelling at 70 km/h, takes to stop.

   (e) It took 40 metres for Jenny to stop, from the time she put her foot on the brake. Use your graph to find the speed at which Jenny was travelling.

Review 1 (a) Copy and complete these coordinates for the relationship y = − x + 2.
(0, 2), (1, . . .), (4, . . .)

(b) Draw the graph of y = − x + 2 for x between −3 and 5.

Review 2 a = 2·5h gives an approximate relationship between area in hectares (h) and acres (a).

(a) Copy and complete this table.

Area in hectares	2	6	10
Area in acres			25

(b) Draw a graph for the relationship a = 2·5h for values of h between 0 and 10.

(c) Use your graph to answer the following questions.

The common near Josef's home has an area of 8 acres.
What is the area of this common in hectares?

Josef spends his holidays on an 8 hectare farm. What is the size of this farm in acres?

Review 3 Temperatures given in °C can be changed to °F by using the relationship F = 1·8C + 32.

(a) Debbie drew the graph of this relationship. She began by plotting the points for which C = 10, C = 40 and C = 100.
Copy and complete these coordinates. (10, 50), (40, . . .), (100, . . .).

(b) Plot Debbie's 3 points. Draw the line that goes through these.

(c) Use your graph to change 75°C to °F.

(d) Use your graph to change 75°F to °C.

PRACTICAL EXERCISE 9:4

Crocodile hunting in Australia?   *Skiing in Switzerland?*
Rodeo riding in Canada?   *Trekking in Nepal?*
Cruising the Greek Islands?

Where would you like to go for a holiday abroad? Decide on a place to visit.
Find the rate of exchange between the £ and the currency you will use on your holiday. Draw a graph to change pounds into this currency.

INVESTIGATION 9:5

LINE EQUATIONS

Either:

Draw the following lines. y = 2x + 1   y = 2x + 2   y = 2x   y = 2x – 1
                                         y = 2x – 2   y = x + 3   y = 2x + 3   y = 3x + 3

Investigate relationships between the numbers in the equations of the lines and the position of the lines on the graph. As part of your investigation, make and test statements.

continued . . .

. . . from previous page

Or:

```
10      MODE 1
20      MOVE 0, 100
30      FOR X = 40  TO  400  STEP 40
40      Y = 2 * X + 100
50      DRAW X, Y
60      NEXT X
70      MOVE 0, 300
80      FOR X = 40  TO  400  STEP 40
90      Y = 2 * X + 300
100     DRAW X, Y
110     NEXT X
120     MOVE 0, 500
130     FOR X = 40  TO  400  STEP 40
140     Y = 2 * X + 500
150     DRAW X, Y
160     NEXT X
170     END
```

Which straight lines does the above program draw?

Adjust the program to draw the lines y = x + 400, y = 2x + 400, y = 3x + 400.
Hint: You will need to rewrite lines 20, 40, 70, 90, 120, 140.

Investigate relationships between the numbers in the equations of the lines and the position of the lines on the screen.

As part of your investigation, make and test statements.

FOR YOUR INTEREST

Discuss one of the following statements in relation to scientists, nurses, bank personnel, technicians, travel agents and traffic engineers.

Some information is always best shown on a graph.

Computers and calculators now make it unnecessary for anyone to understand how to draw graphs.

Make a summary of your discussion. Present this to the class as an illustrated talk or present it in some other way.

1. Derek's solution for the equation $4x + 3 = 17$ was $x = 4$.
   Mike's solution was $x = 7 \cdot 5$.

   Who got the correct solution?

2. Write down the first seven terms of these sequences.

   (a) First term equal to 1. Every term, after the first, is 3 more than the previous term.

   (b) First term 1. Second term 1. Every term, after the second, is found by adding the two previous terms.

3. Copy the code-breaker below.
   Complete the code-breaker by
   finding the letter that represents
   each coordinate.

   For example, **I** represents $(1, -3)$,
   so **I** is filled in as shown.

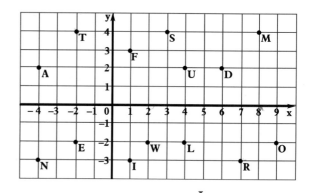

    I   ___ ___ ___ ___   ___ ___ ___   **I**   ___ ___ ___ ___ ___
(1, -3)   (8, 4) (4, 2) (3, 4) (-2, 4)   (-4, -3) (9, -2) (-2, 4)   (2, -2) (7, -3) (1,-3) (-2, 4) (-2, -2)

___   **I**   ___ ___ ___ ___ ___ ___   ___ ___   ___
(4, -2)   (1, -3) (-4, -3) (3, 4) (-2, 4) (-2, -2) (-4, 2) (6, 2)   (9, -2) (1, 3)   (-4, 2)

4. The Patel family went on a touring holiday.
   Each day they travelled 10 fewer kilometres than the
   day before. On the first day they travelled 140km.

   (a) Write down a sequence to show the daily
       distance travelled.

   (b) How far did the Patel family travel on the sixth day?

5. For what value of n is

   (a) $3n = 12$ (b) $\frac{n}{3} = 2$ (c) $n - 3 = 12$ (d) $2n + 3 = 12$?

6. What rule generates these sequences? Test your rule.

   (a) $5, 8, 11, 14, \ldots$ (b) $2, 6, 18, 54, \ldots$ (c) $5, 0\cdot5, 0\cdot05, 0\cdot005, \ldots$

7.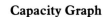

Capacity Graph

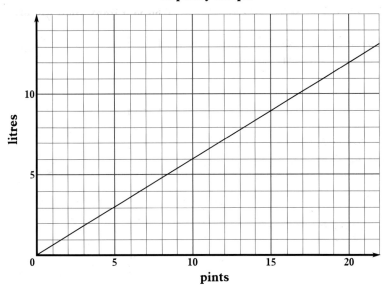

pints

Give the answers to the questions to the nearest whole number.

(a) Neroli made 20 pints of fruit punch.
   How many litres was this?

(b) Another fruit punch recipe was for 8 litres.
   How many pints was this?

8. When John asked Michelle for her house number, Michelle replied, "one subtracted from twice my house number is 47".

(a) Write an equation for h, Michelle's house number.

(b) Solve this equation by a method of your choice, to find h.

9.   **1, 1, 1, 3, 5, 9, 17, . . .**

How is this sequence formed? What is the next term?

10. Draw up a set of axes.
The x-axis should go from –8 to 9 and the y-axis from –9 to 17.

Plot each of **(a)** to **(g)** on this set of axes. In each of **(a)** to **(g)**, join the points in the order in which they are given.

(a)   (– 4, 12), (–3, 15), (–2, 12), (–3, 9), (– 4, 12)

(b)   (–5, 12), (–5, 15), (–6, 13), (– 4, 13)

(c)   (–2, – 4), (–3, –1), (– 4, – 4), (–3, –7), (–2, – 4)

(d)   (4, 15), (5, 12), (4, 9), (3, 12), (4, 15)

(e)   (5, –5), (7, –5), (6, –7), (6, – 4)

(f)   (4, –7), (3, – 4), (4, –1), (5, – 4), (4, –7)

(g)   (8, 16), (8, –8), (–7, –8), (–7, 16), (8, 16)

What picture do you get?

11. Judith scored a total of 65 runs in two cricket matches. In the second match she scored 13 more than in the first match.

Write and solve an equation to find the number of runs Judith scored in the first match.

12. 1, 2, . . .   Continue this sequence in 3 different ways.

13. (a) Copy and complete this table of values for the relationship y = 2x + 1.

x	0	2	4
y			

   (b) Draw the graph of y = 2x + 1 for x between –2 and 4.

14. Copy the cross number.
    Solve the equations given in the clues and complete the cross number.

Across	**Down**
1. 2n – 7 = 15	1. 5 (n – 9) = 15
2. $\frac{2n}{3}$ = 14	3. 2n – 9 = n + 3
4. 5 (2n – 1) = 35	6. $\frac{n}{4}$ = 6
5. 3n – 16 = 50	7. 2n + n = 39
9. 4n – 3 = 3n + 10	8. 2 (2n – 15) = 26
10. $\frac{2n}{7}$ = 12	11. $\frac{n}{2}$ – 6 = 5
13. 2 (n – 9) = 24	12. 6n – 9 = 4n + 11
15. 2 (11 + 3n) = 5 (11 – n)	14. 2 (n – 9) + n = 21

15. d = 5t + 10 gives the distance d, in kilometres, of a plane from Hedgend after t minutes.

   (a) Copy and complete these coordinates for d = 5t + 10.
       (0, 10), (2,), (5,)

   (b) Draw the graph of d = 5t + 10 for t between 0 and 5.

   (c) Use your graph to answer these questions.
       Darryl is on this plane. How far is Darryl from Hedgend after 4 minutes?
       Katherine lives 17·5km from Hedgend. How long does it take before the plane is flying over Katherine's house?

173

16.

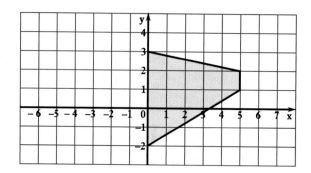

This is one half of a symmetrical shape. The y-axis is an axis of symmetry of the completed shape.

Copy this diagram and complete the shape.

Write down the coordinates of the vertices of the completed shape.

17. (a) Use trial and improvement to find the solution to $x^3 = 15$, accurate to one decimal place.

(b) Use trial and improvement to find the two solutions to the equation $x^2 + 3x - 7 = 0$. Give these solutions accurate to 1 d.p.

18. (a) Write down the sequence which is generated by this program.

```
10   FOR N = 1 TO 6
20   PRINT 4 * N – 3
30   NEXT N
40   END
```

(b) Write a program to print the first 50 terms of the sequence: 10, 12, 14, 16, . . .

SHAPE, SPACE AND MEASURES

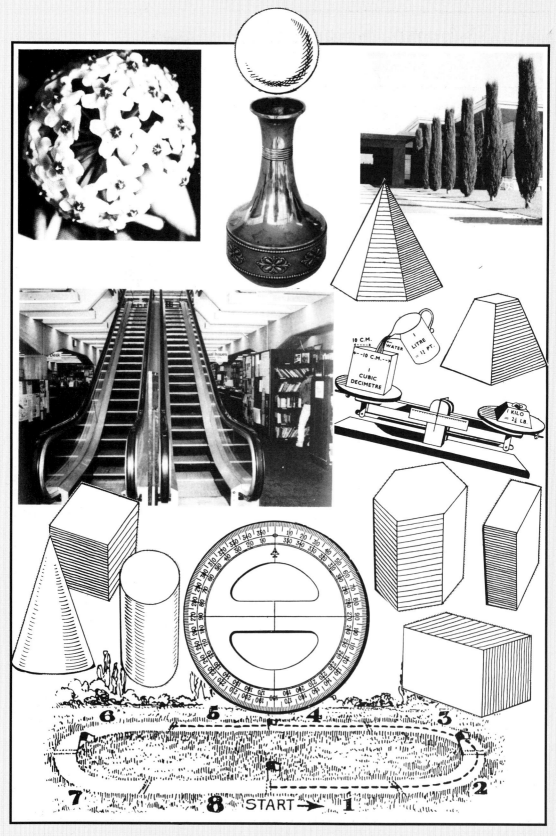

Shape, Space and Measures from Previous Levels

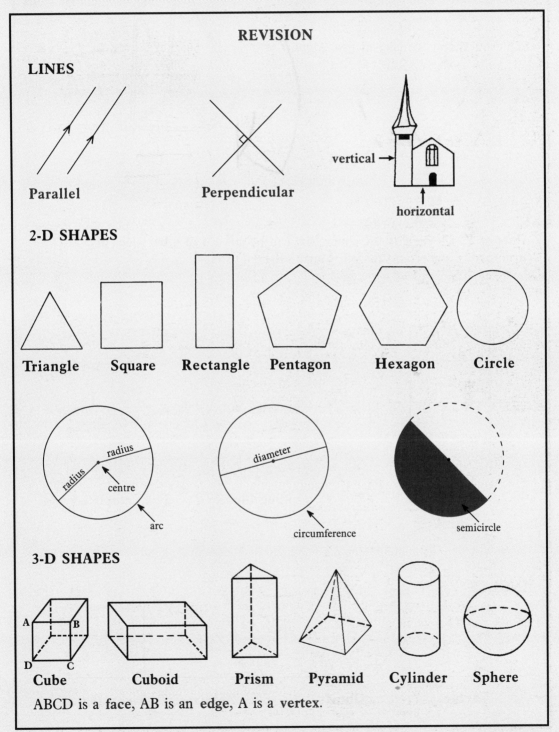

LINES

Parallel

Perpendicular

vertical →

horizontal

2-D SHAPES

Triangle   Square   Rectangle   Pentagon   Hexagon   Circle

radius   radius   centre   arc

diameter   circumference

semicircle

3-D SHAPES

Cube   Cuboid   Prism   Pyramid   Cylinder   Sphere

ABCD is a **face**, AB is an **edge**, A is a **vertex**.

177

continued . . .

. . . *from previous page*

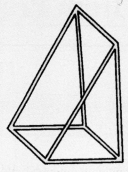

Skeleton shapes consist of just edges.

NETS

A net of a 3-D shape is the shape that can be cut out of a flat piece of cardboard or paper and folded to make the 3-D shape.

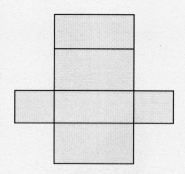

A net for a box

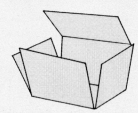

Folding the net

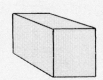

The completed box

ANGLES

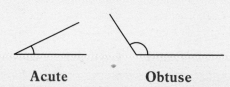

Acute   **Obtuse**

Reflex

Right angle

continued . . .

. . . from previous page

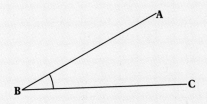

B is the **vertex** of the marked angle. AB and CB are the **arms** of the marked angle.

The marked angle can be labelled as ∠B or ∠ABC.

The angle in a	complete circle	$= 360°$
	half a circle	$= 180°$
	quarter of a circle	$= 90°$
	three-quarters of a circle	$= 270°$

We can **estimate angle size** by comparing with a right angle.

For instance, angle A is about $\frac{1}{3}$ of a right angle.

That is, ∠A is about 30°.

Angle B is a little less than $\frac{1}{3}$ of a right angle.

That is, ∠B is about 20°.

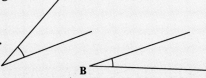

COMPASS DIRECTIONS

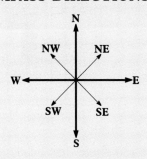

A Northerly wind blows from the North.
A South-Westerly wind blows from the South-West.

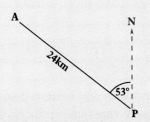

A is 24km from P in the direction N 53°W.

continued . . .

. . . *from previous page*

CONGRUENCE

Congruent shapes are the same size and the same shape. Corresponding lengths are equal; corresponding angles are equal. In congruent 3-D shapes, corresponding faces are identical.

SYMMETRY

A **line of symmetry (axis of symmetry)** divides a 2-D shape into two congruent shapes.
A **plane of symmetry** divides a 3-D shape into two congruent shapes.
A shape has **reflective symmetry** if it has a line or a plane of symmetry.

A shape has **rotational symmetry** if it coincides with itself more than once when it is rotated a complete turn about some point. The point about which it is rotated is called the **centre of rotational symmetry**. The number of times the shape coincides with itself during one complete turn is called the **order of rotational symmetry**.

The **total order of symmetry** of a shape is the sum of the order of rotational symmetry and the number of axes of symmetry.

REFLECTION, TRANSLATION, ROTATION

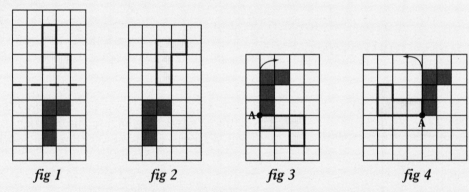

| *fig 1* | *fig 2* | *fig 3* | *fig 4* |

fig 1 illustrates a **reflection** (or **flip movement**). The red shape has been reflected in the dotted line to the shaded shape. The dotted line is called the **mirror line**.

fig 2 illustrates a **translation** (or **straight movement**). The red shape has been translated 1 square to the right and 4 squares up to the shaded shape.

fig 3 and *fig 4* illustrate **rotation** (or **turning movement**). In *fig 3* the red shape has been rotated clockwise about A, through $\frac{1}{4}$ turn or 1 right angle. In *fig 4* the red shape has been rotated anticlockwise about A, through $\frac{1}{4}$ turn.

continued . . .

. . . *from previous page*

MEASURES

Time   1 minute = 60 seconds
           1 hour = 60 minutes
           1 day = 24 hours
           1 year = 12 months
           1 year = 365 days (or 366 days in a leap year)

April, June, September, November have 30 days.
January, March, May, July, August, October, December have 31 days.
February has 28 days except in a leap year when it has 29 days.

All years that are divisible by 4 are leap years, except centuries which are leap years only if they are divisible by 400.

a.m. time is from midnight until noon; p.m. time is from noon until midnight. For instance, 1100 hours is 11a.m., 2300 hours is 11p.m.

Metric Measures

length	km	hm	Dm	**m**	dm	cm	mm
capacity	k*l*	h*l*	D*l*	*l*	d*l*	c*l*	m*l*
mass	kg	hg	Dg	**g**	dg	cg	mg

Each unit on the table is 10 times as large as the unit immediately to its right. The relationships between the metric units in common use are as follows.

Length	**Capacity**	**Mass**	
1km = 1000m	1*l* = 1000m*l*	1kg	= 1000g
1m = 1000mm		1g	= 1000mg
1m = 100cm		1 tonne	= 1000kg
1cm = 10mm			

Some **imperial units** still in common use and the relationships between these units are as follows.

Length	**Capacity**	**Mass**	
1 mile = 1760 yards	1 gallon = 8 pints	1 ton	= 160 stone
1 yard = 3 feet		1 stone	= 14 lb
1 foot = 12 inches		1 lb	= 16oz

Rough approximations between imperial and metric units are:
1kg is about 2 lb (a better approximation is: 1kg is about $2\frac{1}{4}$ lb)
1 litre is about $1\frac{3}{4}$ pints
1 inch is about $2\frac{1}{2}$ cm
5 miles is about 8km
1m is a little longer than 3 feet.

continued . . .

. . . from previous page

CONSTRUCTIONS

Parallel lines may be drawn with a set square and ruler. The diagrams below show how to draw a line through C which is parallel to AB. (The set square is shown shaded.)

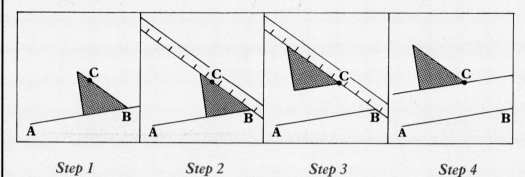

| *Step 1* | *Step 2* | *Step 3* | *Step 4* |

Step 1 Place the set square as shown.

Step 2 Place the ruler as shown.

Step 3 Holding the ruler still, slide the set square along the ruler until C is in the position shown.

Step 4 Remove the ruler. Draw the parallel line.

To **construct a triangle** with sides 5·5cm, 3cm, 3·8cm take these steps.

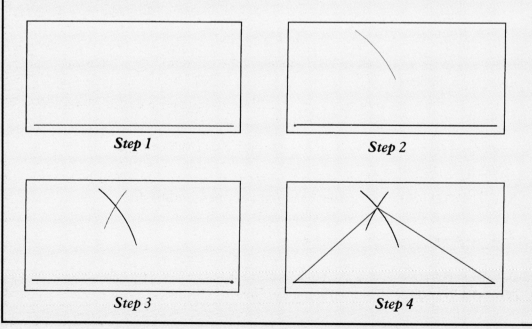

Step 1   *Step 2*

Step 3   *Step 4*

continued . . .

. . . from previous page

Step 1   Draw a line 5·5cm long.

Step 2   Open the compass out to 3cm. Put the compass point on the left-hand end of the line. Draw an arc.

Step 3   Open the compass out to 3·8cm. Put the compass point on the right-hand end of the line. Draw an arc which crosses the arc drawn in Step 2.

Step 4   Complete the triangle.

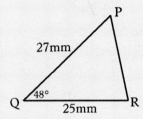

To construct this triangle, take the following steps.

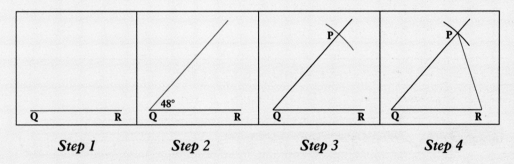

| *Step 1* | *Step 2* | *Step 3* | *Step 4* |

Step 1   Draw a line QR which is 25mm long.

Step 2   Using the protractor and ruler draw the line from Q such that angle Q = 48°.

Step 3   With compass point on Q, and compass opened out to 27mm, draw an arc to meet the line drawn in *Step 2*.

Step 4   Using the ruler complete the side PR of the triangle.

Note This triangle could be constructed without the compass. Then in *Step 3* we just use the ruler to measure 27mm from Q to find P.

PERIMETER, AREA, VOLUME

The distance right around the outside of a shape is called the **perimeter**. Perimeter is measured in mm, cm, m or km.

continued . . .

. . . from previous page

The amount of surface a shape covers is called the **area**. Area is measured in mm², cm², m² or km².

We can count squares to find area. The area of each of these squares is 1cm². Since there are 12 squares in this rectangle, its area is 12cm².

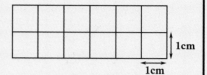

The **volume** of a shape is the amount of space it takes up. Volume is measured in mm³, cm³, m³.

We can count cubes to find volume. There are 72 cubes in this shape. If each cube measures 1cm by 1cm by 1cm, the volume of each is 1cm³. The volume of the shape is then 72cm³.

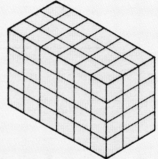

REVISION EXERCISE

1.

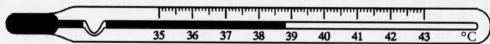

What is the reading on this thermometer?

2. A south-west wind is blowing.
In which direction are these clouds moving?

3.

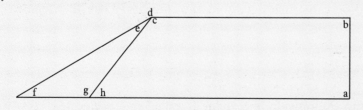

Right	
Acute	
Obtuse	
Reflex	

Name each of the marked angles using the names given in the box.

4.

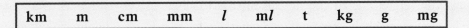

| km | m | cm | mm | *l* | m*l* | t | kg | g | mg |

Which unit of measurement would the following be measured in? (Choose from the units in the box.)

(a) the weight of an apple

(b) the length of a swimming pool

(c) the mass of a daisy seed

(d) the mass of an elephant

(e) the thickness of a fingernail

(f) the capacity of a large frying pan

(g) the distance between two towns

(h) the weight of a child

5.

Use your drawing instruments to make accurate copies of these. (Hint: for 2 of them, begin with a circle.)

Describe how you made these designs using words such as radius, diameter, circumference, arc, semicircle, mid-points, diagonal.

6. Trace these.

Draw the reflections in the dotted mirror lines.

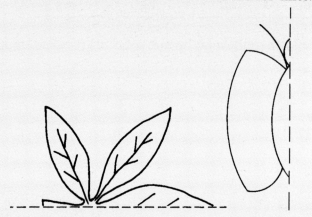
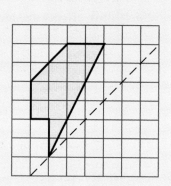

7. Mandy's two brothers weigh 7 stone 10 lb and 9 stone 2 lb.
   What is the difference in their weights?

8. Name the fish that is

   (a) a reflection of fish C

   (b) a translation of fish C

   (c) a rotation of fish C.

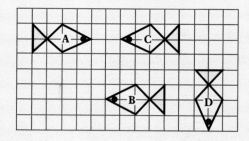

9. Which of these sets of lengths are possible lengths for the sides of a triangle?

   A. 6cm 8cm 10cm   B. 2cm 5cm 8cm   C. 4cm 7cm 3cm

10. Name the marked angle.

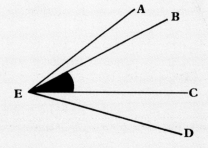

11.

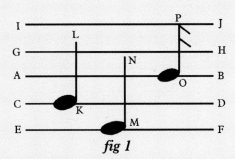

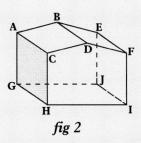

fig 1 *fig 2*

(a) Name the lines in *fig 1* that are parallel to NM.

(b) Name the lines in *fig 1* that are perpendicular to AB.

(c) Name the horizontal lines in *fig 2*.

(d) Name the vertical lines in *fig 2*.

(e) In *fig 2*, which face is parallel to the shaded face?

(f) How many planes of symmetry does *fig 2* have?

12.

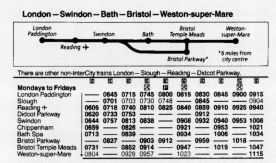

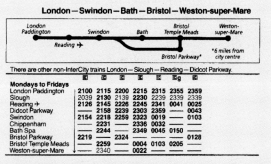

London — Swindon — Bath — Bristol — Weston-super-Mare

There are other non-InterCity trains London — Slough — Reading — Didcot Parkway.

Mondays to Fridays										
London Paddington	——	0645	0715	0745	0800	0815	0830	0845	0900	0915
Slough	——	0701	0703	0730	0748	——	0845	——	——	0904
Reading ✈	0605	0718	0740	0810	0825	0840	0859	0910	0925	0940
Didcot Parkway	0620	0733	0753	——	——	——	0912	——	——	——
Swindon	0644	0757	0813	0838	——	0908	0932	0940	0953	1008
Chippenham	0659	——	0826	——	——	0921	——	0953	——	1021
Bath Spa	0713	——	0839	——	——	0934	——	1006	——	1034
Bristol Parkway	——	0827	——	0903	0912	——	0959	——	1018	——
Bristol Temple Meads	0731	——	0852	0914	——	0947	1019	——	1047
Weston-super-Mare	0804	——	0928	0957	——	1023	——	——	1115

London — Swindon — Bath — Bristol — Weston-super-Mare

There are other non-InterCity trains London — Slough — Reading — Didcot Parkway.

Mondays to Fridays							
London Paddington	2100	2115	2200	2215	2315	2355	2359
Slough	2039	2130	2139	2230	2239	2339	2339
Reading ✈	2126	2145	2226	2245	2341	0041	0025
Didcot Parkway	——	2158	2239	2303	2359	——	0043
Swindon	2154	2218	2259	2323	0019	——	0103
Chippenham	——	2231	——	2336	0032	——	——
Bath Spa	——	2244	——	2349	0045	0150	——
Bristol Parkway	2219	——	2324	——	——	——	0128
Bristol Temple Meads	——	2259	——	0004	0103	0205	——
Weston-super-Mare	——	2340	——	0022	——	——	——

The above timetables are for the early morning and late evening.
Jane travels, by train, from Slough to Swindon.
She arrives in Swindon as near as possible to half past nine in the morning.

(a) Which train does Jane catch at Slough?

(b) How long does this train take to travel from Slough to Swindon?

Later in the day Jane travels on to Bristol Parkway, arriving as near to midnight as possible.

(c) How long has Jane spent in Swindon?

13.

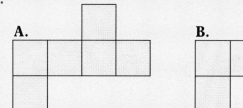 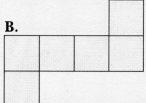 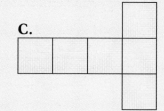

A.   **B.**   **C.**

(a) Which of these nets will fold to make a cube?

(b) Draw another net that will fold to make a cube.

14. Find the missing numbers.

(a) 4cm = · · · mm   (b) 2·6km = · · · m   (c) 0·34m = · · · mm

(d) 1847ml = · · · l   (e) 35g = · · · kg   (f) 0·18t = · · · kg

15. Use your drawing instruments to accurately construct this triangle. On your drawing, measure the size of ∠RPQ. Give your answer to the nearest degree.

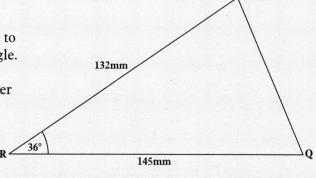

16. (a) How many cubes are there in this shape?

(b) Each cube measures 1cm by 1cm by 1cm. What is the volume of the shape?

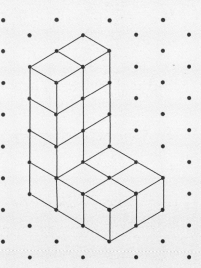

17.

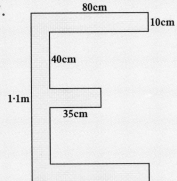

This letter E is painted on a billboard advertising pet food. It is symmetrical.

(a) What is the height of this letter, in cm?

(b) What is the perimeter of this letter?

18. (a) The thickness of the gold in a ring could be

    A. 1mm   B. 5mm   C. 1cm

(b) The capacity of a bottle of lemonade could be

    A. 1·25m*l*   B. 1·25kg   C. 1·25 *l*

(c) The length of the hour hand on a watch could be

    A. 0·5mm   B. 5mm   C. 50mm

(d) The width of a door could be

    A. 75mm   B. 75cm   C. 75m

(e) The weight of a banana could be

    A. 1·5g   B. 15g   C. 150g

(f) The weight of an atlas could be

    A. 1g   B. 1kg   C. 10kg

(g) The weight of a calculator could be

    A. 10g   B. 100g   C. 1kg

(h) The amount of tea in a teacup could be

    A. 50m*l*   B. 150m*l*   C. 0·5*l*

(i) The capacity of a bucket could be

    A. 10m*l*   B. 0·1*l*   C. 10*l*

19. Susan's father made a wall mural that was 8′9″ long. He attached this to a wall that was 11′4″ long.

What length of wall was not covered by the mural?

20. Name all the congruent shapes in this diagram.

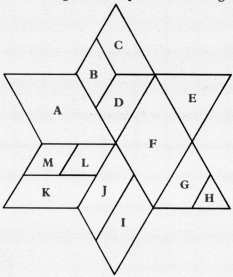

21. (a) About how many litres of water can a 2 gallon bucket hold?

(b) How many pints does the bucket hold?

(c) Darryl lives 20 miles from Swansea. About how many kilometres is this?

(d) Grapes are priced at £2 per kg. Which of the following gives the approximate price per lb of these grapes?

    A. £4   B. £1   C. £3   D. £5

22. (a) How many axes of symmetry does this shape have?

(b) What is the order of rotational symmetry of the shape?

(c) What is the total order of symmetry?

(d) Write down the coordinates of the centre of rotational symmetry.

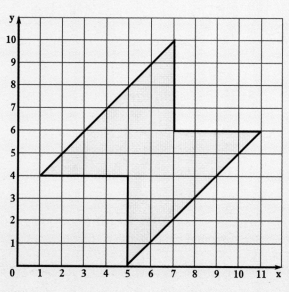

23. Count squares to find the area of these shapes.

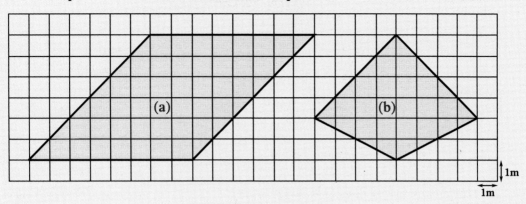

24. Find the missing numbers.

   (a) 78mm + 17cm = · · · cm   (b) $1 \cdot 3l - 543ml = \cdots ml$ (c) 254g + 1·6kg = · · · kg

25. What measurement is shown by the pointer?

   (a)

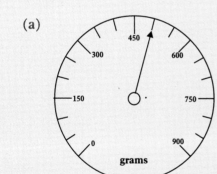

   (b)

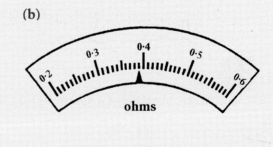

26. (a) Use your protractor to measure the marked angle.

   (b) Copy and complete:
        P is . . . km from Q, in the direction N . . .° . . .

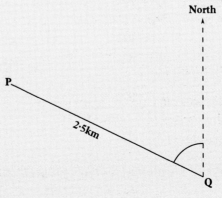

191

27. Name one thing that the three shapes in each of the following lists have in common.

List 1	**List 2**	**List 3**	**List 4**
Pentagon	Prism	Cylinder	Pyramid
Hexagon	Cube	Circle	Hexagon
Triangle	Sphere	Sphere	Rectangle

28. (a) How many edges does this shape have?

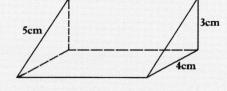

 (b) How many vertices does this shape have?

 (c) Two of the faces are triangular.
    How many other faces are there?

 (d) What is this shape called?

 (e) Use your drawing instruments to make a net for this. Put tabs on every second edge.
    Fold your net to make the shape.

29. (a) What does this LOGO program draw?

```
RT  90
FD  200
PU
BK  100
LT  90
PD
FD  300
LT  90
PU
FD  100
PD
BK  200
```

 (b) Write a different LOGO program that will draw the same shape.

11   Perimeter. Area. Volume   11

DISCOVER, DISCUSS, DO

- The circumference of a circular object, such as a coin or a saucer or the top face of a cylinder, can be found in the following way.

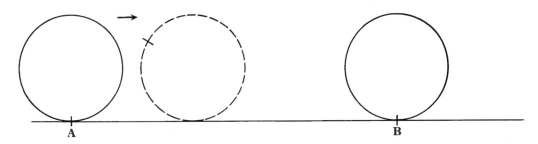

Step 1   Put a mark on the edge of the object.

Step 2   Hold the object upright on a line of your book.
Have the mark on the object on the line. Mark this starting position as A.

Step 3   Roll the object along the line of your book until the mark on its edge is on the line again.
Mark this finishing position as B.

Step 4   Measure the length of AB, in mm.

Use this method to find the circumference of some circular objects.

Discuss how to measure the diameter of the objects as accurately as possible. Measure the diameter, in mm.

List your results for the circumference (C) and the diameter (d) on a table similar to that shown at the top of the next page.

Use your calculator to work out the answer to C ÷ d for each of your objects. Record the answer to C ÷ d in the last column of the table. (Give these calculations to 1 decimal place.)

Discuss your results for $\frac{C}{d}$.

Object	Circumference (mm)	Diameter (mm)	C d
10p coin counter baked beans tin ⋮			

- Use a method, similar to that used on the previous page, to find the circumference of bicycle wheels.

  Work out the ratio $\frac{C}{d}$ for a number of different sized bicycle wheels.

  What do you notice? **Discuss.**

- Another way of finding the circumference of a cylindrical object, such as a baked beans tin, is to measure with a tape measure.

  Another way is to wind a length of cotton around the tin a number of times. Why do you think the cotton is wound around a number of times, rather than just once? **Discuss.**

  Use this last method to find the ratio $\frac{C}{d}$ for a number of tins of different sizes. What do you notice? **Discuss.**

The MEANING of π

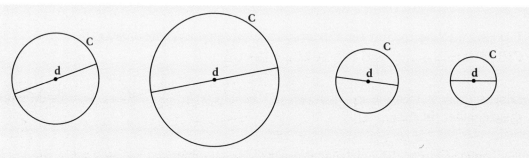

C is the circumference of a circle, d is the diameter. The ratio $\frac{C}{d}$ is the same for any circle, regardless of how big or small the circle is.
This ratio $\frac{C}{d}$ is called π (pronounced as "pi"). To 1 d.p. the value of π is 3·1.

Most calculators have a π key.
On the Casio *fx–82* calculators, which display 8 digits, the value of π is 3·1415927.
This is the value of π, accurate to 7 d.p.
In recent years π has been worked out, accurate to many millions of decimal places, on the computer.

INVESTIGATION 11:1

THE VALUE of π

The time line below shows some of the values that have been used for π, over the years.

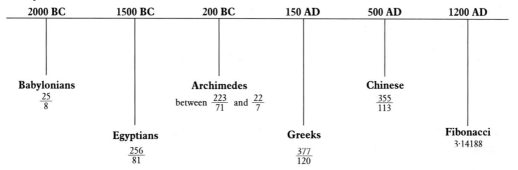

| 2000 BC | 1500 BC | 200 BC | 150 AD | 500 AD | 1200 AD |

Babylonians $\frac{25}{8}$

Archimedes between $\frac{223}{71}$ and $\frac{22}{7}$

Chinese $\frac{355}{113}$

Egyptians $\frac{256}{81}$

Greeks $\frac{377}{120}$

Fibonacci 3·14188

How many decimal places were these values accurate to?

Can you find a fraction that will give the 8th digit more accurately than the fraction the Chinese used? **Investigate.**

CIRCUMFERENCE and AREA of a CIRCLE

Since $\frac{C}{d} = \pi$, then $C = \pi d$.

We can use the formula $C = \pi d$ to calculate the circumference of a circle.

Remember: r is the radius of a circle.
$\qquad d = 2r$

Replacing d by 2r in the formula $C = \pi d$ we get $C = 2\pi r$.

i.e. **C = πd and C = 2πr both give the circumference of a circle.**

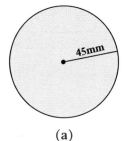
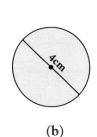

Worked Example Find the circumference of these circles.
Use π = 3·1.

(a)   (b)

Answer (a) C = 2πr   (b) C = πd
           C = 2 × 3·1 × 45   C = 3·1 × 4
           = 279mm   = 12·4cm

DISCUSSION EXERCISE 11:2

● Draw circles of radius 2cm, 3cm, 4cm, 5cm, 6cm on 1cm squared paper.

Count squares to estimate the area of the circles.
Would you expect your estimates to be very accurate? **Discuss.**

Discuss how you could get better estimates for the area.

● Draw a circle on a loose piece of paper.
Cut it into "slices". Rearrange these "slices" as shown.

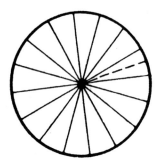
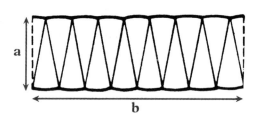

Which of **a** or **b** is equal to the radius of the circle? Which is about the same as half the circumference?

How could you use this to find the area of a circle? **Discuss.**

The **area of a circle** can be calculated using the formula $A = \pi r^2$.

Worked Example   Find the area of these circles.
                 Take $\pi = 3\cdot1$.
                 Give the answers to 1 d.p.

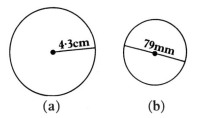

Answer   (a) $A = \pi r^2$
                $A = 3\cdot1 \times 4\cdot3^2$ **Key** $\boxed{3\cdot1}\,\boxed{\times}\,\boxed{4\cdot3}\,\boxed{\text{SHIFT}}\,\boxed{x^2}\,\boxed{=}$
                  $= 57\cdot3\text{cm}^2$ (to 1 d.p.)

        (b) $d = 79\text{mm}$ $r = 39\cdot5\text{mm}$ $A = \pi r^2$
                                                  $= 3\cdot1 \times 39\cdot5^2$
                                                  $= 4836\cdot8\text{mm}^2$ (to 1 d.p.)

EXERCISE 11:3

In each question of this exercise, use $\pi = 3\cdot1$.
Give the answers to 1 d.p. if rounding is necessary.

1. Find the circumference of each of these circles.

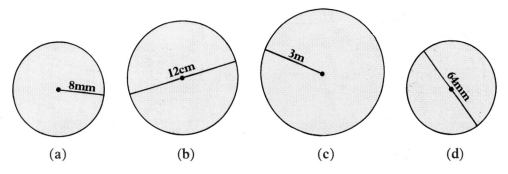

          (a)   (b)   (c)   (d)

2. Find the area of the circles drawn in **question 1**.

3. A Vauxhall car has wheels of diameter 48cm.

    Find the circumference of these wheels.

4. An African Violet is in a 9cm pot. That is, the diameter of the top of the pot is 9cm.

What is the distance around the edge of the top of this pot?

5. A canvas cover is made to fit exactly over a circular goldfish pond. The diameter of this pond is 2·8m.

What is the area of the canvas cover?

6. A circular picture, of diameter 29cm, is covered with glass.

What is the area of the glass?

7. A ribbon is tied around a hat, as shown.

Find the total length of the ribbon, if the bow needs 30cm.

8. In the McMath solar telescope, in Arizona, there are two flat round mirrors. One has a radius of 1m and the other a diameter of 122cm.

What is the difference in the areas of these mirrors?
(Answer in square centimetres.)

9. A circular tablecloth overhangs a circular table, as shown.
Mai-Lin buys 3·4m of braid to sew around the edge.

Is 3·4m enough to sew around the outside edge?

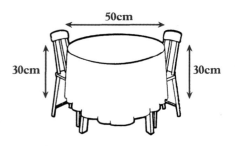

10. Samantha's bicycle has 0·6m diameter wheels.
On the way to school, the front wheel rotates 500 times.

How far does Samantha live from school?

Review 1 Find (a) the circumference

(b) the area of this circle.

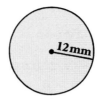

Review 2 The bottom of circular slate table mats is to be covered with cork. The diameter of each table mat is 22cm.
How much cork is needed for each of these table mats?

Review 3 Roger's bicycle has wheels of diameter 68cm.

How many times do the wheels on Roger's bicycle rotate in a journey of 4km?

A. about 200 times   **B.** about 2000 times   **C.** about 20000 times

INVESTIGATION 11:4

ENCLOSING CIRCLES

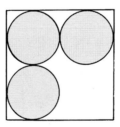

A rectangle is shown drawn around three equal circles.

Investigate how to position three equal circles so that the rectangle drawn around them has the smallest possible area.

What if a rectangle was to be drawn around four equal circles?

What if a rectangle was to be drawn around five equal circles?

What if . . .

What if a circle was to be drawn around the small equal circles?

What if a triangle was to be drawn around the small equal circles?

INVESTIGATION 11:5

RACE TRACK

The shading on the diagram represents a circular race track.

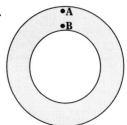

A and B give the positions of two horses which are training on this track. These horses race around this track in such a way that B is always on the inside of A and 4m from A.

Investigate the difference in the distances run by A and B for varying widths of track.

AREA of SQUARE, RECTANGLE and TRIANGLE

DISCUSSION EXERCISE 11:6

•

1cm

1cm

Count squares to find the areas of these rectangles.

Draw some more rectangles on centimetre squared paper.
List the length, the width and the area of each.

Discuss your results with your group or your class. As part of your discussion, make and test statements about the relationship between area, length and width of a rectangle.

- Draw squares of side 2cm and 5cm on centimetre squared paper.

  Count squares to find the areas.

  Draw more squares and find the areas.

  Discuss your results with your group or class.

INVESTIGATION 11:7

GREATEST AREA or PERIMETER

1. These shapes both have perimeter of 12cm.

   Draw other shapes with perimeter of 12cm.

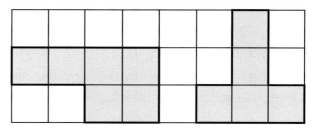

   Investigate to find the shape with the greatest area.

2.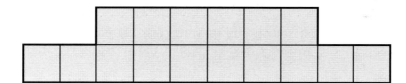

   This shape has an area of 16cm².

   Draw other shapes with area of 16cm².

   Investigate to find the shape with the greatest perimeter.

3. A rectangle has an area of 24cm².

   Investigate to find possible dimensions of this rectangle.

4. Ann displayed her designs on a rectangular wall chart. Her wall chart had the same area as perimeter.

   Investigate to find possible dimensions for Ann's wall chart.

DISCUSSION EXERCISE 11:8

- On a loose piece of paper, draw a triangle.

  Draw a rectangle around the triangle, as shown below. (One side of the triangle becomes a side of the rectangle.)

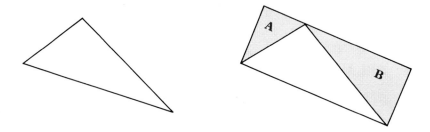

  Cut out the two pieces of the rectangle that are outside the triangle. (Pieces A and B.)

  Can you arrange these two pieces to fit exactly over the triangle?

  Repeat this with triangles of other shapes.

  Discuss your results with your group or your class. As part of your discussion, test the statement "the area of a triangle is half the area of a rectangle."

- Use your results from above to write down the areas of each of the following triangles. (The distance between two dots is 1cm.)
  Discuss your answers.

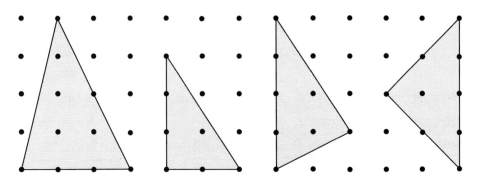

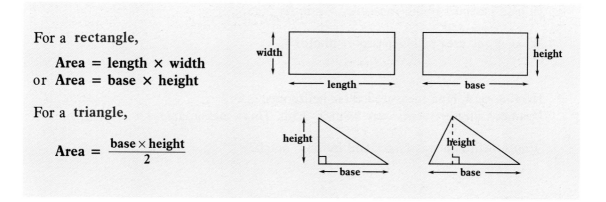

For a rectangle,

Area = length × width
or **Area = base × height**

For a triangle,

$$\text{Area} = \frac{\text{base} \times \text{height}}{2}$$

EXERCISE 11:9

1.

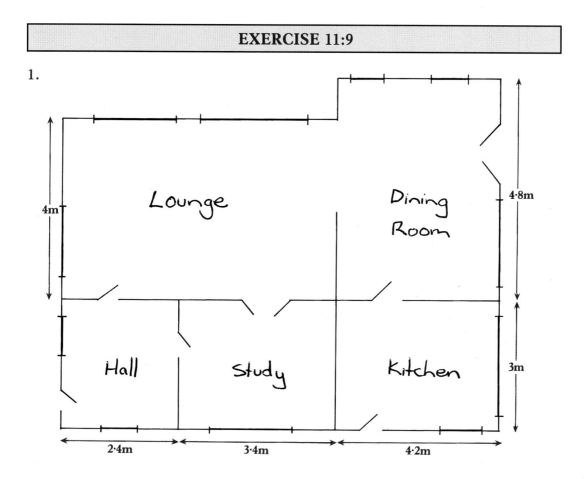

Emma drew this plan of the ground floor of her house.

She then calculated the area of each room.

What answers should Emma get?

2. Riffet's passport photo measures 35mm by 50mm.

   What is the area of her passport photo?

3. Heather and Tina measured their bedrooms.
   Heather's measurements were 3·9m × 3·5m. Tina's measurements were 3·7m square.

   Whose bedroom was larger and by how much?

4. The tiles on Emma's hall floor are 15cm square.

   (a) What is the area of one of these tiles?

   (b) Write the dimensions of Emma's hall in cm (see **question 1**).

   (c) What is the area of the floor of Emma's hall? (Answer in square centimetres.)

   (d) How many tiles are on Emma's hall floor?

5. A table measures 1·5m by 1m.

   (a) Write the dimensions of this table in cm.

   (b) A table cloth overhangs this table by 20cm all round.

   What is the area of this table cloth?

6.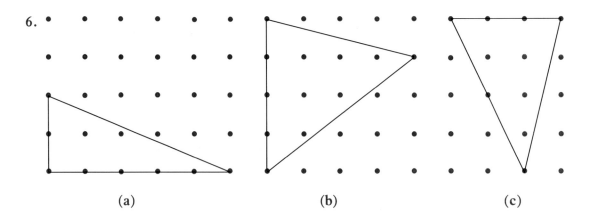

   (a)   (b)   (c)

The dots on this diagram are 1cm apart. Find the area of these triangles.

7.

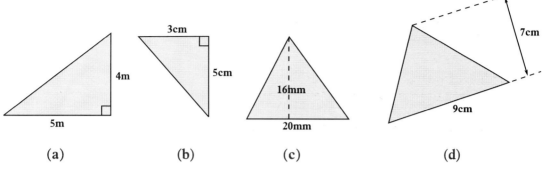

(a) (b) (c) (d)

Calculate the area of these triangles.

8. What is the area of this sail?

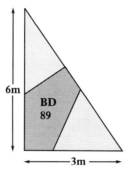

9. The "Bermuda Triangle" is a part of the Atlantic Ocean in which more than 50 ships and 20 planes have mysteriously disappeared.

Find the area of the "Bermuda Triangle" if the base is 1560km and the height is 1320km.

Review 1 The tennis court behind Seadoone Hall measures 24m by 11m.

What is the area of this tennis court?

Review 2 A table top is a square of side 110cm.

Six table mats, each 25cm × 17cm, are placed on this table.

(a) Find the area of the table top.

(b) Find the area covered by each table mat.

(c) Find the area of the table not covered by the table mats.

Review 3 Triangles of pastry, the shape shown, are used to make savouries.

What area of pastry is used for each?

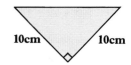

PRACTICAL EXERCISE 11:10

Use a tape or a trundle wheel to measure rectangular shapes around your school.

You could measure the tennis court
          or the soccer field
          or the maths. classroom
          or the gymnasium.

Calculate the perimeter and the area of each shape.

PRACTICAL EXERCISE 11:11

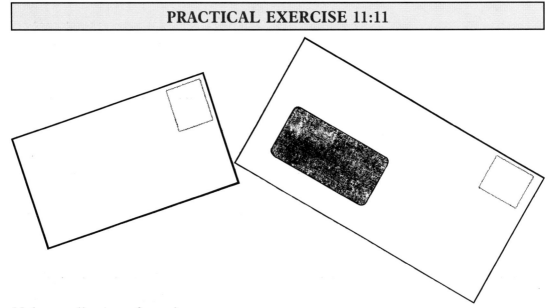

Make a collection of envelopes.
Undo each envelope to find its net. Work out the area of paper used to make each envelope.

Design and make an envelope.

Your design could give the greatest size envelope for the least amount of paper.
You could make your envelope an interesting shape.

AREA of PARALLELOGRAM, TRAPEZIUM and KITE

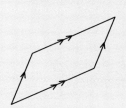

The opposite sides of a **parallelogram** are equal and parallel.

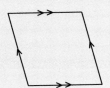

A **rhombus** is a parallelogram which has all sides equal.

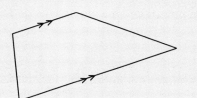

In a **trapezium**, one pair of opposite sides are parallel.

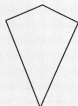

In a **kite**, two pairs of adjacent sides are equal.

DISCUSSION EXERCISE 11:12

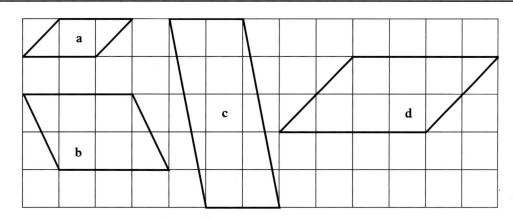

Count squares to find the area of the above parallelograms.

Discuss how the sequence of diagrams given below can be used to find the area of the parallelogram **b**. How does the area of the parallelogram relate to the area of the rectangle ABCD?

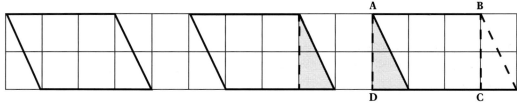

Discuss how to find the area of the parallelograms **a**, **c** and **d** without counting squares.

What if no sides of the parallelogram were horizontal?

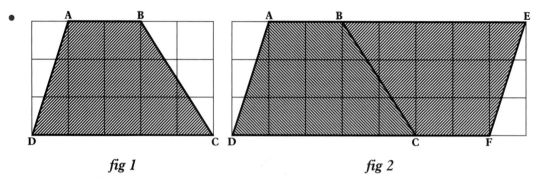

fig 1   fig 2

Is the trapezium BEFC on *fig 2* congruent to the trapezium ABCD? What shape is AEFD?

Count squares to estimate the area of the trapezium ABCD.

Discuss how the diagrams shown can be used to find the area of the trapezium ABCD, without counting squares.

What if the parallel sides of the trapezium were not horizontal? (Consider diagrams such as those below.)

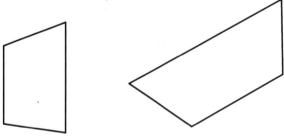

The area of the trapezium ABCD can also be found by dividing the trapezium into a parallelogram and a triangle.
Discuss how this could be done.

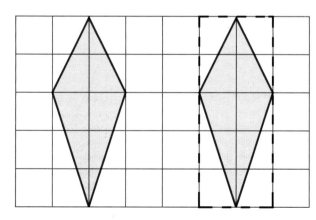

- Discuss the relationship between the area of the kite and the area of the rectangle surrounding the kite.

  Discuss the relationship between the area of the kite and the length of the diagonals.

Area of parallelogram = base × height.

In these diagrams, $\boxed{A = bh}$

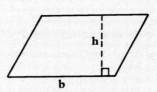 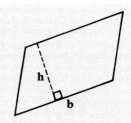

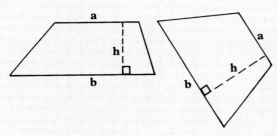

Area of trapezium = half the sum of the parallel sides × height, where the height is the perpendicular distance between the parallel sides.

In these diagrams, $\boxed{A = \frac{1}{2}(a + b) \times h}$

Area of kite = half the product of the diagonals.

In this diagram, $\boxed{A = \frac{1}{2}ab}$

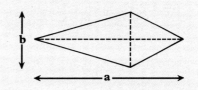

Examples

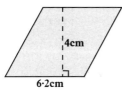 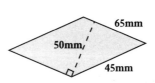 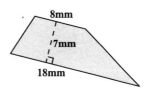

$A = bh$

$\quad = 6{\cdot}2 \times 4$

$\quad = 24{\cdot}8\,\text{cm}^2$

$A = bh$

$\quad = 65 \times 50$

$\quad = 3250\,\text{mm}^2$

$A = \frac{1}{2}(a + b) \times h$

$\quad = \frac{1}{2}(8 + 18) \times 7$

$\quad = 91\,\text{mm}^2$

Worked Example   The area of a kite is 38cm². The length of the longer diagonal is 20cm. What length is the shorter diagonal?

Answer   Using $A = \frac{1}{2}ab$, $\quad 38 = \frac{1}{2} \times 20 \times b$

$\qquad\qquad\qquad\qquad\qquad 38 = 10b$

$\qquad\qquad\qquad\qquad\qquad\; b = 3{\cdot}8\,\text{cm}$

EXERCISE 11:13

1. Find the area of these parallelograms.

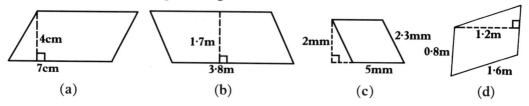

(a)   (b)   (c)   (d)

2. The area of a parallelogram is 20cm². The base is 16cm.
   What is the height of this parallelogram?

3. Even without measurements written on this diagram, we know that the areas of
   the shaded figures are equal. How do we know?

4. Find the area of these trapeziums.

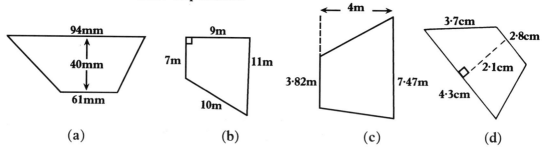

(a)   (b)   (c)   (d)

5. Mike made a kite with diagonals 73cm and 48cm. Find its area.

6.

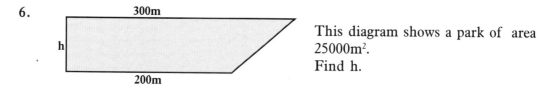

This diagram shows a park of area 25000m².
Find h.

7. This shows the cross-section of a swimming pool. What is the area of this cross section?

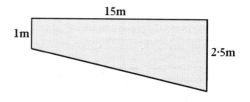

Review 1 Find the area of these.

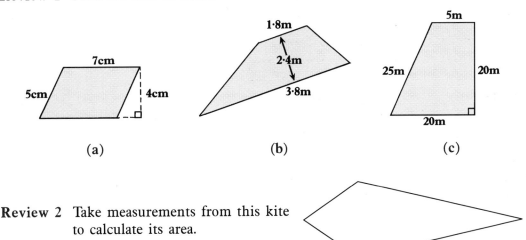

(a)   (b)   (c)

Review 2 Take measurements from this kite
to calculate its area.

Review 3   This diagram represents an end wall of a
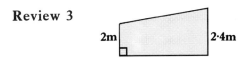   shed. The area of this wall is 26·4m².
What is the length of the wall?

VOLUME of a CUBOID

DISCUSSION EXERCISE 11:14

For this cuboid: length = 5cm
width = 4cm
height = 3cm.

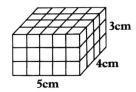

The cuboid has been divided into cubes of side 1cm.
How many cubes are there altogether? What is the volume of this cuboid?

Discuss the following statement "the volume of a cuboid can be found by
multiplying the length by the width by the height."

Test the formula "volume = length × width × height" on other cuboids.

For a **cuboid,** Volume = length × width × height

Example Volume = length × width × height

= 8m × 5m × 3m

= 120m³

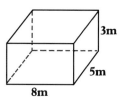

EXERCISE 11:15

1. Find the volume of these.

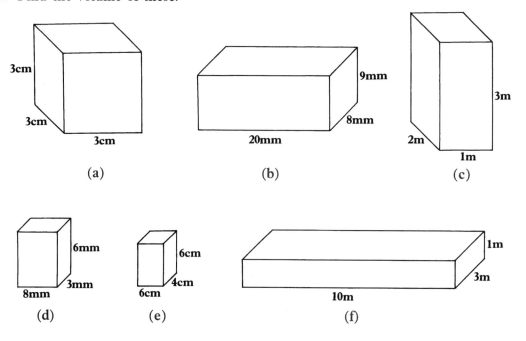

(a)   (b)   (c)

(d)   (e)   (f)

2. A room is 4 metres long, 3 metres wide and 2·7 metres high.

What is the volume of this room?

3. Concrete posts are made by pouring concrete into moulds, such as that shown.

What volume of concrete is there in each post?

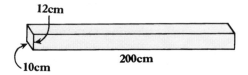

4. A "square" baking dish is in fact a cuboid with a square base, as shown in the diagram.

   How much cake mixture could this "square" dish hold if it was half filled?

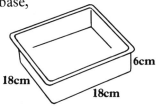

5. Deborah built a sandpit for her sister.
   She made it 350cm long, 240cm wide and 40cm high. Deborah then filled it with sand to within 10cm of the top.

   What volume of sand did Deborah put in this sandpit?

6. A box has dimensions 10cm by 8cm by 6cm.

   Dice, such as those shown, are to be packed into this box.

   How many dice will this box hold?

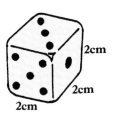

Review 1 Find the volume of these.

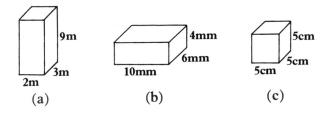

(a) (b) (c)

Review 2 Each of the small cubes in a Rubik's cube has a side of 18mm.

   (a) What is the volume of each small cube?

   (b) What is the volume of the Rubik's cube?

INVESTIGATION 11:16

MAKING BOXES

This net can be drawn on cardboard and folded to make a box of volume 24cm³. The dimensions of this box are 3cm × 4cm × 2cm.

What other dimensions could a box of volume 24cm³ have? **Investigate.**

Design nets for these other dimensions.
Which of these nets uses the smallest amount of cardboard?
Investigate.

What if the volume was 48cm³?

What if the volume was 30cm³?

What if the volume was 36cm³?

What if . . .

FOR YOUR INTEREST

Paint   For two coats of paint, allow 1 litre for every 8 square metres.

Curtain material   Width needed: twice the width of the windows
length needed: length of windows + 20cm extra

Wallpaper

height of room in metres	WALLPAPER CHART													
	distance round the room in metres (m)													
	9	10	11	13	14	15	16	18	19	20	21	23	24	25	26
2·00m – 2·30m	4	5	5	6	6	7	7	8	8	9	9	10	10	11	12
2·31m – 2·50m	5	5	6	6	7	7	8	8	9	9	10	11	11	12	13
2·51m – 2·70m	5	6	6	8	8	8	9	10	11	11	12	13	13	13	14
2·71m – 3·00m	6	6	7	8	9	9	10	11	12	12	13	14	14	15	16
3·01m – 3·20m	6	7	8	8	10	10	10	12	12	13	13	14	15	16	16
	Number of rolls needed													

The quantities given above are recommended for decorating.

Use this information to do a project on decorating a room in your house, or school, in the colour scheme of your choice.

As part of your project, take measurements, draw plans, work out how much paint, wallpaper, curtain material etc. that you will need and find the total cost.

DISCOVER, DISCUSS, DO

- What is the meaning of the word "parallel"?

  What is the meaning of the word "intersect"?

  Where, around your school, do you find examples of parallel lines?
  Where, in your community, do you find parallel lines?
  Discuss with your neighbour or group or class.

  Where, around your school, do you find examples of intersecting lines?
  Where, in your community, do you find intersecting lines? **Discuss.**

- Choose an activity such as playing football, going shopping, disco dancing, taking a photograph, playing a card game etc. **Discuss** what parallel and intersecting lines you would be likely to find.

- Try and draw truly parallel lines. How could you test whether your lines are truly parallel?

- Design a street plan for a village using parallel and intersecting lines.

ANGLES made with INTERSECTING LINES

DISCUSSION EXERCISE 12:1

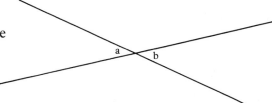

● 1. Use your protractor to measure the
size of the angles marked **a** and **b**.

2. Repeat 1 for these diagrams.

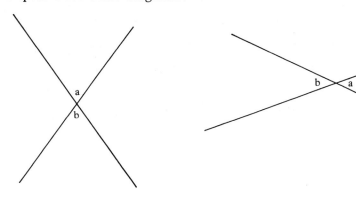

Discuss your answers for **1** and **2** with your neighbour or group or class.
Make a statement about the sizes of **a** and **b**.
Test your statement by drawing more diagrams similar to those in **1** and **2**
and measuring **a** and **b**.

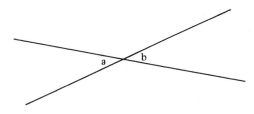

How could the following statement be
completed?

Without measuring the size of the
angles **a** and **b**, I know that a = . . .

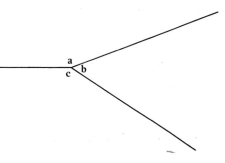

● 1. Use your protractor to measure
the size of the angles marked **a**,
b and **c**.
Find the sum **a** + **b** + **c**.

2. Repeat **1** for these diagrams.

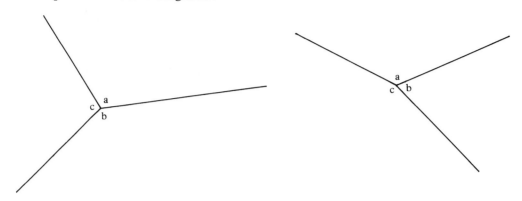

Discuss your answers for **1** and **2**.

Make a statement about the sum **a** + **b** + **c**.

Test your statement by drawing more diagrams similar to those in **1** and **2**, measuring the angles and finding the sum **a** + **b** + **c**.

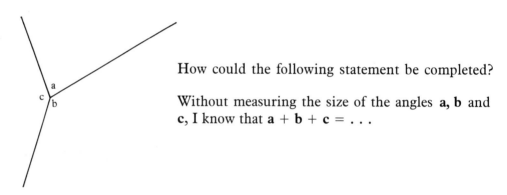

How could the following statement be completed?

Without measuring the size of the angles **a, b** and **c**, I know that **a** + **b** + **c** = . . .

In each of the diagrams above there were three angles (**a, b** and **c**) around the point.

What if there were more than three angles such as in the following diagrams?

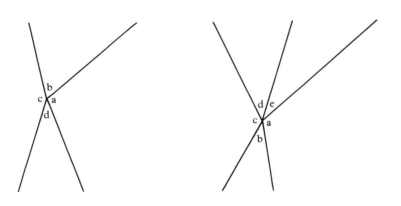

218

- 1. Use your protractor to measure the
  size of the angles marked **a** and **b.**
  Find the sum **a + b.**

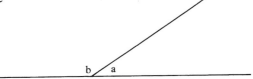

2. Repeat **1** for these diagrams.

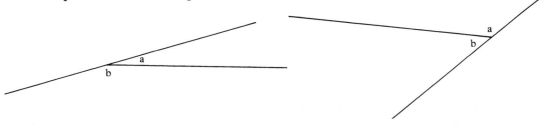

Discuss your answers for **1** and **2** with your neighbour or group or class.
Make a statement about the sum **a + b.**
Test your statement by drawing more diagrams similar to those in **1** and **2,**
measuring and finding the sum **a + b.**

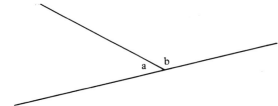

How could the following statement be
completed?

Without measuring the size of the angles
a and **b,** I know that **a + b** = . . .

In each of the diagrams above there were just two angles (**a** and **b**) on the
straight line.

What if there were more than two angles such as in the following diagrams?

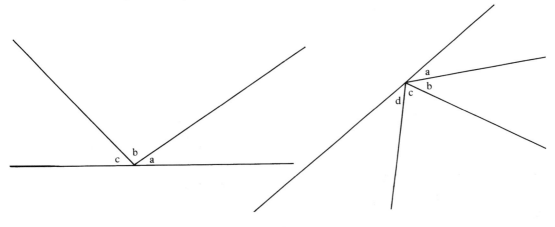

Angles at a point add to 360°. Use this fact to justify your statement about the sums of the marked angles in the diagrams on the previous page.

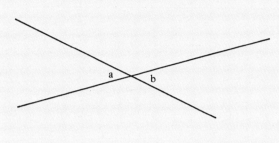

Angles such as **a** and **b** are called **vertically opposite angles**.

They are the two angles which are opposite one another (not beside each other) when two lines intersect.

| **Vertically opposite angles are equal.** |

Whenever we use this fact, we must say so. Instead of writing out the full reason "Vertically opposite angles are equal", we may use the abbreviated reason: **vert. opp.** ∠s.

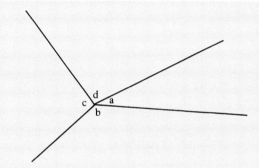

Angles such as **a, b, c** and **d** are called **angles at a point**.
They are the angles around a point.

| **Angles at a point add to 360°.** |

Whenever we use this fact, we must say so. Instead of writing out the full reason "Angles at a point add to 360°", we may use the abbreviated reason: ∠s at a point.

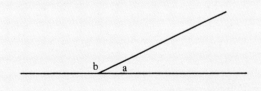

Angles such as **a** and **b** are called **adjacent angles on a straight line**.
"Adjacent" means "beside" and these angles are beside each other.

| **Adjacent angles on a straight line add to 180°.** |

Whenever we use this fact, we must say so. Instead of writing out the full reason "Adjacent angles on a straight line add to 180°", we may use the abbreviated reason: **adj. ∠s on line.**

Worked Example Calculate the value of f in the following diagrams.

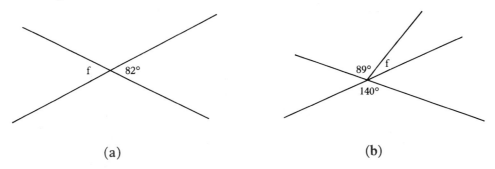

(a) (b)

Answer (a) $f = 82°$ (vert. opp. $\angle$s)

  (b) Since the 140° angle is vertically opposite the angle consisting of both 89° and f together, then:
$$f + 89° = 140° \text{ (vert. opp. } \angle s)$$
$$f = 51° \text{ (subtracting 89° from both sides)}$$

Worked Example Calculate the value of **z** in the following digrams.

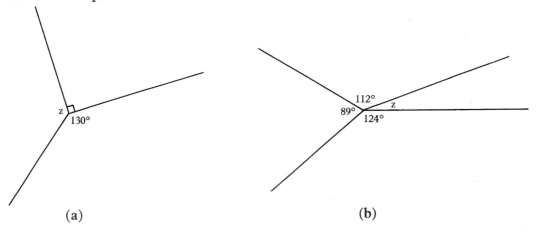

(a) (b)

Answer (a) $z + 130° + 90° = 360°$ ($\angle$s at a point)
$$z + 220° = 360°$$
$$z = 140° \text{ (subtracting 220° from both sides)}$$

  (b) $z + 112° + 89° + 124° = 360°$ ($\angle$s at a point)
$$z + 325° = 360°$$
$$z = 35° \text{ (subtracting 325° from both sides)}$$

Worked Example   Calculate the size of the angle marked as **x** in these diagrams.

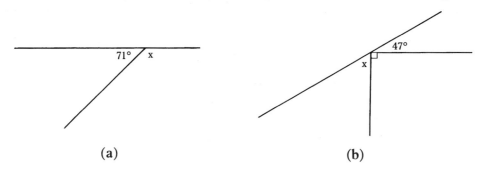

(a)   (b)

Answer   (a) $x + 71° = 180°$ (adj. $\angle$s on line)

$\qquad\qquad\quad x = 109°$ (subtracting 71° from both sides)

(b) $x + 90° + 47° = 180°$ (adj. $\angle$s on line)

$\qquad\quad x + 137° = 180°$

$\qquad\qquad\qquad x = 43°$ (subtracting 137° from both sides)

Worked Example   Write and solve equations to find the value of **x** and **y**.

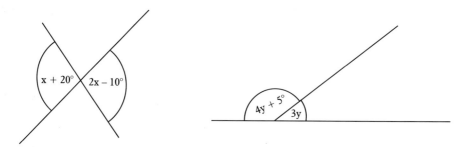

Answer $\qquad\qquad 2x - 10° = x + 20°$ (vert. opp. $\angle$s)

$\qquad\qquad\qquad x - 10° = 20°$ (subtracting x from both sides)

$\qquad\qquad\qquad\qquad x = 30°$ (adding 10° to each side)

$\qquad\qquad 4y + 5° + 3y = 180°$ (adj. $\angle$s on line)

$\qquad\qquad\quad 7y + 5° = 180°$

$\qquad\qquad\qquad\qquad 7y = 175°$ (subtracting 5° from both sides)

$\qquad\qquad\qquad\qquad y = 25°$ (dividing both sides by 7)

Note   All of the equations in the Worked Examples were solved using the Balance Method. They could have been solved in other ways.

EXERCISE 12:2

1. In each of the following, **x** can be calculated as 100°. Which of the reasons in the box would you use to justify your answer?

> **A.** Adjacent angles on a line
> **B.** Angles at a point
> **C.** Vertically opposite angles

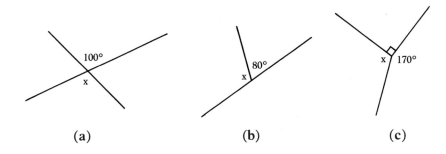

(a)   (b)   (c)

2. Trace the diagram at the right.
   Calculate the value of each unknown on the left.
   Draw a line from the dot (•) beside each diagram on the left to the correct answer.
   How many lines cross the shaded region?

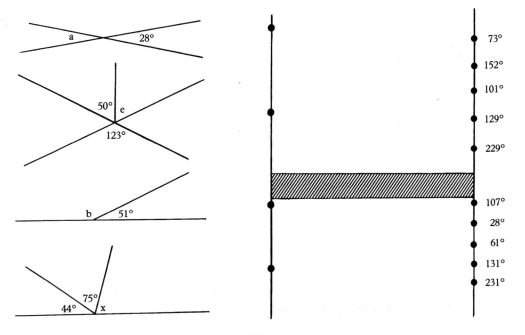

3. Calculate the value of **c** and **d**.

4. Calculate the value of each unknown. Give one of the reasons in the box in **question 1** to justify your answer.

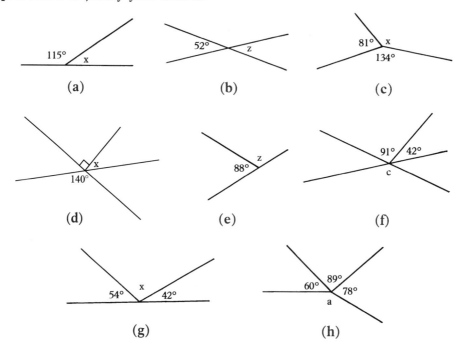

5. Calculate the value of each of the unknowns.

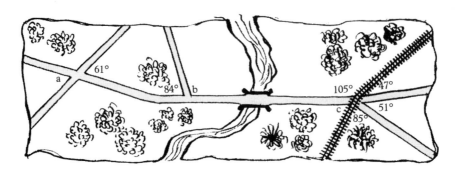

6. Calculate the value of x.

(a)

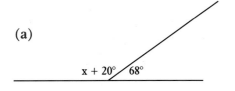

(b)

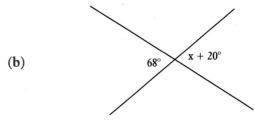

(c)

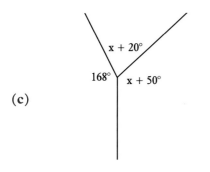

(d)

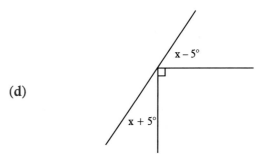

(e)

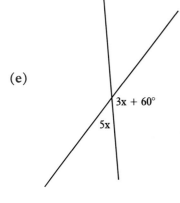

(f)

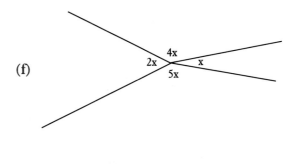

(g)

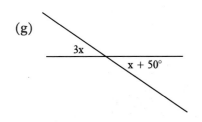

(h)

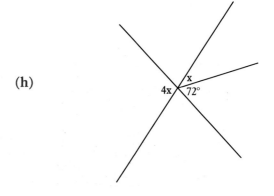

Review 1 Copy the crossnumber.

Calculate the value of each unknown.
Using these values, complete the crossnumber.

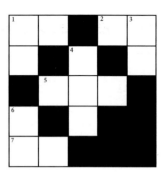

Across	Down
1. c	1. h
2. d	3. e
5. g	4. f
7. b	6. a

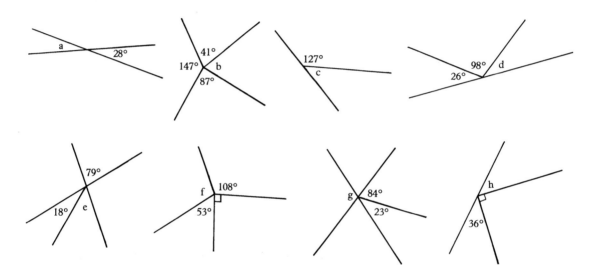

Review 2 Which of these reasons did you use
to find each of a, b, c, . . ., h in
Review 1?

A.	vert. opp ∠s
B.	∠s at a point
C.	adj. ∠s on line

Review 3 Calculate the value of x.

(a)

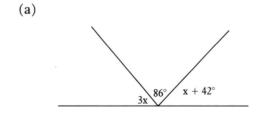

(b)

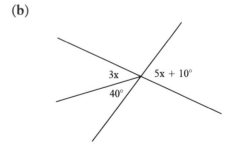

ANGLES made with PARALLEL LINES

DISCUSSION EXERCISE 12:3

● 1. Use your protractor to measure the size of the angles marked **a** and **b**.

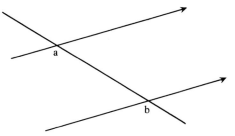

2. Repeat 1 for these diagrams.

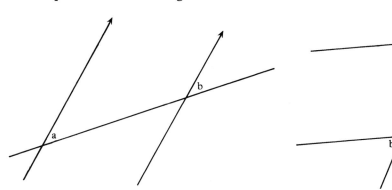

Discuss your answers to **1** and **2** with your neighbour or group or class. Make a statement about the sizes of **a** and **b**.

Notice that in each of the diagrams in **1** and **2**, the angle marked **a** can be translated onto the angle marked **b**. That is, angle **a** can be slid (without any rotating or turning) onto angle **b**.

Discuss how you could test the statement you made about the sizes of **a** and **b**. (***Hint:*** You might consider using tracing paper.)

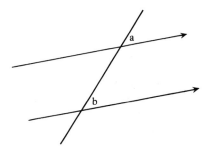

How could the following statement be completed?

Without measuring the size of angles **a** and **b**, I know that **a** = . . .

● 1. Use your protractor to measure the size of the angles marked **a** and **b**.

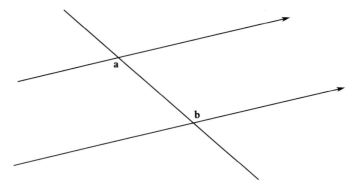

2. Repeat **1** for these diagrams.

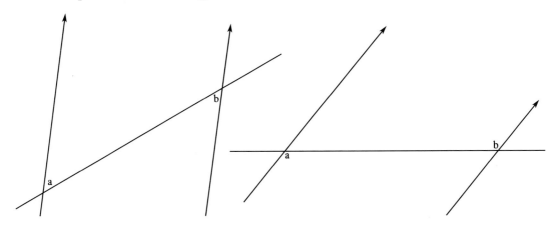

Discuss your answers to **1** and **2**.
Make and test a statement about the sizes of **a** and **b**.

Notice that in each of the diagrams in **1** and **2**, the angle marked **a** can be rotated onto the angle marked **b**.

Discuss how you could test the statement you made about the sizes of **a** and **b**.

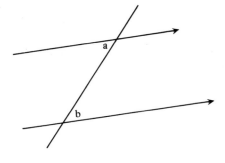

How could the following statement be completed?

Without measuring the size of the angles **a** and **b**, I know that **a** = . . .

● 1. Use your protractor to measure the size of the angles marked **a** and **b**.

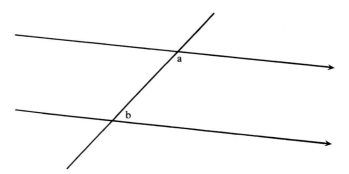

2. 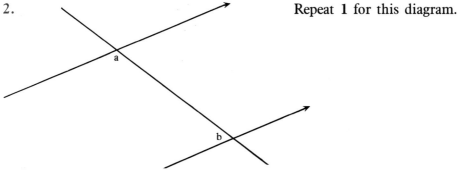   Repeat **1** for this diagram.

Discuss your answers to **1** and **2**.
Make a statement about the sizes of **a** and **b**.

Notice that in the diagrams in **1** and **2**, the angles marked **a** and **b** are both inside the parallel lines and both on the same side of the line that crosses the parallel lines.

Discuss how you could test the statement you made about the sizes of angles **a** and **b**.

How could the following statement be completed?

Without measuring the size of the angles **a** and **b**, I know that **a** + **b** = . . .

A line which crosses parallel lines is called a **transversal**.
In this diagram, AB is a transversal.

Angles such as **a** and **b** are called **corresponding angles**. Corresponding angles are in corresponding positions. One corresponding angle can be **translated** onto the other.

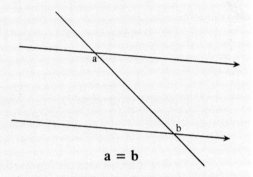

Corresponding angles are equal.

$a = b$

Whenever we use this fact, we must say so. Instead of writing out the full reason "Corresponding angles are equal" we may use the abbreviated reason: **corr.** $\angle$s.

Angles such as **a** and **b** are called **alternate angles**.
Alternate angles are both inside the parallel lines and on opposite sides of the transversal.
One alternate angle can be **rotated** onto another alternate angle.

Alternate angles are equal.

$a = b$

Whenever we use this fact, we must say so. Instead of writing out the full reason "Alternate angles are equal" we may use the abbreviated reason: **alt.** $\angle$s.

Angles such as **a** and **b** are called **interior angles**.
Interior angles are both inside the parallel lines and on the same side of the transversal.

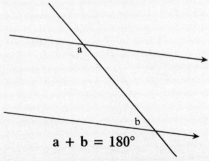

Interior angles add to 180°.

$a + b = 180°$

Whenever we use this fact, we must say so. Instead of writing out the full reason "Interior angles add to 180°" we may use the abbreviated reason: **int.** $\angle$s.

Example

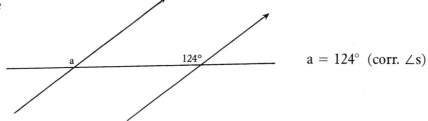

a = 124° (corr. ∠s)

Example

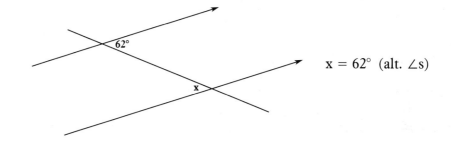

x = 62° (alt. ∠s)

Example

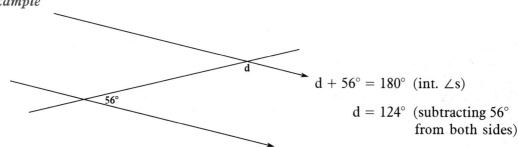

d + 56° = 180° (int. ∠s)

d = 124° (subtracting 56° from both sides)

Worked Example Write and solve equations to find the value of **a** and **x**.

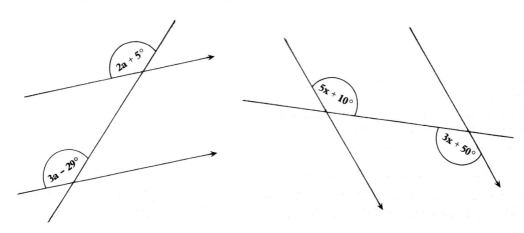

Answer $3a - 29° = 2a + 5°$ (corr. $\angle$s)
           $a - 29° = 5°$ (subtracting 2a from both sides)
                $a = 34°$ (adding 29° to each side)

        $5x + 10° = 3x + 50°$ (alt. $\angle$s)
          $2x + 10° = 50°$ (subtracting 3x from both sides)
                $2x = 40°$ (subtracting 10° from both sides)
                 $x = 20°$ (dividing both sides by 2)

EXERCISE 12:4

1. Name the angle that is alternate to the marked angle.

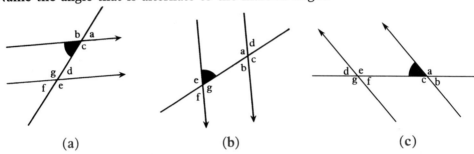

        (a)   (b)   (c)

2. Name all the pairs of corresponding angles in each of the following diagrams. The diagrams represent a section of trellis and a roof.

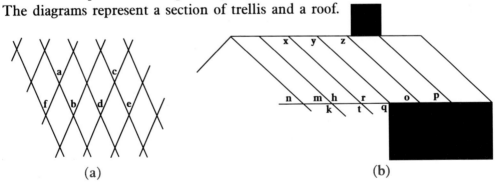

        (a)   (b)

3. In the diagrams for **question 1** which angles are interior angles?

4. Find the size of the marked angles. Give a reason.

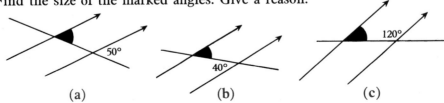

        (a)   (b)   (c)

(d)

59°

(e)

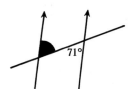

71°

5. Name all the angles that are equal to

(a) e

(b) b

(c) k

(d) d.

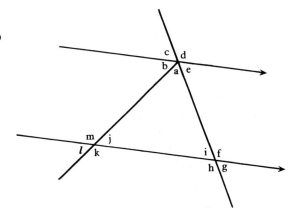

6.

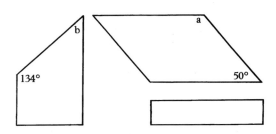

The trapezium, parallelogram and rectangle found on the logo have been drawn at the right. Find the value of **a** and **b**.

134°   50°

7. Find the size of **x**.

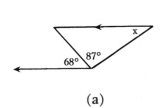

68° 87°

(a)

47° 72°

(b)

47°

(c)

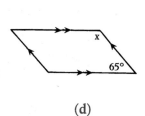

65°

(d)

8. Write and solve equations to find the value of n.

(a)

(b)

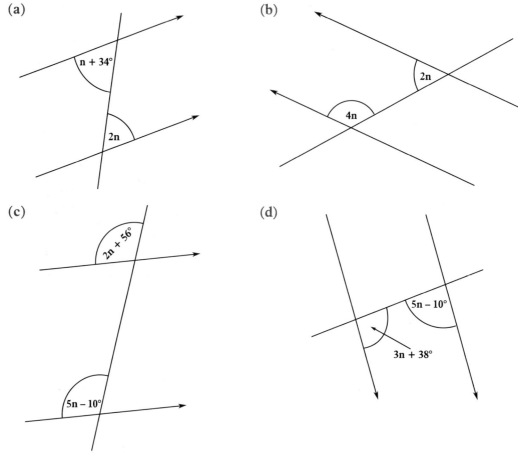

(c)

(d)

9. (a) Explain why the lines AB and CD are not parallel.

(b) Name a pair of parallel lines. Give a reason for your answer.

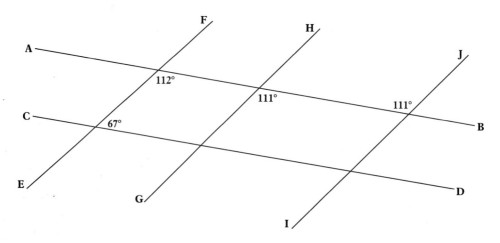

Review 1

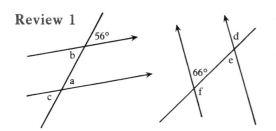 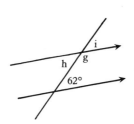 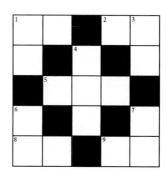

Work out the values of **a**, **b**, **c**, **d**, **e**, **f**, **g**, **h** and **i** from these diagrams. Use these values to complete the crossnumber.

Copy the crossnumber.

Across	**Down**
1. a	1. b
2. d	3. i
5. f	4. g
8. h	6. c
9. e	7. b

Review 2 Explain why the lines HG and FE are parallel.

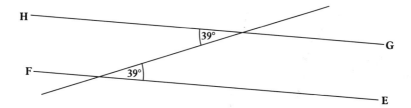

Review 3 Write and solve equations to find the value of x.

(a)

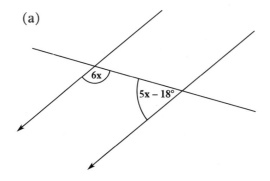

(b)

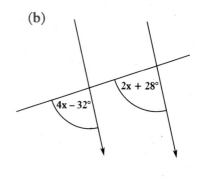

There is often more than one way of finding an unknown angle. We can use any of
vertically opposite angles
adjacent angles on a straight line
angles at a point
corresponding angles
alternate angles
interior angles.

In the following exercise you may use any of these angle relationships.

EXERCISE 12:5

1. Find the value of **a, b, c, d, e** and **f.**

   (a)   (b)

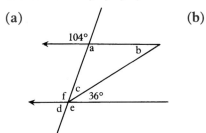 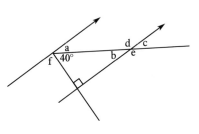

2.

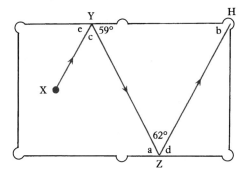

The arrows show the path of a
billiard ball from X to H.
XY and ZH are parallel paths.
Find the values of **a, b, c, d** and **e.**

3. Find the size of the angles marked a, b, c, d, e, f, g.

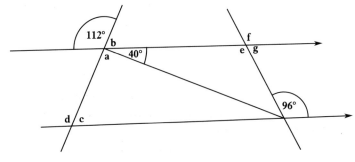

Review 1

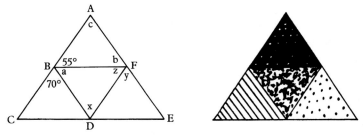

The triangles on the left are the same size and shape as the triangles on the right. The lines BF and CE are parallel. AE and BD are parallel as are DF and CA. Find the size of **x, y, z, a, b, c.**

Review 2 Find the size of the angles marked as **a, b, c, d, e, f.**

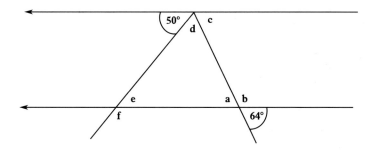

FOR YOUR INTEREST

Discuss one of the following statements. Find examples to support your point of view.

In nature there are no truly parallel lines.

There are more examples around us of intersecting lines than of parallel lines.

Buildings will not stay standing unless the sides are truly parallel.

Everyone in the building industry must understand parallel and intersecting lines.

Present the results of your discussion to the class. You may choose to make a poster, conduct a mock interview, join with another group to debate one of the statements or make a booklet or tape.

DISCOVER, DISCUSS, DO

- Think for a moment about how many times each day you see triangles in the environment around you. **Discuss** with your neighbour or group or class.

- Think now about "what if triangles didn't exist". How would the world look? What are all the things which couldn't exist if we didn't have triangles? **Discuss**.

- Design a bungalow using as many triangles as possible.

- Design an earring or piece of jewellery using triangles.

- Make some other stars using triangles.

INTERIOR ANGLES of a TRIANGLE

DISCUSSION EXERCISE 13:1

●

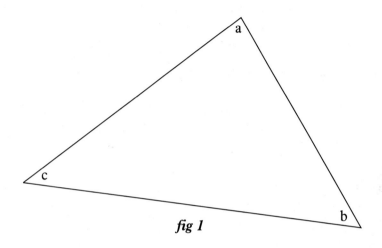

fig 1

On a loose piece of paper draw a triangle similar to that shown above.

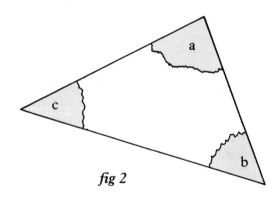

fig 2

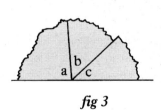

fig 3

Now tear off each of the corners, as shown in *fig 2*.

Place the torn off corners side by side, as shown in *fig 3*.

What statement can you make about the sum **a** + **b** + **c**?
Discuss with your neighbour or group or class.

● Test your statement about the sum **a** + **b** + **c** for some other triangles.

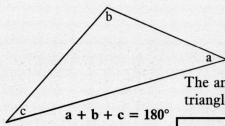

The angles a, b, c are called the **interior angles** of a triangle. They are the angles inside the triangle.

The sum of the interior angles of a triangle is 180°.

We often speak of the "angle sum of a triangle". By this we mean "the sum of the interior angles".

Whenever we use the fact that the angles inside a triangle add to 180°, we must say so. Instead of writing out the reason in full, we may use ∠ sum of Δ.

Worked Example   Find the value of n and x.

(a) 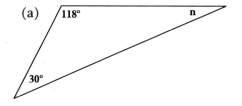   (b)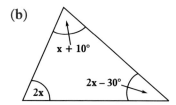

Answer (a) n + 30° + 118° = 180° (∠ sum of Δ)
n + 148° = 180°
n = 32° (subtracting 148° from both sides)

(b) 2x + x + 10° + 2x – 30° = 180° (∠ sum of Δ)
5x – 20° = 180°
5x = 200° (adding 20° to both sides)
x = 40° (dividing both sides by 5)

EXERCISE 13:2

1. Find the value of **x**.

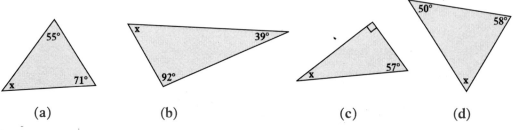

(a)   (b)   (c)   (d)

2. Find the size of a.

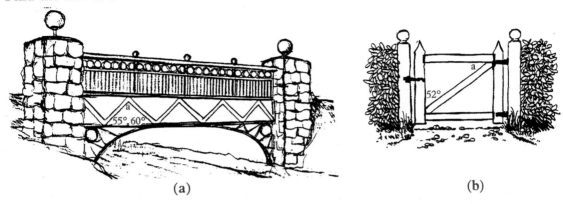

(a)   (b)

3. Find the value of **n**. Hence find the size of the angles.

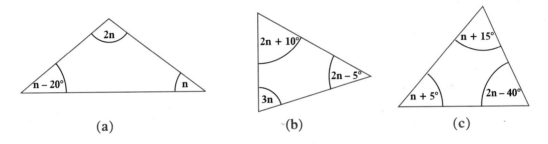

(a)   (b)   (c)

Review 1 Find the value of **x**.

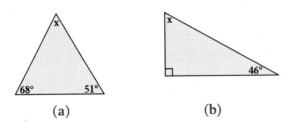

(a)   (b)

Review 2 Find the value of **a**. Hence find the size of the angles.

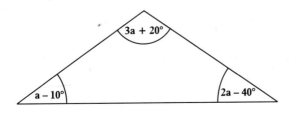

241

ANGLES in SPECIAL TRIANGLES

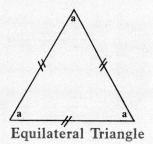

Equilateral Triangle

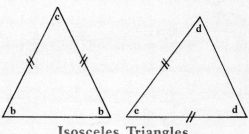

Isosceles Triangles

An **equilateral triangle** has all its sides equal and all its angles equal. Each angle is 60°.

An **isosceles triangle** has two equal sides and two equal angles. The unequal side is sometimes called the **base**. The equal angles are at either end of the base. They are sometimes called the **base angles**.

Whenever we use the fact that the base angles of an isosceles triangle are equal, we must say so. Instead of writing this reason in full we may use the abbreviated reason: **base ∠s isosc. Δ**.

Worked Example Find the size of the marked angles.

(a)

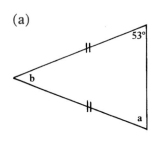

(b)

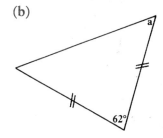

Answer (a) a = 53° (base ∠s, isosc. Δ)
$$b + 53° + 53° = 180° \ (\angle \text{ sum of } \Delta)$$
$$b + 106° = 180°$$
$$b = 74° \text{ (subtracting 106° from both sides)}$$

(b) The unmarked angle equals **a**. (base ∠s, isosc. Δ)
$$a + a + 62° = 180° \ (\angle \text{ sum of } \Delta)$$
$$2a + 62° = 180°$$
$$2a = 118° \text{ (subtracting 62° from both sides)}$$
$$a = 59° \text{ (dividing both sides by 2)}$$

Worked Example

The equal sides of this isosceles triangle are 2x + 3 and 3x – 1.

(a) Find x.

(b) Find the length of the equal sides.

Answer   (a) 3x – 1 = 2x + 3
            x – 1 = 3 (subtracting 2x from both sides)
            x = 4 (adding 1 to both sides)

(b) One of the equal sides is of length 2x + 3.
     Since x = 4, 2x + 3 = 2 × 4 + 3
                        = 11
The equal sides are each of length 11 units.

EXERCISE 13:3

1. Find the size of **a**.

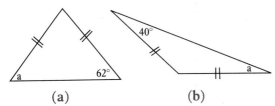   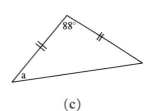   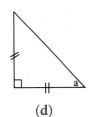

(a)   (b)   (c)   (d)

2. Find the size of the angles marked **x** and **y**.

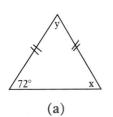   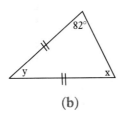   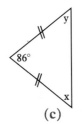   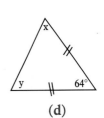

(a)   (b)   (c)   (d)

3. The marked angles are equal.

(a) Find n.

(b) Find the length of the equal sides.

4. 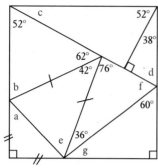 Trace this diagram.

(a) Find the value of each unknown on the diagram.

(b) If the value of the unknown is less than 60°, shade the triangle that contains the unknown.

(c) What is special about all the shaded triangles?

Review Calculate the size of **x**.

(a) 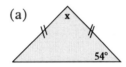 (b) 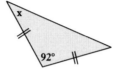 (c)

  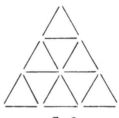

INVESTIGATION 13:4

EQUILATERAL TRIANGLE PATTERNS

fig 1 *fig 2* *fig 3*

fig 1 has side of length 1 match.

fig 2 has side of length 2 matches.

fig 3 has side of length 3 matches.

Investigate these equilateral triangle patterns. (Build up at least another two triangles before beginning your investigation.)
You might like to consider things such as:
    the number of matches needed to build up each triangle
    the number of small equilateral triangles within each triangle
    the number of equilateral triangles of any size within each triangle.

PUZZLES 13:5

? ?

1. Draw two equilateral triangles by drawing just five lines.

2. Draw two equilateral triangles by drawing just four lines.

? ?

EXTERIOR ANGLE of a TRIANGLE

DISCUSSION EXERCISE 13:6

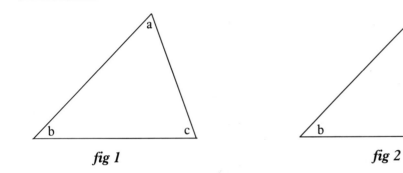

fig 1   *fig 2*

The triangle in *fig 1* is shown again in *fig 2* with one side extended to form another angle **d**.

Investigate the relationship between **a**, **b** and **d**. (*Hint:* On a loose piece of paper, draw a triangle similar to *fig 1*. Tear off the angles **a** and **b**.)

Continue your investigation by extending the other sides of the triangle as shown in *fig 3* and *fig 4*.

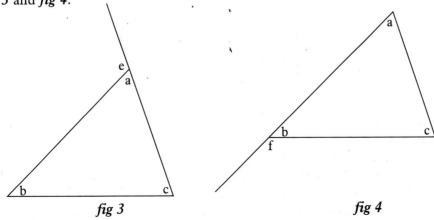

fig 3   *fig 4*

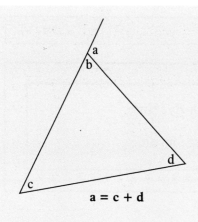

An **exterior angle** of a triangle is the angle between an extended side (often called a produced side) and the adjacent side. **a** is an exterior angle in this diagram.

> **An exterior angle is equal to the sum of the two interior, opposite angles.**

a = c + d

Whenever we use this fact, we must say so. Instead of giving the full reason we may use the abbreviated reason: ext. ∠ of Δ.

Worked Example Find the value of **x**.

(a)

(b)

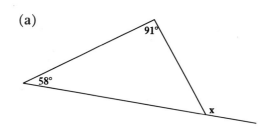

Answer (a) x = 58° + 91° (ext ∠ of Δ)
x = 149°

(b) x + 42° = 93° (ext ∠ of Δ)
x = 51° (subtracting 42° from both sides)

Worked Example Find the size of **a** and **b**.

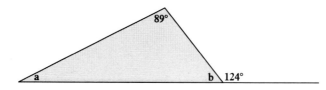

Answer a + 89° = 124° (ext ∠ of Δ)
a = 35° (subtracting 89° from both sides)

b + 35° + 89° = 180° (∠ sum of Δ)
b + 124° = 180°
b = 56°

Notice that b could also be found using adjacent angles on a line.

Example To find **a**, we must find the angle marked with a dot (•).

Both the base angles of the isosceles triangle total 110°.
Hence the angle marked with the dot (•) must equal 55°.

Then a = 70° + 55° (ext. ∠ of Δ)
        a = 125°

EXERCISE 13:7

1. Find the value of **e**.

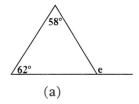 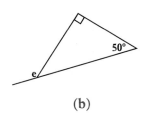 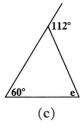 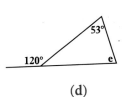

   (a)   (b)   (c)   (d)

2. Find the value of **x** and **y**.

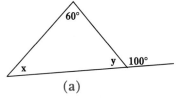 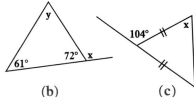 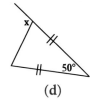

   (a)   (b)   (c)   (d)

3. Copy this diagram.

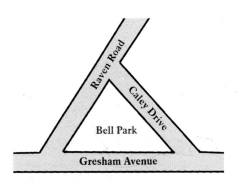

   (a) The angle between Caley Drive and
       Raven Road is 105°. Which of the two
       angles between Caley Drive and
       Raven Road will this be?
       The angle between Caley Drive and
       Gresham Avenue is 60°. Which angle
       is this? Write these angles on your
       diagram.

   (b) Calculate the angles at the three corners of Bell Park.

(c) A path runs across Bell Park from Caley Drive to Gresham Avenue. This path is at right angles to Caley Drive.
Draw in one possible position for this path.
Calculate the angle at which this path meets Gresham Avenue.

Review Find the value of **e, f, x, y, z.**

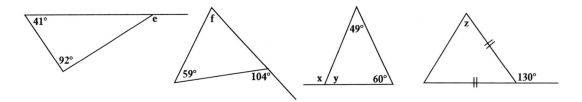

TESSELLATIONS of TRIANGLES

A shape is **tessellated** when it is moved around so that it completely fills a space, leaving no gaps. It may be moved by translating it or reflecting it or rotating it or some combination of these. When we tessellate a shape we form a **tiling pattern**.

Example The shaded figure has been tessellated.

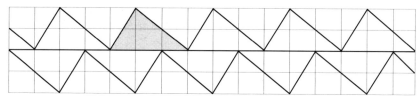

Example

This triangle can be tessellated to cover this rectangular area in the ways shown below and in many other ways.

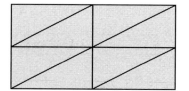
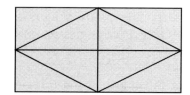

DISCUSSION and PRACTICAL EXERCISE 13:8

1.

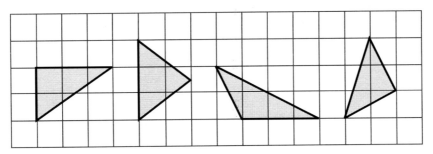

Choose one of the triangles shown.
On squared paper, tessellate this triangle to tile an area.
Colour your design, using at most 3 colours.

Do all triangles tessellate? **Investigate** and **discuss**.

2. Polyiamonds are shapes made from equilateral triangles. Any two adjacent triangles have an edge in common.

fig 1　　*fig 2*　　*fig 3*　　　*fig 4*　　　*fig 5*　　　*fig 6*

Using 1 triangle we get 1 polyiamond as in *fig 1*.
Using 2 triangles we get 1 polyiamond as in *fig 2*.
Using 3 triangles we get 1 polyiamond as in *fig 3*.
Using 4 triangles we get 3 different polyiamonds as in *fig 4, fig 5, fig 6*.

How many different polyiamonds can be made from　(a)　5 triangles
　　　　　　　　　　　　　　　　　　　　　　　　　　(b)　6 triangles?

Note A reflection or a rotation of a polyiamond already found does not give a new polyiamond.

For example;　 　are the same polyiamond.

3. Choose one of the polyiamond outlines shown below or draw another. On isometric "dotty" paper, tessellate this polyiamond to tile an area. Colour your tessellation, using at most 4 colours.

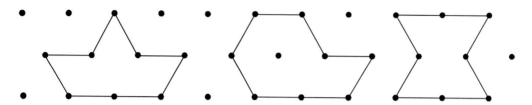

Do all polyiamonds tessellate? **Investigate** and **discuss**.

4. Design a poster, basing the design on the tessellation of triangles.

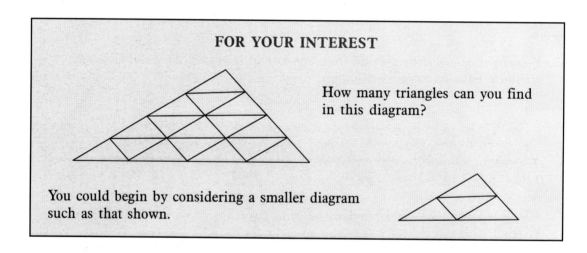

FOR YOUR INTEREST

How many triangles can you find in this diagram?

You could begin by considering a smaller diagram such as that shown.

Quadrilaterals and Polygons

DISCOVER, DISCUSS, DO

- What words, other than quadrilateral and polygon, can you think of that contain "quad" or "poly" or "lateral"? What do these words mean? **Discuss.**

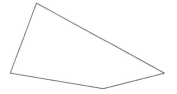 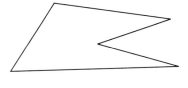 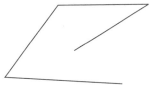

Which of these shapes are closed shapes? **Discuss.**
Which of these shapes are quadrilaterals? **Discuss.**

- Look around you in the classroom or in the school grounds. Look in books and magazines. Find shapes that you know the name of. Sketch these shapes and name them. Think about why the shapes are given particular names. **Discuss.**

- Without using its name, describe a shape to the rest of your group. Can the group name your shape from your description?

Was it difficult to describe some shapes without using their names?

What sorts of things did other students in the group tell you about the shapes they described that made it easy for you to identify the shapes?

NAMING POLYGONS

A 3-sided polygon is a triangle.   A 4-sided polygon is a quadrilateral.
A 5-sided polygon is a pentagon.   A 6-sided polygon is a hexagon.
A 7-sided polygon is a heptagon.   An 8-sided polygon is an octagon.
A 9-sided polygon is a nonagon.   A 10-sided polygon is a decagon.

A **regular** polygon has all its sides equal and all its angles equal.

EXERCISE 14:1

1. Name these shapes.

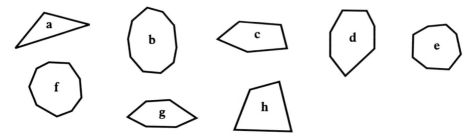

2. Which of these shapes are regular?

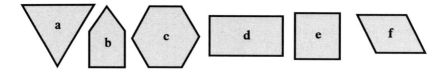

Review

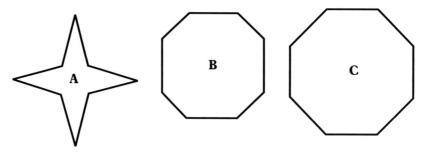

(a) Are all the above shapes octagons?

(b) Which of the above shapes are **regular** octagons?
     Give reasons for your answer.

INVESTIGATION and GAME 14:2

PENTOMINOES: the investigation

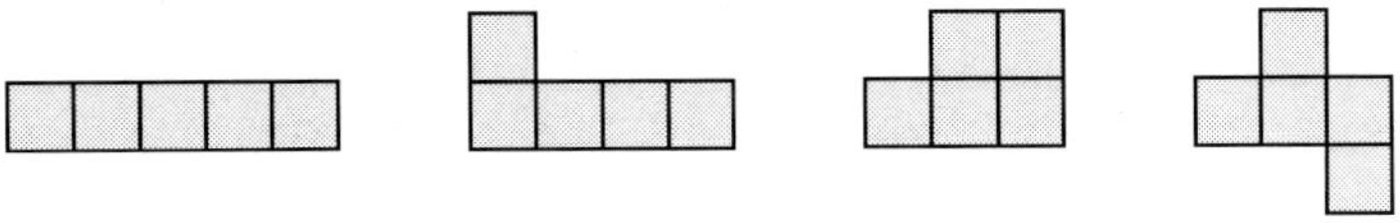

Pentominoes consist of 5 squares, placed edge to edge.
There are 12 pentomino shapes, 4 of which are drawn above.
What do the other 8 pentomino shapes look like?
Note A reflection or a rotation of a pentomino already drawn is not a new shape. For instance, the shapes drawn below are the same pentomino shape.

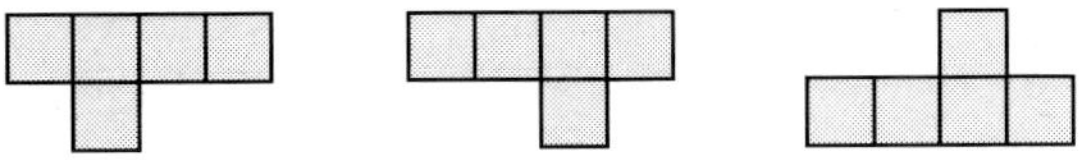

Make the set of 12 pentominoes. You could use heavy paper or thin card.

Fit the 12 pentominoes together to make as many different rectangles as possible.

Is it possible to make all the rectangles shown below, using some or all of the pentominoes? **Investigate.**

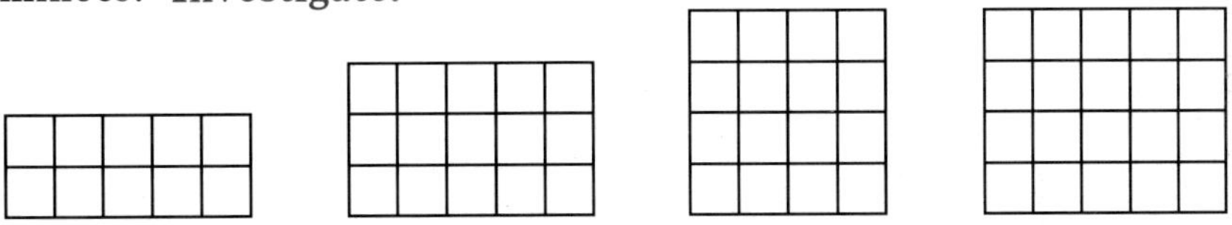

Is it possible to make some of these rectangles in more than one way? **Investigate.**

PENTOMINOES: a game for two players

Equipment   A set of 12 pentominoes for each student.
A large square drawn up in a similar way to a chessboard. Each of the 64 small squares must be the same size as each of the squares on the pentominoes.

The Play   The players take it in turn to place their pieces on the large square. The winner is the last player able to place one of his or her pentominoes on the board.

PRACTICAL EXERCISE 14:3

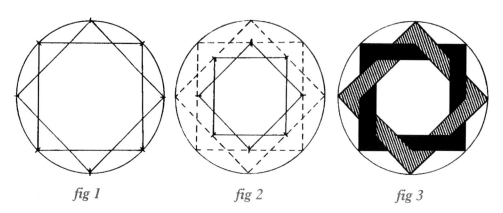

fig 1   *fig 2*   *fig 3*

These diagrams show how an interlocking square design can be made.

Step 1   This step is shown in *fig 1.*

A circle is drawn.

Eight equally spaced points are marked around the circle. (The protractor can be used to get these. They are at 45° intervals.)

Every second point is joined to get two squares.

Step 2   This step is shown in *fig 2*, in which the two squares drawn in Step 1 are shown dotted.

The mid-points of every side of the two squares are marked.

Every second mid-point is joined to get two more squares.

Step 3   This step is shown in *fig 3.*

The design is coloured to get an interlocking squares effect.

Either make an interlocking square design or an interlocking pentagonal design or an interlocking hexagonal design.

To make an interlocking pentagonal design, begin with 10 equally spaced points around a circle; to make an interlocking hexagonal design, begin with 12 equally spaced points.

GAME 14:4

TRIANGLES – a game for 2 students.

Equipment   A piece of paper marked with 6 dots placed
so that no three are in a straight line.
A black pen for one student, a red pen for
the other.

The Play   The first student joins 2 dots with a line.
The second student then joins another 2 dots with a line.
The students continue to take it in turn to join 2 dots.

The first student who is forced to complete a triangle in his or
her colour is the loser.

For instance:

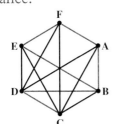

Suppose this is the position near the end of the
play. It is now the turn of the student using the
red pen.
This student must now join either E to A or F
to B and in either case must lose. (If E and A
are joined, the red triangle EFA is completed;
If F and B are joined, the red triangle FAB is
completed.)

Note This is the game of SIM if the 6 points are the vertices of a regular
hexagon.

SPECIAL TRIANGLES and QUADRILATERALS

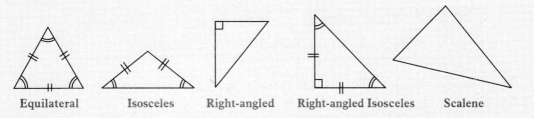

| Equilateral | Isosceles | Right-angled | Right-angled Isosceles | Scalene |

An **equilateral triangle** has all its sides equal and all its angles equal.
An **isosceles triangle** has two equal sides and two equal angles. The equal angles
are opposite the equal sides.
A **right-angled triangle** has one angle equal to 90°.
A **right-angled isosceles** triangle is both right-angled and isosceles.
A **scalene triangle** has no equal sides and no equal angles.

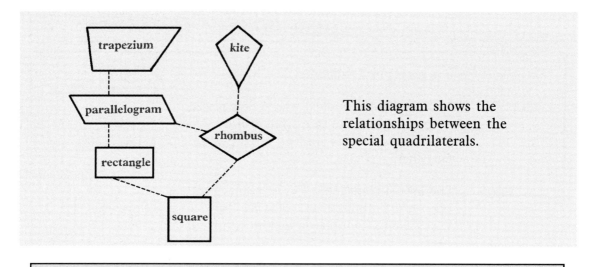

This diagram shows the relationships between the special quadrilaterals.

EXERCISE 14:5

1. Name these triangles as scalene, equilateral, isosceles, right-angled, or right-angled isosceles.

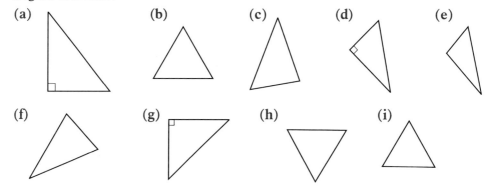

(a) (b) (c) (d) (e)

(f) (g) (h) (i)

2. What special name is given to a regular 4-sided polygon?

3.

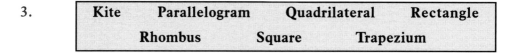

| Kite | Parallelogram | Quadrilateral | Rectangle |
| Rhombus | Square | Trapezium |

Which name best describes the following shapes? Choose from the names in the box above.

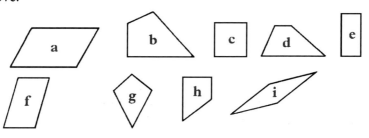

4. (a) Find the value of a.

(b) How long are the sides of this square?

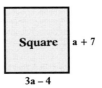

Square a + 7

3a − 4

Review 1 Choose the best name for each of the following.

(a)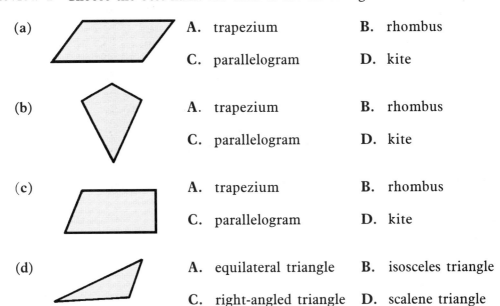

    A. trapezium   **B.** rhombus

    C. parallelogram   **D.** kite

(b)

    A. trapezium   **B.** rhombus

    C. parallelogram   **D.** kite

(c)

    A. trapezium   **B.** rhombus

    C. parallelogram   **D.** kite

(d)

    A. equilateral triangle   **B.** isosceles triangle

    C. right-angled triangle **D.** scalene triangle

Review 2 What special name is given to a regular 3-sided polygon?

DISCUSSION EXERCISE 14:6

Discuss the following statements which may be true or false.

Statement 1.   All rectangles are squares.
Statement 2.   All squares are rectangles.
Statement 3.   All squares are rhombuses.
Statement 4.   All kites are quadrilaterals.
Statement 5.   All quadrilaterals are parallelograms.
Statement 6.   Some rectangles are squares.
Statement 7.   Some parallelograms are kites.
Statement 8.   Some quadrilaterals are trapeziums.
Statement 9.   Some rhombuses are squares.

INVESTIGATION 14:7

QUADRILATERALS on the COMPUTER

```
10    MODE  1
20    MOVE  200,  620
30    DRAW  200,  900
40    DRAW  480,  900
50    DRAW  680,  420
60    DRAW  200,  620
70    MOVE  850,  800
80    DRAW  850,  100
90    DRAW  1050,  100
100   DRAW  1050,  400
110   DRAW  850,  800
120   END
```

This program draws two special quadrilaterals. Name them.
How could you adjust the program to also draw the diagonals of these quadrilaterals?
Investigate.

```
        Program 1                    Program 2
10    MODE 1                  10    MODE  1
20    MOVE 200,  400          20    MOVE  300,  200
30    DRAW 200,  800          30    DRAW  600,  200
40    DRAW ...,  ...          40    DRAW  900,  500
50    DRAW ...,  ...          50    DRAW  ...,  ...
60    DRAW ...,  ...          60    DRAW  ...,  ...
70    END                     70    END
```

For Program 1
Investigate ways of completing this program to draw a square.
Were you able to find more than one way?

What if the program was completed to draw a rectangle?

What if the program was completed to draw a trapezium?

For Program 2
Investigate ways of completing this program to draw a parallelogram. Is there more than one way to do this?

What if the program was completed to draw a trapezium?

PUZZLE 14:8

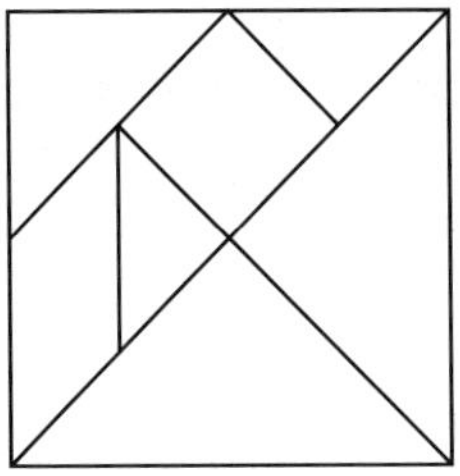

fig 1 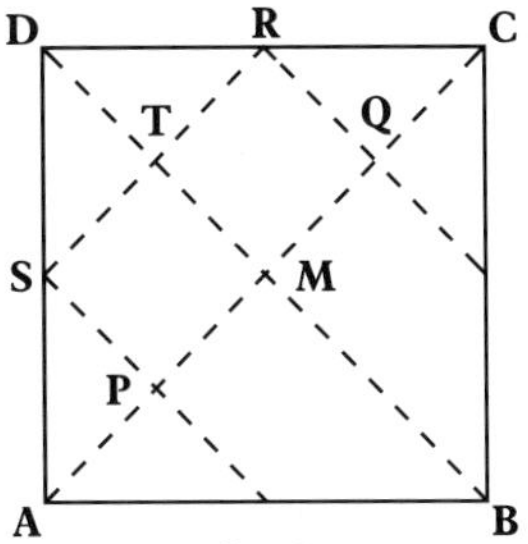   *fig 2*

fig 1 shows the 7 pieces of a tangram puzzle.

fig 2 illustrates how these 7 pieces can be found by paper folding:

Take a piece of square paper.
Fold to get the diagonals.
Fold D onto M, getting SR.
Fold A onto M to find P.
Fold C onto M to find Q.

Now join SR, TP, TM, RQ, AC and MB.
Cut out the 7 pieces.

Use all 7 pieces to make these shapes: a rectangle
a parallelogram
a triangle
a trapezium
a regular hexagon
a hexagon that isn't regular.

Make this pentagonal tangram.
Begin by drawing a regular pentagon on a loose
piece of paper. (One way of doing this is to begin
by putting 5 equally spaced marks around a
circle. How could you do this? **Discuss**.)
Fold your pentagon to get the 10 pieces. **Discuss**
what folds to make. Cut out the 10 pieces.

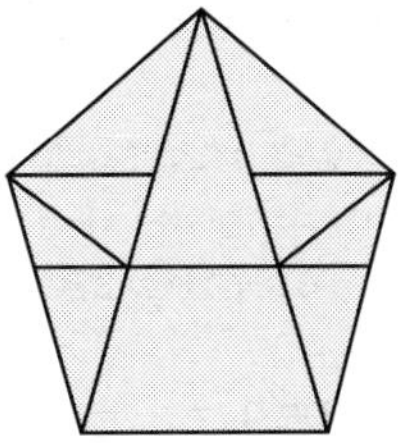

Use all 10 pieces to make: a triangle
a square.

PROPERTIES of SPECIAL QUADRILATERALS and OTHER POLYGONS

INVESTIGATION 14:9

SYMMETRY

A square has 4 axes of symmetry. Where are these axes of symmetry?

Find the axes of symmetry of the other special quadrilaterals shown above. You may find it helpful to copy the shapes, then fold about possible lines of symmetry. Don't forget to fold about diagonals.

A rectangle has rotational symmetry of order 2. What is the order of rotational symmetry of the other special quadrilaterals?

As part of your investigation, make and test statements such as the following (which may be true or false).

Statement 1. The opposite angles of a rhombus are equal.
Statement 2. The diagonals of a parallelogram are equal.
Statement 3. The diagonals of a kite bisect the angles.

Extend your investigation to other polygons such as the regular hexagon, the regular pentagon, the isosceles triangle etc.

 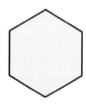

EXERCISE 14:10

---

1. Name all the special quadrilaterals which have

   (a) 2 axes of symmetry   (b) 4 axes of symmetry   (c) 1 axis of symmetry

   (d) no axes of symmetry   (e) all angles equal   (f) all sides equal.

2. (a) A quadrilateral with just one pair of parallel sides is a
      A. parallelogram B. kite   C. trapezium D. rhombus.

   (b) A quadrilateral with just one line of symmetry is a
      A. parallelogram B. kite   C. square   D. rhombus.

   (c) A quadrilateral with equal diagonals that are also perpendicular is a
      A. rhombus   B. rectangle C. kite   D. square.

   (d) A quadrilateral with parallel sides and equal diagonals is a
      A. rhombus   B. rectangle C. kite   D. parallelogram.

Review What do the quadrilaterals in each of these lists have in common?

List A	List B	List C	List D
rhombus	rectangle	rhombus	rectangle
square	square	square	rhombus
		kite	square
			parallelogram

DISCUSSION EXERCISE 14:11

Make lists of the special quadrilaterals that have a particular property. For instance, make a list of all the quadrilaterals that have opposite sides equal. **Discuss.**

You may like to draw up and complete tables, such as the one below, as part of your discussion.

	Diagonals equal	Diagonals perpendicular	Diagonals bisect each other	Diagonals bisect the angles
Parallelogram				
Rectangle				
Square				
Rhombus				
Kite				

INTERIOR ANGLES of a POLYGON

To find the sum of the angles in a polygon we can proceed as follows:

Step 1 From one vertex, draw all the diagonals to divide the polygon into triangles. This is shown in the diagram.

Step 2 Find the sum of the angles in all of these triangles.

Worked Example Find the sum of the angles in the polygon shown above.

Answer This polygon can be divided into 6 triangles.
Sum of the angles in 6 triangles = 6 × 180°
= 1080°

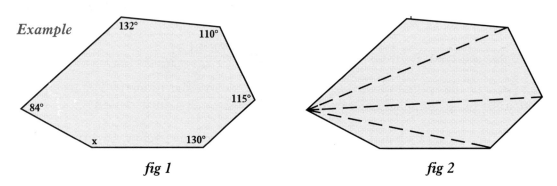

Example

fig 1   *fig 2*

To find the size of the angle marked as x, proceed as follows:

The polygon in *fig 1* can be divided into 4 triangles; see *fig 2*.
The sum of the angles in this polygon is 4 × 180° = 720°
x + 84° + 132° + 110° + 115° + 130° = 720°
x + 571° = 720°
x = 149°

EXERCISE 14:12

1.

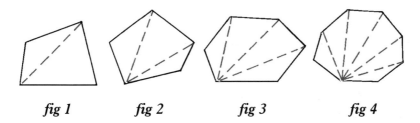

fig 1   *fig 2*   *fig 3*   *fig 4*

Using the above diagrams, complete these statements.

(a) A quadrilateral can be divided into . . . triangles.

(b) A pentagon can be divided into . . . triangles.

(c) A hexagon can be divided into . . . triangles.

(d) An octagon can be divided into . . . triangles.

2. Use the diagrams in **question 1** to find the sum of the angles in

(a) a quadrilateral   (b) a pentagon   (c) a hexagon   (d) an octagon.

3. (a) If a 7-sided polygon was divided into triangles, by drawing all the diagonals from one vertex, how many triangles would there be?

(b) What is the sum of the angles in a heptagon?

4. Find the sum of the angles in a 12-sided polygon.

5. Find the size of the angle marked as **x**.

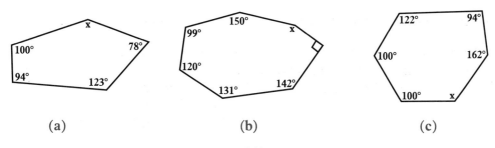

(a)   (b)   (c)

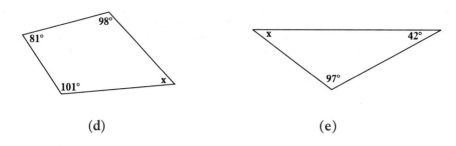

(d)   (e)

6. (a) A **regular** polygon has equal angles. Is this statement true?

   (b) Sketch a **regular** hexagon.

   (c) Find the sum of the angles in a hexagon.

   (d) How many angles are there in a hexagon?

   (e) Find the size of each of the angles in a **regular** hexagon.

7. Find the size of each of the angles in   (a) a regular octagon

                                              (b) a regular 10-sided polygon

                                              (c) a regular 15-sided polygon.

Review 1 Find the value of x.

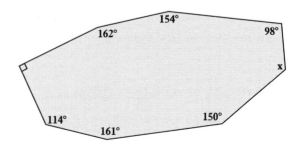

Review 2   (a) Sketch a regular pentagon.

                 (b) Find the size of each of the angles in a regular pentagon.

INVESTIGATIONS 14:13

POLYGONS and TRIANGLES

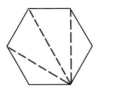 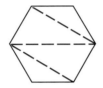

fig 1   *fig 2*   *fig 3*

fig 1 and *fig 2* both show a 6-sided polygon divided into 4 triangles.

fig 3 shows a 6-sided polygon divided into more than 4 triangles.
Are there other ways of dividing a polygon into triangles? **Investigate.**

POLYGONS and RIGHT ANGLES

Is it possible to have 2 right angles in a triangle?

Is it possible to have 2 right angles in a quadrilateral? Is it possible to have 3? Is it possible to have 4?

What is the greatest number of right angles it is possible to have in a 5-sided polygon?

What if the polygon had 6 sides?
What if the polygon had 7 sides?
What if . . .

Investigate to find the maximum possible number of right angles in polygons with different numbers of sides.

DIAGONALS and REGIONS

The diagram shows the diagonals of a pentagon.

These diagonals divide the pentagon into 11 regions, 10 of which are triangular in shape while the other is the shape of a pentagon.

Investigate the regions into which the diagonals of other polygons divide the polygon.

EXTERIOR ANGLES of a POLYGON

DISCUSSION EXERCISE 14:14

For the polygons that you consider in this exercise, it would be a good idea to either mark them out on the floor in chalk or on the ground using a length of string.

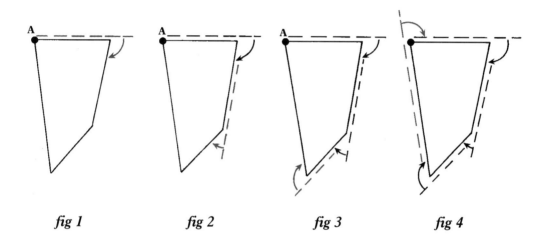

| *fig 1* | *fig 2* | *fig 3* | *fig 4* |

Mark out a quadrilateral similar to that shown in the above diagrams.

Take a walk, beginning at one vertex of the polygon (marked as A).

Walk along one side of the polygon, continuing to walk a little further in the same direction. Then turn as shown in *fig 1*.

Now walk along the next side of the polygon, continuing to walk a little further in the same direction. Then turn as shown in *fig 2*.

Continue walking and turning as shown in *fig 3* and *fig 4*.

Through what size angle have you turned altogether?

What can you say about the sum of the four exterior angles of this quadrilateral?

What if the quadrilateral was of quite a different shape?

What if you walked anticlockwise instead of clockwise?

What if you walked around a triangle instead of a quadrilateral?

What if you walked around a pentagon instead of a quadrilateral?

Make and test a statement about the sum of the exterior angles of any polygon.

EXERCISE 14:15

1.

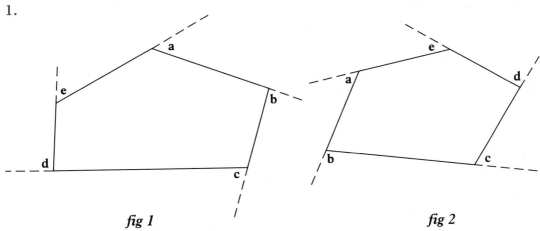

fig 1   *fig 2*

a + b + c + d + e = . . . How should this statement be completed for   (a) *fig 1*

(b) *fig 2?*

2. Calculate the value of **a.**

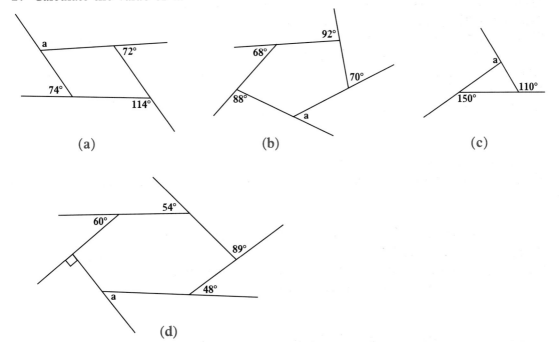

(a)   (b)   (c)

(d)

3. Copy and complete these statements.

    (a) This regular polygon has . . . sides.

    (b) This regular polygon has . . . equal exterior angles.

    (c) The sum of all the exterior angles equals . . .

    (d) Each exterior angle equals . . .

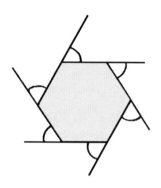

4. Find the size of each exterior angle of a

    (a) regular pentagon   (b) regular 20-sided polygon   (c) equilateral triangle.

Review Calculate the value of **x**.

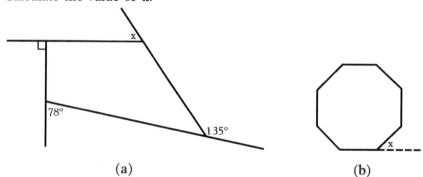

        (a)   (b)

INVESTIGATION 14:16

DRAWING POLYGONS

How many sides has a regular polygon which has an exterior angle of 40°?

What if each exterior angle was 72°?
What if each exterior angle was 15°?
What if each exterior angle was 80°?
What if each exterior angle was 50°?
What if . . .

continued . . .

. . . from previous page

LT   90
FD 200
LT   72
FD 200
LT   72
FD 200
LT   72
FD 200
LT   72
FD 200

What shape does the above LOGO program draw?

Can you write a more efficient LOGO program to draw the same shape?

Sketch some polygons.
Investigate to find programs to draw your polygons.

TESSELLATIONS

PRACTICAL EXERCISE 14:17

1. Make 4 copies of the small shape.

   Tessellate these to tile the large area.

 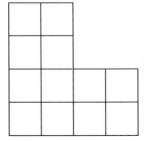

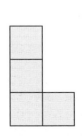 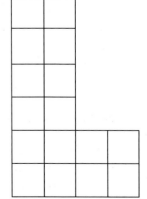

(a)   (b)

2. Tessellate one of the quadrilaterals shown below, or a quadrilateral of your choice, to tile an area. Colour your design using not more than 4 colours.

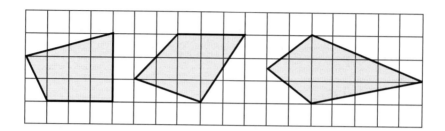

3. On thin card, draw and cut out a rhombus.

   Use this rhombus to create the shape shown.

   Tessellate this shape.

   Instead of colouring 2 out of 3 rhombuses as shown, you may wish to colour 1 out of 3.

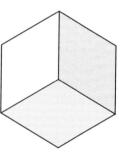

4. Make a cardboard template which can be used for a tessellation design as follows:

  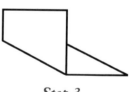

   Step 1   *Step 2*   *Step 3*

   Step 1   Draw and cut out a square.

   Step 2   Remove a portion of the square.

   Step 3   Replace this portion elsewhere on the square.

   You may wish to remove more than one portion. You may remove as many portions as you like as long as you replace them elsewhere.

   You may wish to remove curved portions.

   Once you have made your template, use it to tile an area, perhaps the back cover of your maths. exercise book. Colour your design using no more than four colours.

5. Many designs on wallpaper, fabric and floor coverings involve tessellations. Make a mural for the classroom from a collection of samples of wallpaper or fabric or floor coverings.

INVESTIGATION 14:18

TESSELLATING POLYGONS

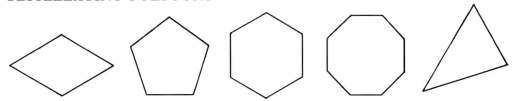

Investigate the following statements, which may be true or false.

Statement 1. All quadrilaterals tessellate.
Statement 2. A regular pentagon will not tessellate.
Statement 3. A regular hexagon will tessellate.

Make and test a statement about a regular octagon or about a non-regular hexagon or about any other polygon you choose.

As part of your investigation, make and test statements about the angles of the shapes.

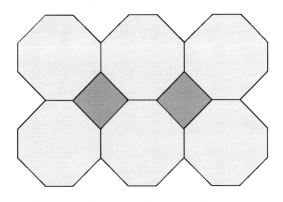

Interesting tessellations can be made by tessellating two shapes.

For instance, an octagon and a square as shown here.

Would it be possible to tessellate an octagon and an equilateral triangle in this way?

Investigate to find shapes that will tessellate in this way.

To help in your investigation, consider the angles of the shapes.

PRACTICAL EXERCISE 14:19

Design a paving stone.
Make a cardboard template of your paving stone.

Go into the school grounds.
Experiment with your paving stone template to tile an area in different ways.

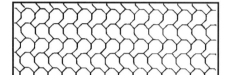 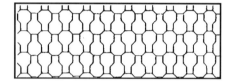

FOR YOUR INTEREST

Choose one of the following statements. Find examples to show whether the statement is correct or incorrect.

You should do some research, perhaps in your High Street or your library or local DIY shop.

Make and test a similar statement of your own. Your statement must be about quadrilaterals and/or polygons.

The façade (the front view from the street) of any building is a combination of quadrilaterals and other polygons.

Square shapes are more common than triangular shapes.

The trapezium is the most common shape used on wallpaper.

In everyday life, the shape that is most often tessellated is the regular hexagon.

Give a presentation to your class on your findings. This presentation could be a talk or a video. If it is a talk prepare a poster that you can refer to or make transparencies for the overhead projector.

2-D Representation of 3-D Shapes

DISCOVER, DISCUSS, DO

- Take an object such as a small bucket (without a handle) or a glass.

Look directly down on the bucket.
The view will be similar to that shown.

Look at the bucket from the side.
The view will be similar to that shown.

Now place the bucket on top of a book.
Which of the views shown is from the top and
which is from the side?

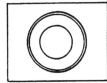

Choose objects that are in the classroom.
Discuss with your neighbour or group how you could draw the view from above
and the view from the side. As part of your discussion, draw these views. Does it
matter which side you view the object from? **Discuss.**

Which objects in the classroom look similar when viewed from above? **Discuss.**

Which objects in the classroom look similar when viewed from the side? **Discuss.**

- Do objects which have the same view from above also have the same view from
  the side? **Discuss.** As part of your discussion, make and test statements.

- What do you think the West and South elevations of this bungalow might look
  like? **Discuss.**

EAST ELEVATION   NORTH ELEVATION

TOP, FRONT, BACK, SIDE VIEWS

To draw the top, front, back and side views of a solid we think of the solid as a skeleton shape. That is, we think of the solid as consisting of just edges.

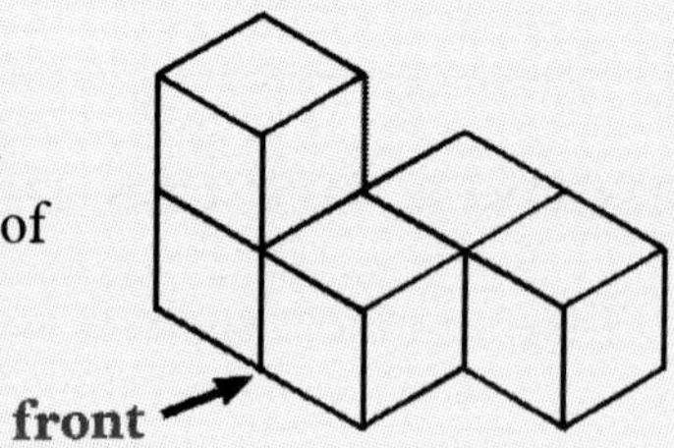

front

For the above 3-D shape, if we look from the **front** the view we see is

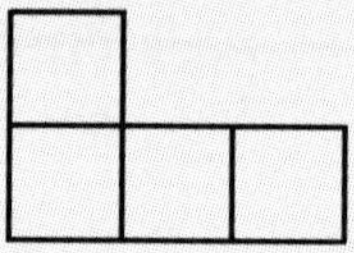

If we look from the **back**, the view we see is

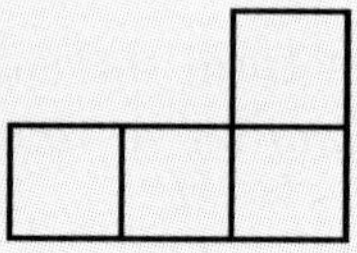

If we look from the **top**, the view we see is

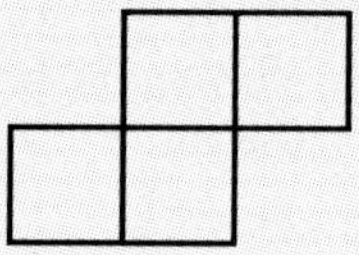

If we look from the **right** side, the view we see is

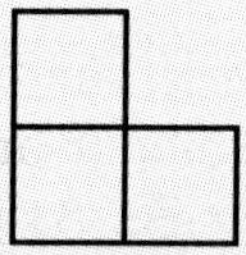

If we look from the **left** side, the view we see is

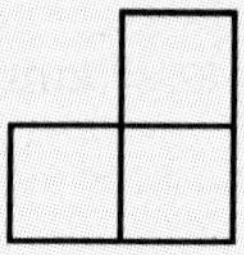

PRACTICAL and DISCUSSION EXERCISE 15:1

- Build some 3-D shapes using cubes. Draw the views from the top, front, back, left and right. (You could use square dot paper.) **Discuss** the views you have drawn.

- *Work in pairs.*　　Use cubes to build a 3-D shape.
　　　　　　　　　　Draw the views from the top, front, back, left and right.
　　　　　　　　　　Ask your partner to build the shape from your drawings.

EXERCISE 15:2

1.

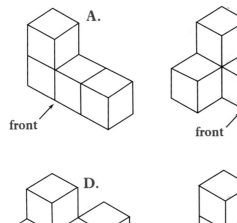
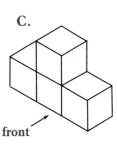
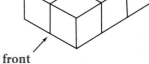
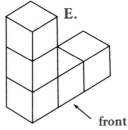
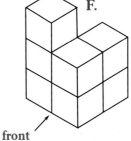
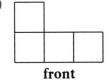

The views from the front, back, top, left and right of these 3-D shapes are shown below. Which views belong to which shape?

(a)

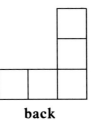
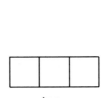
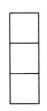

| front | back | top | left | right |

(b)

| front | back | top | left | right |

(c)

| front | back | top | left | right |

(d)

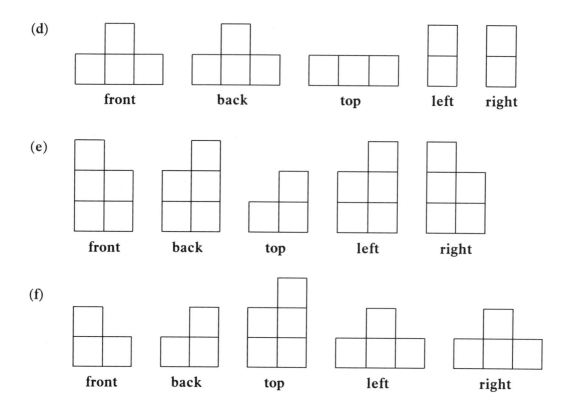

(e)

(f)

2. Draw the front, back, top, left and right views of these shapes.

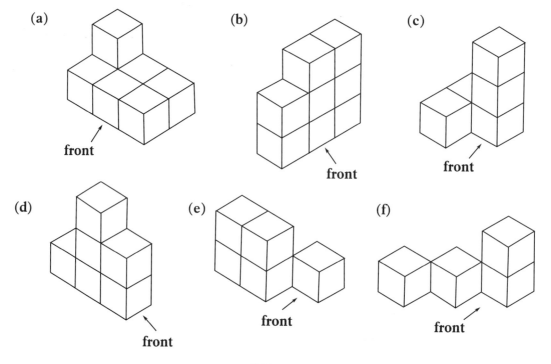

(a)

front

(b)

front

(c)

front

(d)

front

(e)

front

(f)

front

Review Draw the front, back, top, left and right views of these shapes.

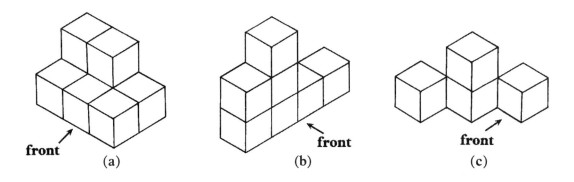

(a)   (b)   (c)

PRACTICAL and DISCUSSION EXERCISE 15:3

- What can you say about the front and back views of a 3-D shape?

  What can you say about the left and right views of a 3-D shape?

  Discuss. As part of your discussion you could look at the diagrams in **Exercise 15:2**.

  Chantelle claimed that a 3-D shape could be drawn by giving just 3 views. Is she correct? Which 3 views? **Discuss.**

- Use cubes to build these shapes. Sketch your shapes.

Shape 1

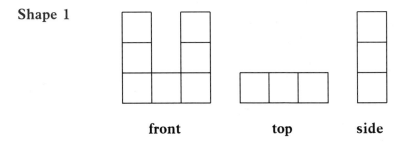

front   top   side

Shape 2

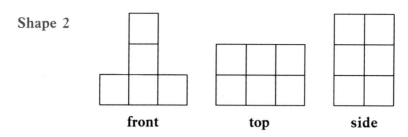

front   top   side

- Which of these is it possible to build? Is there more than one way to build some of them? **Discuss.**

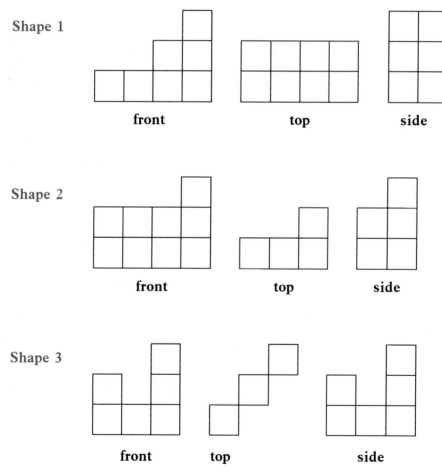

Shape 1

front   top   side

Shape 2

front   top   side

Shape 3

front   top   side

- ***Work with a partner.*** Use cubes to build some 3-D shapes.
  Draw the view from the front, top and side.
  Ask your partner to build the shape from your drawings.

PLANS and ELEVATIONS

The view from the top is often called the **plan**.

Look down to find the plan

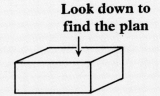

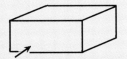

Look from the front to find the front elevation.

The view from the front is often called the **front elevation**.
Note: The view from the back is a reflection of the front elevation.

The view from one side is often called the **side elevation**.

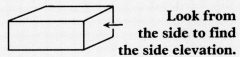

Look from the side to find the side elevation.

Note: The left side is a reflection of the right side.

Example The plan, front elevation and side elevation for the shape on the left are shown on the right.

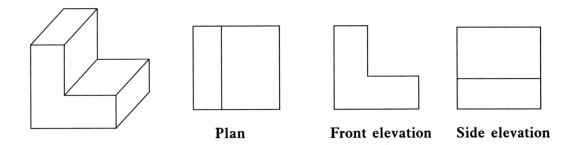

Plan **Front elevation** **Side elevation**

To help make it easier to see which edges have been drawn on the plan, on the front elevation and on the side elevation, the edges have been numbered below.

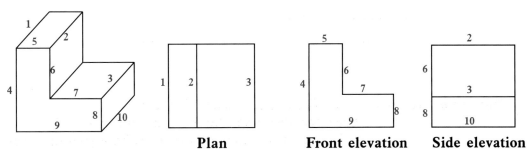

Plan **Front elevation** **Side elevation**

DISCUSSION EXERCISE 15:4

You may wish to build models or skeleton models of the shapes in this exercise to help in your discussion. You could use some commercial material such as Multilink or Clever Sticks.

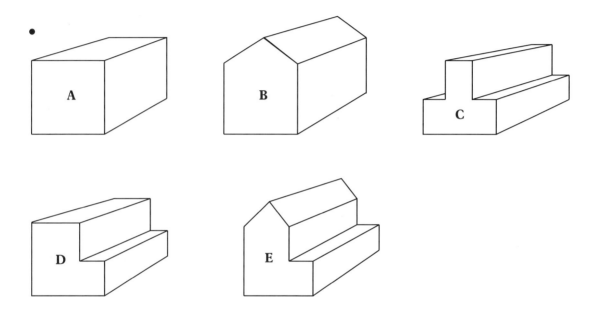

Which of the above shapes have the same plan? **Discuss.**

Which have the same front elevation? **Discuss.**

Which have the same side elevation? **Discuss.**

- Sketch other shapes which have the same side elevation as this one. **Discuss.**

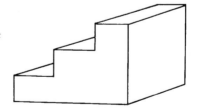

Sketch other shapes which have the same front elevation as this one. **Discuss.**

PRACTICAL EXERCISE 15:5

1. Build models of the shapes which have plans and elevations as shown below. You could build solid models or skeleton models.

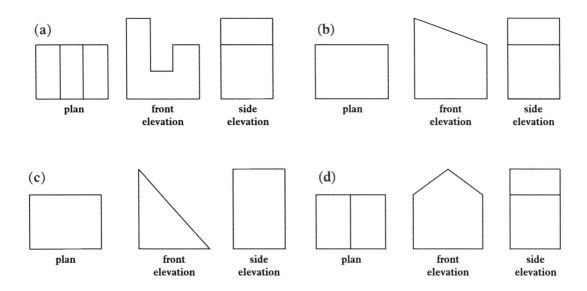

(a)   plan   front elevation   side elevation   (b)   plan   front elevation   side elevation

(c)   plan   front elevation   side elevation   (d)   plan   front elevation   side elevation

2. Build solid or skeleton models.

   Draw the plan and front elevation and side elevation of each model.

3. Draw some plans and elevations. From these, build models.

4. Choose a building in the school grounds or a piece of equipment in the gymnasium or workshop.

   Draw the plan, front elevation and side elevation.

   Have other students identify the building or piece of equipment from your drawings.

5. Use cardboard to make a model of one of the school buildings.

   Draw the plan and front and side elevations on a sheet of paper. Display these along with the model.

USING ISOMETRIC PAPER to DRAW 3-D SHAPES

Isometric means "same measure".
On an isometric drawing of a 3-D shape, lengths which are equal on the shape are also equal on the drawing.
An isometric drawing of a 3-D shape will make the shape appear slightly distorted.

To make an isometric drawing of a 3-D shape we can use either isometric graph paper or isometric dot paper.
Vertical edges of the 3-D shape should be drawn as vertical lines.

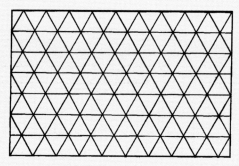

Isometric graph paper

Isometric dot paper

Examples The isometric drawings shown below are of a cube and shapes built from cubes.

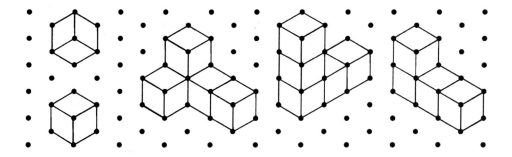

The steps taken to draw a cube are

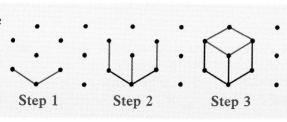

Step 1   Step 2   Step 3

INVESTIGATION 15:6

CUBES

How many different shapes can be built using 4 cubes?
Build as many as possible. Make an isometric drawing of each shape.

What if you used 3 cubes?
What if you used 5 cubes?
What if . . .

INVESTIGATION 15:7

OPTICAL ILLUSIONS

Did you notice that one of the cubes drawn in the example on the previous page can be viewed in two ways? Depending on the way you look at it, it could be a cube viewed from below or if it is viewed from the front it could be a cube that is missing three faces. Can you see both of these?

Can you draw other optical illusions using isometric paper?
Does one view always have to be from below? **Investigate.**

DISCUSSION EXERCISE 15:8

These isometric drawings
show two prisms; one on a
rectangular base and the other
on a triangular base.
How would you make an
isometric drawing of a prism
on a pentagonal base? **Discuss.**

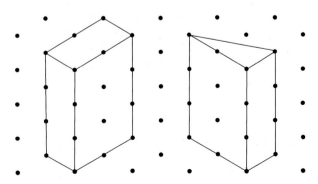

What if the base was a hexagon?
What if the base was an octagon?
What if the base was a trapezium?
What if . . .

PRACTICAL EXERCISE 15:9

1.

 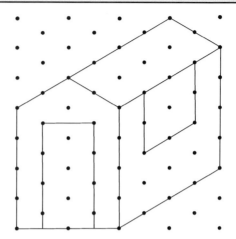

Judith made this isometric drawing of the shed in her garden.

Design another garden shed. Draw your design on isometric paper.

2. Design a bungalow.
   Draw the plan, the front elevation and the side elevation.

   You could also draw some of the rooms on isometric dot paper as shown below. You could also draw plans of the rooms on square dot paper as shown below. You might like to include furniture.

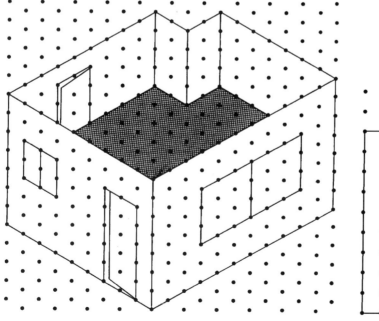 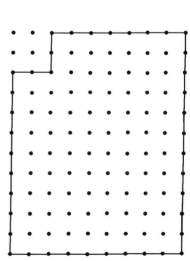

3. Choose one of your school buildings.

Measure each room of this building.

Make a scale drawing of the floor plan of this building.

Draw a 2-D representation of the building.

FOR YOUR INTEREST

-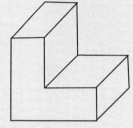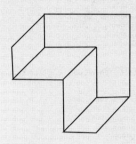

    The diagram on the left has been turned upside down to get the diagram on the right.

    Find or draw other 3-D shapes that look completely different when they are rotated.

-   A famous artist, Escher, drew many 3-D optical illusions. Find some examples of Escher's drawings.

DISCOVER, DISCUSS, DO

- Gavin had some photos enlarged at Kate's Camera Shop.
  Mardi enlarged a magazine article on the school photocopier.

  Think of other everyday examples where the word "enlarged" is used. **Discuss.**

- Amanda made a scale drawing of a small leaf for her biology homework. Her drawing was three times the actual size.
  A dress pattern in a magazine had the instruction "make each pattern piece 10 times the size shown".

  Think of everyday examples where the drawing of an object is larger than life size. **Discuss.**

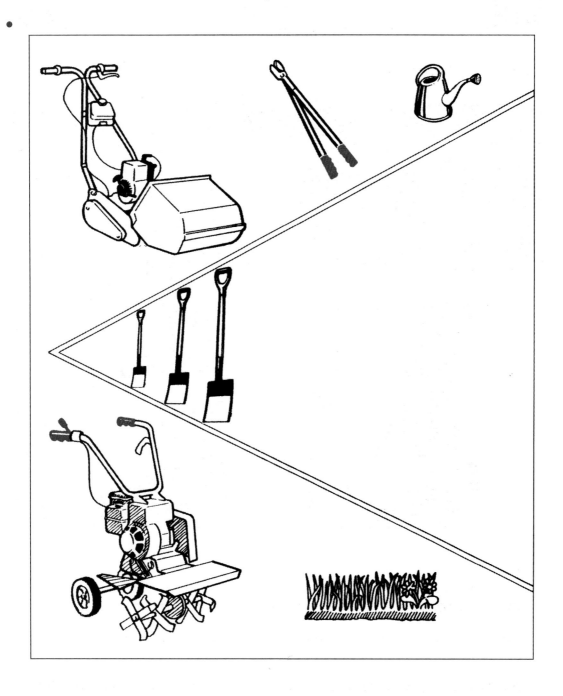

Beatrice was illustrating the cover of her project on gardening. She began the centrepiece of spades as shown. She completed this centrepiece with more spades, one smaller and the rest bigger.

Discuss various ways Beatrice may have done this. As part of your discussion, copy the centrepiece with the three spades between the double lines. Complete this drawing.

SCALE FACTOR of an ENLARGEMENT

If a shape is enlarged so that each length becomes twice the size it was on the original, we say the **scale factor** of the enlargement is 2.

If a shape is enlarged so that each length becomes three times the size it was on the original, we say the **scale factor** of the enlargement is 3 etc.

We read A → A′ as "A maps onto A′" or "A becomes A′". This means the image of A is A′. A and A′ could be points. A and A′ could be shapes.

Examples

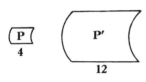

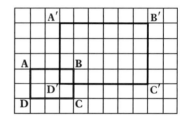

fig 1   **fig 2**

fig 1 shows the shape P enlarged to the shape P′.
The length of 12 units on the enlargement P′, corresponds to a length of 4 units on the original P. That is, each length on P′ is 3 times as long as the corresponding length on P. The scale factor for this enlargement is 3.

fig 2 shows the shape ABCD enlarged to the shape A′B′C′D′.
Each length on the enlargement A′B′C′D′ is 2 times as long as the corresponding length on the original ABCD.
The scale factor for this enlargement is 2.

EXERCISE 16:1

1.

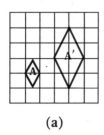

(a)   (b)   (c)

In these diagrams A has been enlarged to A′. What is the scale factor of each of these enlargements?

2.

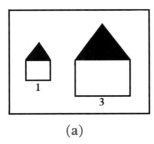

(a)

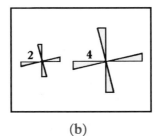

(b)

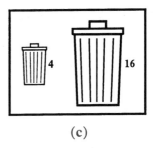

(c)

In each of these diagrams the smaller shape has been enlarged to the larger shape. **Use the dimensions given** to find the scale factor of each of these enlargements. (The diagrams are not drawn to scale.)

3.

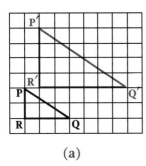

(a)

(b)

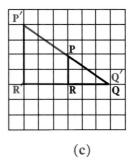

(c)

PQR → P′Q′R′ under an enlargement.

State the scale factor for each enlargement.

Review

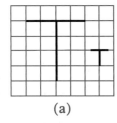

(a)

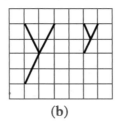

(b)

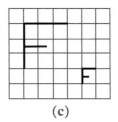

(c)

Each shape on the right has been enlarged to the shape on the left.

Give the scale factor for each of these enlargements.

CENTRE of ENLARGEMENT

DISCUSSION EXERCISE 16:2

●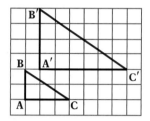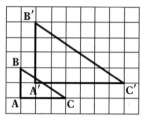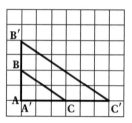

In each of the above diagrams, the triangle ABC has been enlarged to the triangle A'B'C'.

For each enlargement, the scale factor is 2.

What is the difference between these enlargements? **Discuss.**

Could you begin with the same triangle ABC, enlarge it by a scale factor of 2, and get the enlargement in any other positions? **Discuss.**

● Begin with the rectangle shown.
"Enlarge this rectangle by a scale factor of 3". Is this a sufficient instruction for you to be able to draw the image the right size and in the right position? **Discuss.**

● What instructions do you need to be able to draw an enlargement of the right size and in the right position? **Discuss.** As part of your discussion, make and test statements.

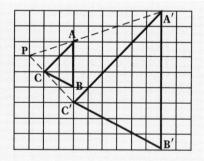

The triangle ABC has been enlarged to the triangle A'B'C'. The scale factor of the enlargement is 3.

Join A'A and C'C. The point P, where these lines meet, is known as the **centre of enlargement.**

DISCUSSION EXERCISE 16:3

● For the previous example, could the centre of enlargement be found by finding where the lines A'A and B'B meet? Must the lines A'A, B'B, C'C meet at the same point? **Discuss.**

- Sketch enlargements where the centre of enlargement is inside the original shape. Sketch enlargements where the centre of enlargement is at one of the vertices of the original shape. **Discuss.**

EXERCISE 16:4

1. Copy this diagram onto squared paper.

   The small shape on the right has been enlarged to the large shape on the left.

   Draw in lines on your diagram to locate the centre of this enlargement.

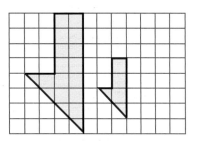

2.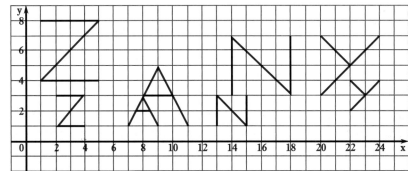

   Copy this diagram.

   Each of the letters Z, A, N, Y has been enlarged.
   Locate the centre of enlargement for each of these enlargements.
   Write down the coordinates of each of these centres of enlargement.

Review

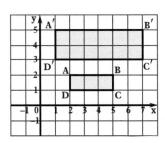

Copy this diagram.

Locate the centre of enlargement for the enlargement
ABCD →A′B′C′D′.

What are the coordinates of this centre of enlargement?

DRAWING ENLARGEMENTS

To draw an enlargement of a shape we need to know both the scale factor and the centre of enlargement.

We need the scale factor to make the enlargement the right size.

We need the centre of enlargement to position the enlargement correctly.

The following steps should be taken to make an enlargement of a shape:

Step 1   Draw a line from the centre of enlargement to each point on the shape.

Step 2   Extend each of these lines to get the corresponding point on the image. The distance from the centre of enlargement to the point on the image equals the distance from the centre of enlargement to the point on the original shape multiplied by the scale factor.

For instance, if the scale factor is 2, then the length from the centre of enlargement to any point on the image is twice the length from the centre of enlargement to the corresponding point on the original.

Step 3   Draw the image shape by joining all the points found in *Step 2*.

Example   The "stick-person" on the left has been enlarged to the "stick-person" on the right by following the previous steps.

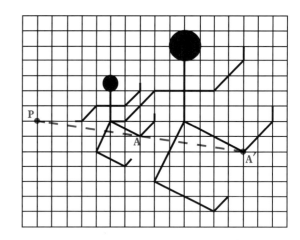

The centre of enlargement is **P**; the scale factor is 2.

The dotted line shows how A′, the image of point A, was found: P was joined to A, then the line PA was extended to A′ so that PA′ = 2PA.

The image of every other point was found in the same way. Then all the image points were joined.

EXERCISE 16:5

1.

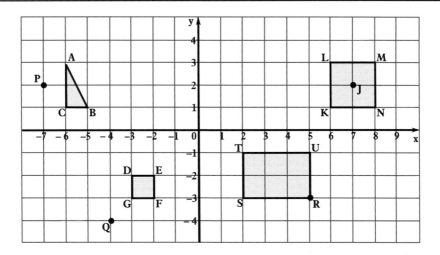

Copy this diagram.

(a) Using P as the centre of enlargement, enlarge the triangle ABC by a scale factor of 3. Write down the coordinates of the vertices of the image triangle.

(b) Enlarge the square DEFG by a scale factor of 4, centre of enlargement Q. Write down the coordinates of D′, E′, F′ and G′.

(c) With R as centre of enlargement, enlarge the rectangle RSTU by a scale factor of 3. What are the coordinates of the vertices of the image rectangle?

(d) KLMN → K′L′M′N′ under an enlargement, centre J, scale factor 2.
Draw the square K′L′M′N′.
Give the coordinates of K′, L′, M′ and N′.

2.

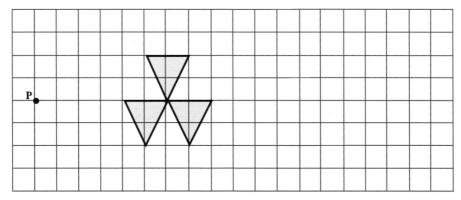

Copy this diagram.
Using P as the centre of enlargement, enlarge the shaded shape by a scale factor of 2.

3.

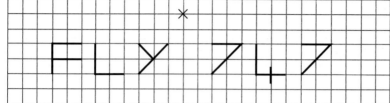

Copy this diagram.
Enlarge it by a scale factor of your choice.
A suggested centre of enlargement has been marked with a cross.
You may use another centre of enlargement if you wish.

4. Draw a shape of your choice.
Choose a centre of enlargement. Choose a scale factor.
Draw the enlargement of your shape.

Review Copy this diagram.

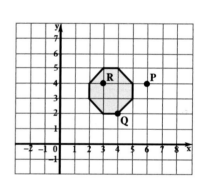

Draw three enlargements of the shape, all
with scale factor 2.
For the first enlargement use P as the
centre of enlargement, for the second use
R and for the third use Q.

Write down the coordinates of the vertices
of each of the three image shapes.

PRACTICAL EXERCISE 16:6

A pantograph is an instrument which is used to enlarge a drawing.
Find out how a pantograph is constructed and how it is used to make an
enlargement.
You could make a pantograph using meccano.
You could use your meccano pantograph to make an enlargement of a drawing.

REFLECTIONS using LOGO

DISCUSSION and PRACTICAL EXERCISE 16:7

● The following LOGO instructions will draw the shaded shape.

RT   90
FD   80
LT   60
FD   150
RT   60
FD   30
LT   35
FD   262
HOME

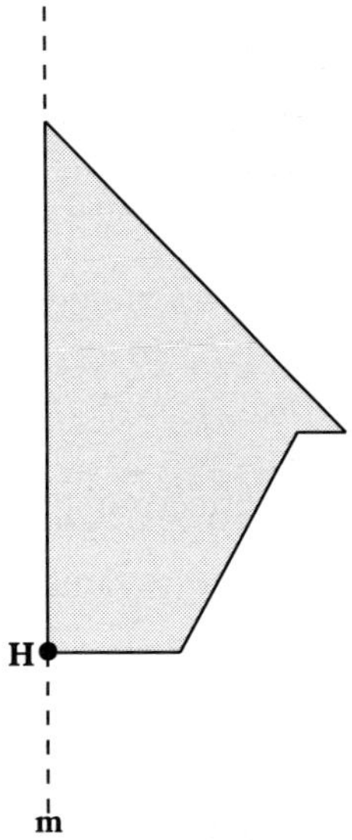

What LOGO instructions are needed to reflect this shape in the vertical mirror line m?
Discuss.

As part of your discussion, draw the shape and its reflection.

●

PU		
RT 90	RT 90	
FD 100	FD 100	
PD	PD	
LT 10	.	
FD 100	.	
LT 140	.	
FD 400	.	
LT 90	.	
FD 200	.	
RT 90	.	
FD 150	.	
LT 135	.	
FD 120	.	
PU	.	
HOME	.	

The instructions on the left will draw the top half of a fish.

This fish has a horizontal mirror line. **Discuss** how to complete the instructions on the right to draw the bottom half of the fish.

As part of your discussion, draw the fish.

● **Shape 1**	PU		**Shape 2**	PU	
	LT	90		RT	90
	FD	40		FD	40
	PD			PD	
	FD	200		FD	200
	RT	135		LT	135
	FD	282		FD	282
	LT	135		RT	135
	FD	200		FD	200
	PU			PU	
	HOME			HOME	

Draw these two shapes.
Write another two programs to draw another path and its reflection in a vertical mirror line.

What if a reflection in a horizontal mirror line was wanted?

● If your school has a CAD (Computer Aided Design) package use this to draw shapes or paths and their reflections.

ROTATIONS using LOGO

DISCUSSION AND PRACTICAL EXERCISE 16:8

● What shape is drawn by the instruction REPEAT 4 [FD 200 RT 90]
What if the instruction was REPEAT 3 [RT 120 FD 200]

What does the REPEAT instruction do? **Discuss.**

● What shape is drawn by: REPEAT 6 [FD 200 BK 200 RT 60]
Is the same shape drawn by: REPEAT 6 [FD 200 HOME RT 60]
What shape is drawn if REPEAT 6 is replaced by REPEAT 8 and RT 60 is replaced by RT 45?
What if REPEAT 6 is replaced by REPEAT 12 and RT 60 is replaced by RT 30?
What if REPEAT 6 and RT 60 are replaced by . . .

What shape is drawn if BK 200 is left out?
What if BK 200 is left out and REPEAT 6 and RT 60 are replaced by . . .

- In the diagrams below, a rectangle has been rotated.

  What instructions might you give the turtle to draw these? **Discuss.**

  As part of your discussion draw these diagrams.

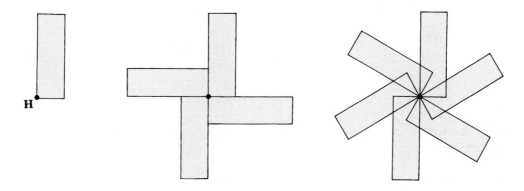

- What instructions might you give the turtle to draw this "spoke"? **Discuss.**

  The "spoke" is to be rotated to make the diagrams below.

  What instructions, which include REPEAT statements, might you give the turtle? **Discuss.**

  As part of your discussion draw these diagrams.

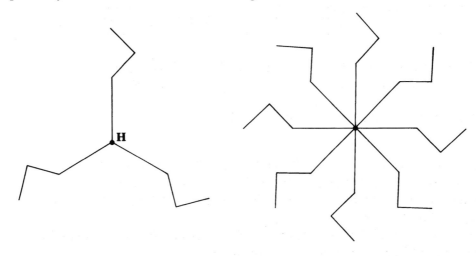

- Write LOGO instructions to draw other paths and shapes.
  Rotate these to make interesting diagrams.

You can instruct the turtle to draw shapes.

You can also make the turtle *remember* how to draw shapes.

For instance, if you want to draw a number of congruent rectangles on the screen, the first step is to teach the turtle what a rectangle is:

Type   TO RECTANGLE

Now type in your instructions. For instance:

FD	300
RT	90
FD	100
RT	90
FD	300
RT	90
FD	100
RT	90
END	

The message   RECTANGLE DEFINED   will appear on the screen. From now on, until you switch off the computer, the turtle will know how to draw the rectangle.

DISCUSSION AND PRACTICAL EXERCISE 16:9

- Naseem typed   TO RECTANGLE
  REPEAT 2 [FD 300   RT 90   FD 100   RT 90]
  END

She said this gave the same rectangle as above? Was she correct? **Discuss.**

Naseem said she could draw the diagram with 4 rectangles that is on **Page 297** as follows.

        TO RECTANGLE
        REPEAT 2 [FD 300   RT 90   FD 100   RT 90]
        END
        REPEAT 4 [RECTANGLE   RT 90]

Is Naseem correct? **Discuss.** As part of your discussion, type in Naseem's instructions.

Write similar instructions to draw the diagram with 6 rectangles that is on **Page 297.**

- Jim wrote instructions to teach the turtle to remember another shape. He then drew and rotated his shape. His instructions were:

```
TO SHAPE
FD 100
RT 90
FD 240
HOME
END
SHAPE
LT 120   SHAPE
```

What was Jim's shape? What did the "picture" of Jim's shape and its rotation look like? **Discuss.** As part of your discussion, type in Jim's instructions.

- Choose another shape or path. Teach the turtle to remember your path or shape. Then have the turtle draw your path (or shape) and one or more rotations of it.

TRANSLATIONS using LOGO

DISCUSSION AND PRACTICAL EXERCISE 16:10

- Type in these instructions.

```
TO SHAPE
FD   200
RT   90
FD   100
RT   90
FD   50
PU
HOME
PD
END
SHAPE
PU
FD   150
RT   90
FD   50
LT   90
SHAPE
```

What do these instructions do? **Discuss.**

- Write instructions to draw another path (or a shape) and one or more translations of it.

INVESTIGATION 16:11

TESSELLATIONS using LOGO

- Teach the turtle to draw a rectangle of your choice. Use your RECTANGLE instruction to make tiling patterns. You could begin with one of the following patterns.

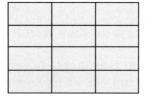 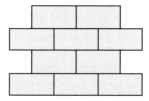

- Teach the turtle how to draw a hexagon.
  Use your HEXAGON instruction to make a tiling pattern.

- Teach the turtle to draw and tessellate a triangle using both translation and rotation.

  What instructions would you need to give to reflect your triangle as well as translate and rotate it? **Investigate.**

ENLARGEMENTS using LOGO

REPEAT 4 [FD 100   RT 90]
REPEAT 4 [FD 200   RT 90]
REPEAT 4 [FD 300   RT 90]

The above instructions will draw the pattern of squares.
This same pattern of squares may also be drawn by first
teaching the turtle to draw squares with sides of any length.
This is done as follows:

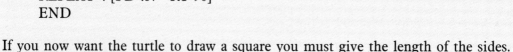

TO SQUARE :N
REPEAT 4 [FD :N   RT 90]
END

If you now want the turtle to draw a square you must give the length of the sides.
For instance, to draw the above pattern of squares, *type*:   SQUARE   100
SQUARE   200
SQUARE   300

DISCUSSION AND PRACTICAL EXERCISE 16:12

- What LOGO instructions would draw the small square and the enlargements of it in these diagrams? **Discuss.**

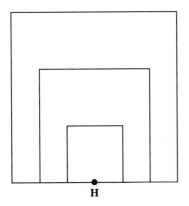
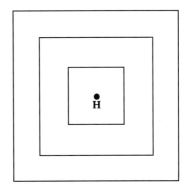

- Choose another shape.
  Write instructions to draw this shape and enlargements of it, using different centres of enlargement and different scale factors.

FOR YOUR INTEREST

- Photographers, cartographers (map makers), town planners, boat builders, opticians, exhibition designers, artists, craftworkers, film makers and graphic designers are some of the people who use enlargement and other transformations in their work.

  Discuss one of the following statements in relation to one or more of these people.

  The computer has replaced the need to understand enlargement and other transformations.

  I find many examples of reflection, rotation, translation and enlargement in my work.

- Discuss the following statement.

  A model should be made, and displayed, of all proposed new buildings, shopping precincts, motorways etc.

  Present a summary of your discussion to the class.

1. Name the shapes in this diagram.

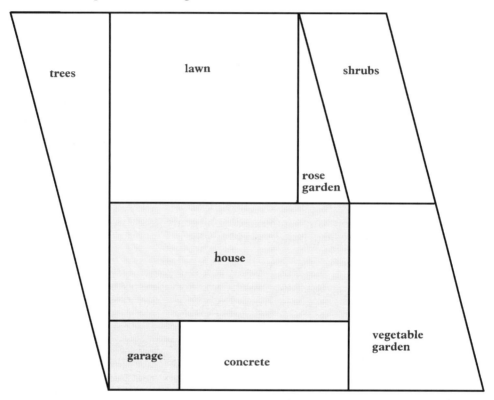

2. Square tiles of side 300mm are to be used to pave a terrace which is 9 metres long and 3 metres wide.

   (a) Write the dimensions of this terrace in mm.

   (b) How many tiles will be needed?

3. Take $\pi = 3\cdot1$.
   Kieran had the Irish crest printed on the back of a t-shirt. The diameter of the circle was 20cm.

   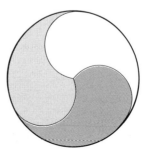

   (a) Find the area of the design.

   (b) Find the circumference.

4.

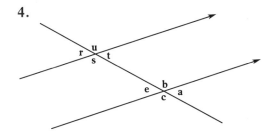

Corresponding angles	a	c	e	r	s
Alternate angles	b	c	e	s	
Interior angles	e	s	t	u	

Copy the table given above.

On the top line, cross out all the letters which give pairs of corresponding angles. On the middle line, cross out all the letters which give pairs of alternate angles. On the bottom line, cross out all the letters which give pairs of interior angles.

You should have a total of 5 letters not crossed out. Rearrange these 5 letters to spell a word to do with angles.

5. Are the following statements true or false?

(a) A regular polygon has all its sides and angles equal.

(b) A hexagon is a 5-sided polygon.

(c) An octagon is an 8-sided polygon.

(d) A regular 4-sided polygon is called a rhombus.

(e) The sum of the exterior angles of any polygon is 360°.

(f) The sum of the interior angles of any polygon is 360°.

(g) A kite has no axes of symmetry.

(h) A square has 4 axes of symmetry.

6. (a)   **(b)**   **(c)**

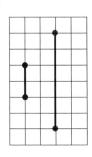 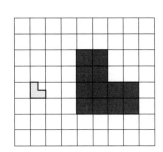 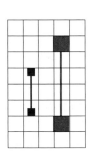

In each of the above diagrams, the shapes on the left have been enlarged to the shapes on the right. State the scale factor for each of the enlargements.

7. Copy this "code-breaker".

8	7	6	5	4	3	2	1

Name these shapes.

    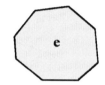

Complete the "code-breaker" using the following clues.

1. The first letter of shape **d**.
2. The last letter of shape **a**.
3. The first letter of shape **c**.
4. The third letter of shape **e**.
5. The letter that occurs most often in the names of the shapes.
6. and 8. The two letters that are not in the name for shape **b** but are in the names of all of the other shapes.
7. The letter that occurs twice in shape **e**.

What does the "code-breaker" read, reading from right to left?
(Note: you may have to swap the letters you placed under **6.** and **8.**)

8. What volume of sand will this matchbox hold?

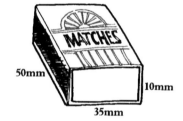

9. Find the value of **x** and **y**.

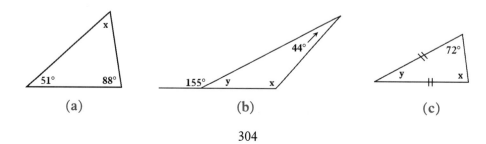

(a)   (b)   (c)

10. (a)

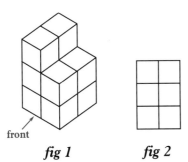

fig 2. shows the view from the left of the shape in **fig 1.**

Use square dot paper or grid paper to draw the views from the front, top, back and right.

fig 1   **fig 2**

(b) A shape is built from 6 cubes. The views from the front, back, top, left and right are shown.
Use isometric paper to draw this shape. You might like to build the shape and sketch it first.

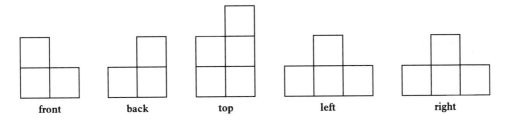

front   back   top   left   right

11. Work out the value of **e** for each of the diagrams in **Box A**. Match with the answers from **Box B**, then fill in this chart e.g. **1 → L** so **L** is filled in as shown.

8	2	4	1	5		3	5	8	6	7	2	6
			L									

Box A

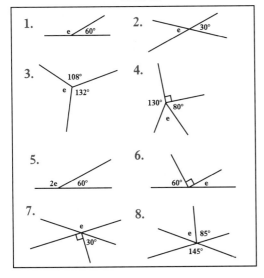

1. e 60°
2. e 30°
3. 108° e 132°
4. 130° 80° e
5. 2e 60°
6. 60° e
7. e 30°
8. e 85° 145°

Box B

A. 60°; vert. opp. ∠s
E. 60°; adj. ∠s on a line
G. 60°; ∠s at a point
L. 120°; adj. ∠s on a line
O. 120°; vert. opp. ∠s
R. 120°; ∠s at a point
N. 30°; vert. opp. ∠s
S. 30°; adj. ∠s on a line

12. Copy this graph.

    Using I as the centre of enlargement, enlarge the shape ABCD by a scale factor of 3.

    Write down the coordinates of A′, B′, C′ and D′ (the images of A, B, C and D).

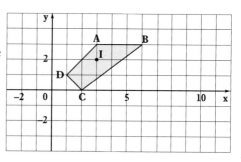

13. (a) The quadrilateral in which all the angles are equal and all the sides are equal is a

    A. Rectangle   **B.** Square   **C.** Rhombus   **D.** Parallelogram.

    (b) The diagonals are at right angles in a

    A. Rectangle and Square   **B.** Rectangle and Rhombus

    C. Square and Rhombus   **D.** Rectangle and Parallelogram.

    (c) The diagonals are equal in a

    A. Rectangle and Rhombus   **B.** Square and Rhombus

    C. Rectangle and Square   **D.** Rectangle and Parallelogram.

14. Find the size of the angles marked as a, b, c, d and e.

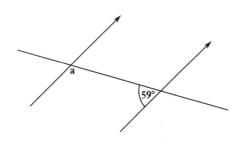

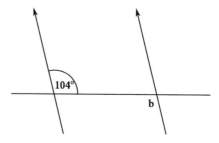

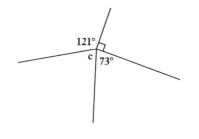

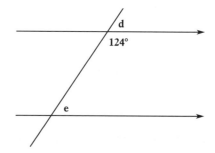

15.

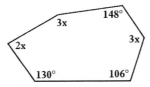

Find the value of x.

16. Isla stacked bricks like the one shown. When she had finished, her pile was 3m long, 40cm wide and 0·8m high. How many bricks were in Isla's pile?

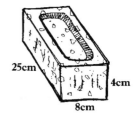

17. The distance between each dot is 1cm. Find the area of each shape.

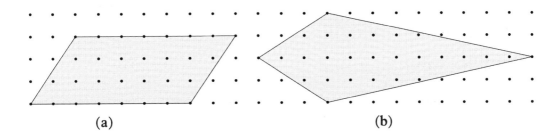

(a) (b)

18.

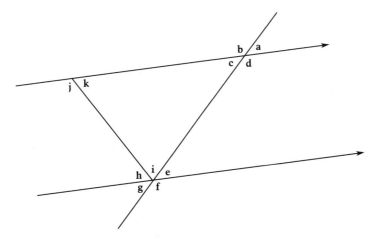

Name all the angles that are equal to   (a) d   (b) c   (c) h.

19.

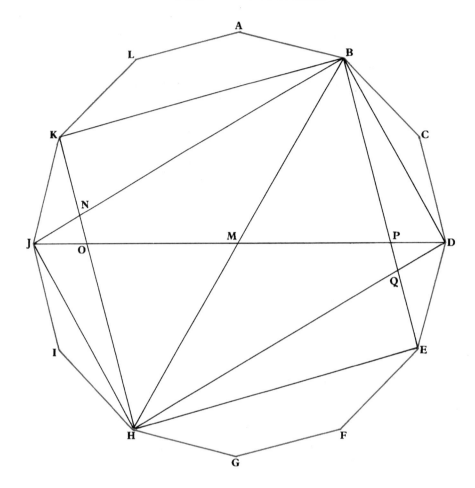

(a) Is the polygon which forms the outline of this "picture" a regular polygon? Explain your answer.

(b) One isosceles triangle is BCD. Name five others.

(c) Name three scalene triangles.

(d) Name two equilateral triangles.

(e) Name four right-angled triangles.

(f) BEHK is a square. Are there other squares in this "picture"? If so, name them.

(g) What name is given to the polygon BDEH?

(h) Name two hexagons.

(i) Name a heptagon, an octagon and a nonagon.

20.

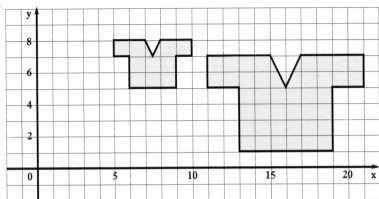

Copy this graph.

The sweat shirt on the left has been enlarged to the sweat shirt on the right.

(a) What is the scale factor for this enlargement?

(b) Draw lines on your graph to locate the centre of enlargement.
Write down the coordinates of the centre of enlargement.

21. Find the area of these.

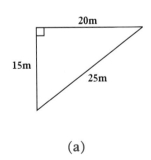

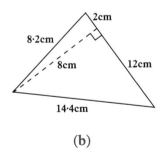

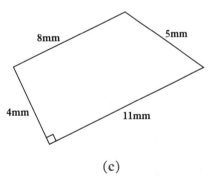

(a)   (b)   (c)

22. (a) Calculate the size of an exterior angle of a regular 18-sided polygon.

(b) Calculate the size of an interior angle of a regular 18-sided polygon.

(c) Can a regular polygon be drawn with each exterior angle equal to 54°?
Give reasons for your answer.

23. Match the shapes with the sketches of their plans and elevations.

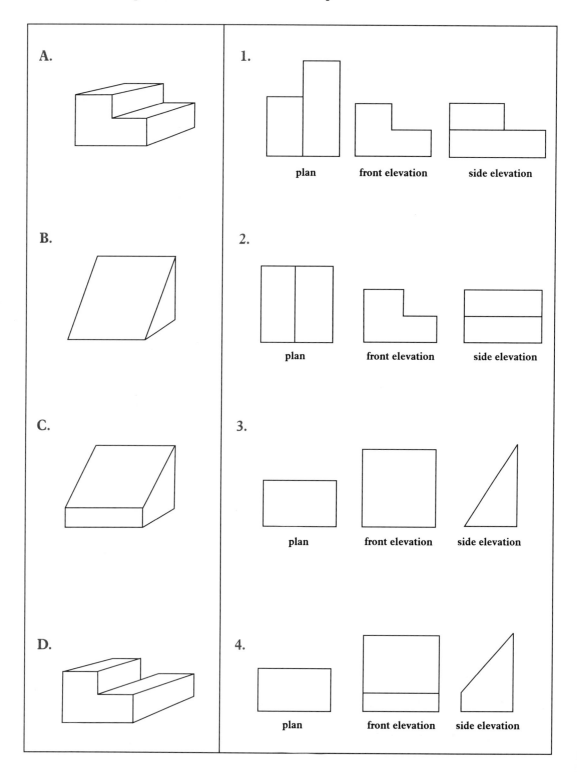

24. Find the value of **n.** Hence find the size of the angles.

(a)

(b)

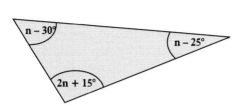

25. A school office is twice as long as it is wide. Its area is 72m².
    Use trial and improvement, or some other method, to find the length of this office.

26. Write and solve equations to find the value of x.

(a)

(b)

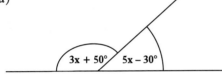
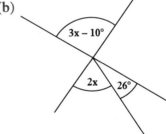

27.

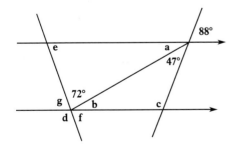

Find the value of each unknown.

28. (a) Write and solve an equation to find the value of x.

    (b) How long is this rectangle?

(3x + 2)cm

Rectangle

(2x + 5)cm

29.

This shape is made from 5 cubes. Two pairs are joined by a common edge.
Use isometric paper to draw a different shape made from 5 cubes in which 2 pairs are joined by just a common edge.

30.(a) RT 45

FD 200

REPEAT 6 [FD 200 RT 90]

LT 135

FD 80

REPEAT 20 [FD 10 RT 18]

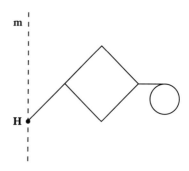

The LOGO instructions on the left draw the shape on the right.
Write instructions to draw the reflection of this shape in the mirror line m.

(b) Damien taught the turtle to remember how to draw a square. He then instructed the turtle to draw this diagram.
Copy and complete Damien's instructions.

TO SHAPE
REPEAT 4 [FD 200 RT . . .]
. . .
REPEAT . . . [SHAPE RT . . .]

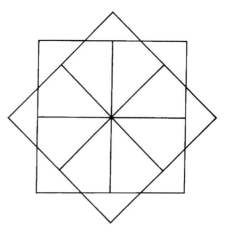

31.

Using "dotty" isometric paper, tessellate one of these polyiamond outlines. Colour your design, using at most 4 colours.

HANDLING DATA

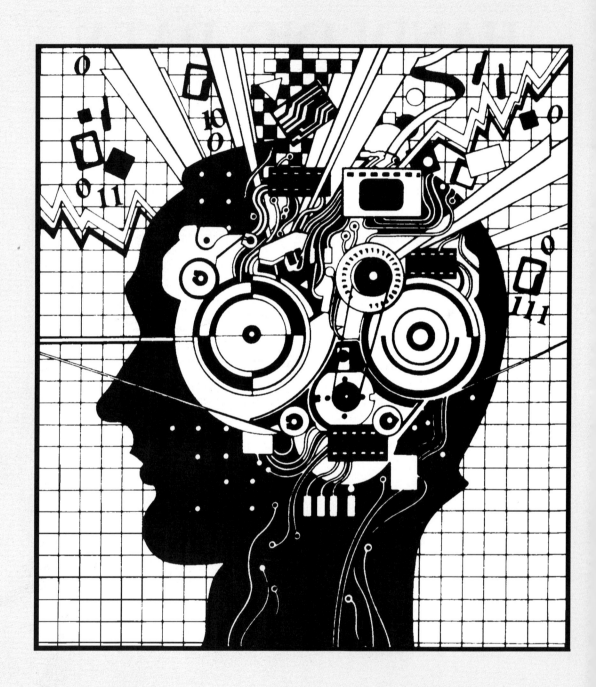

Handling Data from Previous Levels

REVISION

GRAPHS and FREQUENCY TABLES

This **pictogram** shows the number of teams in a sports competition.

9 teams are playing Football.
6 teams are playing Hockey.
5 teams are playing Badminton.

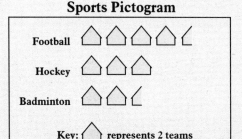

Sports Pictogram

Transport	Walk	Cycle	Train	Bus	Car	Other
Frequency	6	2	3	5	3	1

The **frequency table** shows how the students in one class come to school. This information is also shown on the **block graph** below.

Frequency is always on the vertical axis.

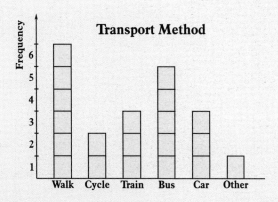

We can make conclusions from this graph.
For instance, the same number of students come to school by car as by train.

continued ...

. . . from previous page

This **bar chart** or **bar graph** shows the number of hours of sunshine on each of the days of one week.
On Monday there were 3 hours of sunshine, on Tuesday 4 hours, on Wednesday 4 hours, on Thursday 3 hours, on Friday 8 hours, on Saturday 6 hours and on Sunday 5 hours.

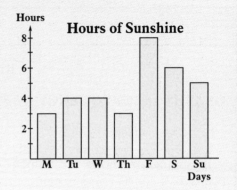

27 29 28 30 29 27 27 29 28 29 27 30 29 28 27 28 29 29 27

The figures in this list give the number of biscuits in 19 packets. These figures are summarised on the **tally chart**.

On the tally chart, a stroke is made as each figure is recorded (a diagonal stroke is used for every 5th entry). Once all the figures have been recorded, the strokes are added to get the frequency. Because this tally chart also has the frequency it can also be called a **frequency table**.

Biscuits Tally Chart

Number	Tally	Frequency
27	⦀⦀⦀ I	6
28	IIII	4
29	⦀⦀⦀ II	7
30	II	2

The data on the tally chart is graphed on this **bar-line graph**.

On the bar-line graph the height of each vertical line gives the frequency.

f stands for frequency.

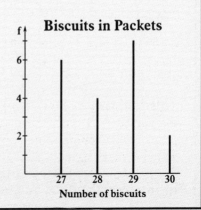

continued . . .

. . . from previous page

This data gives the number of times the letter e appears in each sentence on the last page of "The Clan of the Cave Bear".

1 2 2 1 6 10 2 8 3 3 5 5 3 1
6 7 3 9 3 4 5 2 4 9 11 15 0 8

The data has been **grouped** into 6 categories on this combined tally chart and frequency table. Categories are sometimes called **class intervals.** When we group data we always have each class interval the same width.

e's Frequency Table

Number of e's	Tally	Frequency
0–2	卌 ‖‖	8
3–5	卌 卌	10
6–8	卌	5
9–11	‖‖‖	4
12–14		0
15–17	‖	1

The information on the tally chart is graphed on this **frequency diagram.**

A frequency diagram has the bars joined as shown.

Grouped data is graphed on a frequency diagram rather than a bar graph or bar-line graph.

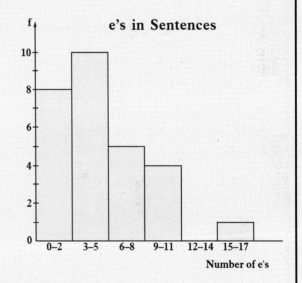

In hospital, Jane's temperature was taken every 4 hours.

At 8a.m. it was 37°C, at Noon it was 38°C, at 4p.m. it was 37·5°C and at 8p.m. it was 37·8°C.

This **line graph** shows these temperatures. It was drawn by plotting the temperatures at 8a.m., Noon, 4p.m., 8p.m. and joining the points with straight lines.

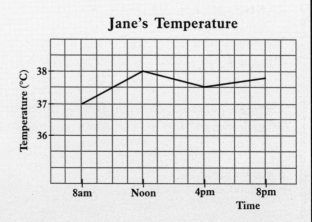

continued . . .

317

. . . from previous page

Pie Charts are circle graphs.
The circle is divided into sections.
The number of degrees in the angle at the centre of each section represents the frequency.

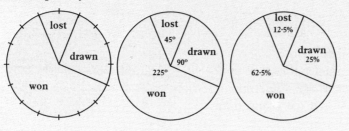

Hockey Matches

Won	15
Lost	3
Drawn	6

DIAGRAMS

A class was surveyed about board games played.
This **Venn diagram** shows that
  4 played both Scrabble and Monopoly
  6 played Scrabble but not Monopoly
  9 played Monopoly but not Scrabble
  2 played neither Scrabble nor Monopoly.

Scrabble Monopoly

6 4 9

2

In this **Carroll Diagram,** two aspects of the daily weather in May are shown.
It was cold and raining on 8 days, cold but not raining on 2 days, mild and raining on 5 days, mild and not raining on 16 days.

May Weather

8	2	cold
5	16	mild
raining	not raining	

RANGE. MEAN. MEDIAN. MODE

The **range** of a list of data is the difference between the greatest and smallest data values. For instance, the range of 3, 2, 6, 2, 5, 3, 7 is $7 - 2 = 5$.

There are three measures of **average** often used. They are, the **mean,** the **median** and the **mode**. The mean is commonly called the average.

$$\text{Mean} = \frac{\text{sum of all data values}}{\text{number of data values}}$$

For instance, the mean of 1, 2, 4, 6, 10 is $\frac{1+2+4+6+10}{5} = 4{\cdot}6$.

continued . . .

. . . *from previous page*

The **mode** is the data value that occurs most frequently.
For instance, the mode of 2, 5, 3, 5, 4, 1 is 5.
A set of data may have more than one mode or no mode.
For instance 2, 5, 3, 4, 1 has no mode; 2, 5, 3, 5, 4, 3 has two modes, both 5 and 3.

The **median** is the middle value of a set of data which is written in order.
For instance, to find the median of 2, 5, 3, 5, 4, 1, 7 we write the data in order
as 1, 2, 3, 4, 5, 5, 7. The median is 4.
If there is an even number of data values, the median is the mean of the
middle two values. For instance, the median of 7, 8, 8, 9, 14, 15 is $\frac{8+9}{2} = 8 \cdot 5$.

DATABASES

A **computer database** is a program which organises large amounts of
information. From a database many different lists can be printed out.

For instance:

Name	Age	Birthmonth	School Year	Teacher	Previous School	
Tony Abellton	8	May	4	Cowie	None	
Carina Akande	7	November	3	Merton	None	
David Alabaster	9	September	4	Patel	Brightwater	
Jason Andrews	8	February	4	Patel	None	
Kirsty Andrews	5	October	1	Langham	None	

This could be part of a database on which Riverton Primary School keeps
information about their students.

One line of information is called a **record**.
For instance, Tony Abellton   8   May   4   Cowie   None   ... is a record.

The **fields** in the above database are: Name, Age, Birthmonth, School Year,
Teacher, Previous School, . . .

SURVEYS

The steps taken to **conduct a survey** are:

Step 1   **Decide** on the purpose of the survey.

Step 2   **Design** an observation sheet.

Step 3   **Collect** the data on the observation sheet.

Step 4   **Organise** the data onto tables and graphs or into a computer
database.

Step 5   **Analyse** the data i.e. write some conclusions.

continued . . .

. . . from previous page

PROBABILITY

A game is **fair** if each player has the same chance of winning.
A game is **unfair** if one player has less chance of winning than another.

The chance of an event happening can be described by one of:

certain, very likely, likely, unlikely, very unlikely, impossible

For instance, if today is Monday the 3rd of June:

It is certain that tomorrow will be Tuesday.
It is very likely that there will be some cloud, sometime today.
It is likely that it will be sunny sometime tomorrow.
It is unlikely to rain all day tomorrow and the next day.
It is very unlikely that it will snow tomorrow.
It is impossible that tomorrow will be Friday.

There is an **even chance** of an event happening if the chance of the event happening is the same as the chance of the event not happening.
For instance, there is an even chance of getting a head when a coin is tossed.

There is a **better than even chance** of an event happening if the event is more likely to happen than not to happen.

There is a **less than even chance** of an event happening if the event is less likely to happen than not to happen.

The probability of an event that is certain to happen is 1.
The probability of an event that will never happen is 0.
The probability of any other event is between 0 and 1.

0				1
no chance	poor chance	even chance	good chance	certain

Choosing at **random** means every item has the same chance of being chosen.

Equally likely outcomes are outcomes which have the same probability of occurring.

continued . . .

. . . from previous page

Probability may be calculated.

For equally likely outcomes, P (an event occurring) = $\dfrac{\text{Number of favourable outcomes}}{\text{Number of possible outcomes}}$

For instance, the probability of getting a prime number when a die is tossed is calculated as follows.

Possible outcomes are 1, 2, 3, 4, 5, 6. Number of possible outcomes = 6.
Favourable outcomes are 2, 3, 5. Number of favourable outcomes = 3.

P (prime number) = $\frac{3}{6}$ or $\frac{1}{2}$.

Probability may be estimated from experiments.

P (an event occurring) = $\dfrac{\text{Number of times the event occurs}}{\text{Number of trials}}$

For instance, if a drawing pin is dropped a number of times

P (drawing pin landing on its side) = $\dfrac{\text{Number of times drawing pin landed on its side}}{\text{Number of times drawing pin was dropped}}$

REVISION EXERCISE

1.

Number of books read

Angela   📖 📖 📖 📖 📖

Belen   📖 📖 📖 📖 📖 📖

Catherine   📖 📖 📖

Derek   📖 📖

Elena   📖 📖 📖 📖

Key: 📖 represents 2 books

This pictogram shows the number of books read by 5 students during the summer holidays.

(a) How many books did Catherine read?

(b) How many books did these students read altogether?

2. Do you think there will be a good chance or a poor chance of getting two heads when you toss a fair coin twice?

3. Jason gathered data on the star-sign of the students in his class. As he gathered the data he drew these block graphs.

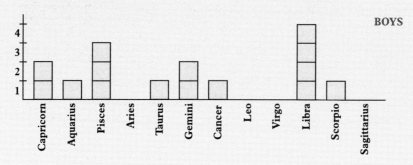

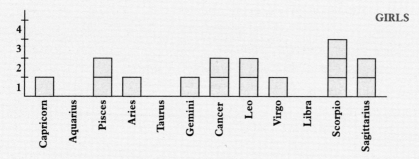

(a) How many girls have star-sign Cancer?

(b) How many students have star-sign Capricorn?

(c) How many more girls than boys have star-sign Scorpio?

(d) Which is the most common star-sign for the students in Jason's class?

(e) How many students are there in this class?

4. In 1000 tosses of a coin, heads came up 47 times. Do you think it is likely that this is a fair coin? Explain your answer.

5. Beth interviewed a number of students about their preferred holiday destination.
She included this diagram in her analysis.

21	65	**Boys**
32	82	**Girls**
Abroad	**U.K.**	

(a) How many girls preferred a destination abroad?

(b) How many students preferred to holiday in the U.K?

(c) How many students did Beth interview?

6. A die is tossed.
Use one of "even chance", "better than even chance",
"less than even chance" to describe the chance of
these events happening.

(a) an odd number   (b) a six   (c) a number smaller than 5

7. Dale was doing an investigation on cricket. This data shows the runs made by
Alex Hale in the 48 matches he played.

```
43  25   0  34  11  21  47  25  27  42  35  51   0   9  17  28
29  15  38   7   4  24  52  32  31  22   8  17  28  26  31  19
18  15  21  29  28  55   9   0  18  41  34   0  14   4  32  29
```

(a) Use your calculator to find the mean.

(b) What is the mode?

(c) What is the median?

8. Every chocolate in a box is wrapped.
Alexis chooses one of these chocolates.

Find the probability that the chocolate Alexis chooses is

(a) wrapped   (b) not wrapped.

9.
```
31°  14°  17°  12°  15°  16°   9°  24°  11°  13°  17°  18°   3°  17°   9°
 8°  15°  18°  21°  23°  18°   3°  14°  19°  21°  28°  17°  34°  18°  11°
17°  28°  14°   8°  18°  12°  11°   7°  19°  17°  25°  27°  16°   9°  22°
36°  25°   6°  22°  37°  12°   9°  23°  14°  30°  21°  15°  13°  11°   2°
```

This data gives the temperatures on September 1st in different cities throughout
the world.

(a) Find the range of this data.

(b) Draw up a tally chart and
frequency table for this
data. Choose sensible class
intervals.

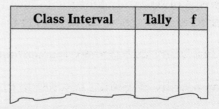

Class Interval	Tally	f

(c) Draw a frequency diagram
for this data.

323

10. This graph shows the population (to the nearest 1000) of a town at 5 yearly intervals, and the projected population in future years.

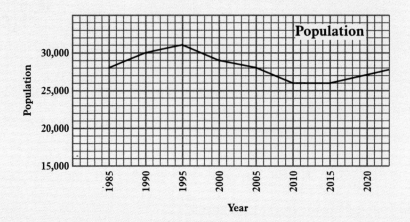

(a) What was the population in 1995?

(b) What is the projected population for the year 2020?

(c) In what year is the population expected to be the same as in 1985?

(d) What was the increase in population between 1985 and 1995?

(e) What is the expected decrease in population between 2000 and 2020?

(f) This graph is misleading. Why?

(g) It seems that the population in the middle of 1987 was 29,000. Is this necessarily so? Explain your answer.

11. Could you calculate each of the following probabilities or would you need to conduct a survey (or an experiment) to find them?

(a) probability that the next person going into the library wears glasses

(b) probability of getting two heads when a coin is tossed twice

(c) probability that the next student to come into class has no brothers

12.

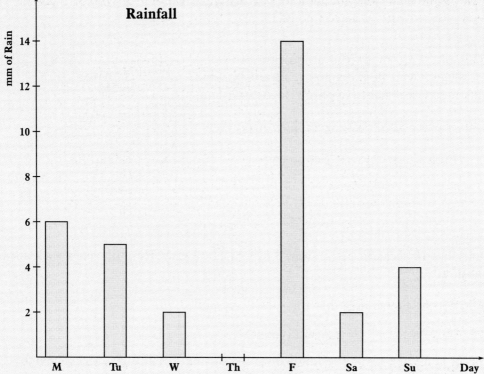

Rainfall

mm of Rain

(a) What was the rainfall on Tuesday?

(b) Which was the wettest day?

(c) How much more rain was there on Monday than on Sunday?

(d) Did it rain every day?

(e) Find the total rainfall for the week.

(f) One conclusion we can make from this graph is "nearly half of the rain for the week fell on Friday".
Make another conclusion from this graph.

(g) Neroli claimed that the average daily rainfall was about 4·7mm. Liam claimed it was 5·5mm.
Who is right, Neroli or Liam?

13. A die is tossed twice. Both times the number 6 came up.

What is the probability of getting another 6, if this die is tossed again?

14. List all the ways you can get a total of 6, when two dice are tossed together.

15. This pie chart shows the proportion of passengers who flew Economy, First Class and Business Class from Heathrow to Amsterdam.

    Out of every 2000 passengers, how many flew

    (a) First Class   (b) Economy?

    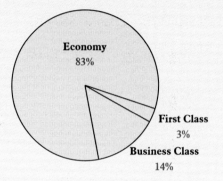

16. Tony has 10 socks in his drawer, 3 of which are grey. He pulls out a sock at random.

    What is the probability that the sock Tony pulled out is grey?

17. Susan and Greg made the following runs during a 3-innings cricket match.
    Susan: 11, 37, 15   Greg: 28, 31, 10

    (a) Who had the better batting average, Susan or Greg?

    (b) Did Susan or Greg have the larger range?

    (c) Who do you think is the better player? Explain your answer.

18. 25 small discs, numbered from 1 to 25, are placed in a bag.
    One of these discs is chosen at random.

    What is the probability that the disc chosen will be numbered with a multiple of 3?

19. Karen entered the data from her survey, on leisure activities, into a computer database.

    Give three examples of lists that Karen could have printed.

DISCOVER, DISCUSS, DO

- What do you already know about displaying data? **Discuss.**

- What data is displayed on the graph and table below?
  Do you think the data is displayed well? Can you think of better ways to display the data?
  Discuss.

Holidays[1]: by destination
Millions and Percentages

	1976	1981	1986	1988
Domestic holidays taken by				
residents of Great Britain (millions)	75	72	71	73
of which holidays of 4 or				
more nights	38	40	39	38
Destination of holidays abroad taken				
by residents of the United				
Kingdom(percentages)				
Austria	2	3	3	3
Belgium or Luxembourg	3	2	3	2
France	20	27	21	18
Germany (Fed. Rep.)	2	3	2	2
Greece	5	7	8	8
Irish Republic	6	4	2	3
Italy	7	6	4	3
Netherlands	3	2	2	2
Spain [2]	30	22	31	31
Switzerland	2	2	2	2
All in Europe	91	87	91	88
United States	2	5	3	4
Other countries	7	8	6	7
Total (= 100%) (millions)	7	13	18	21

1 A holiday is defined as a visit of 1 or more nights made for holiday
  purposes. Business trips and visits to friends and relatives are excluded.
2 From 1981 includes Balearic and Canary Isles, but in earlier years only
  includes Balearic Isles.

Source: Key Data 1990/91

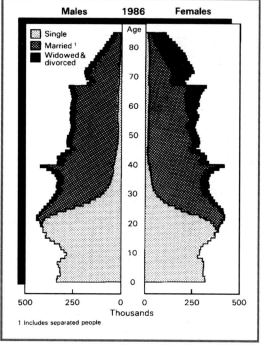

Population: by sex, age and marital status, 1986
England and Wales

1 Includes separated people

Source: Kay Data 1989/90

- In what places in your community do you see data displayed?
  What sorts of tables or charts or graphs are used?
  Why do you think the data is displayed in this way? Could the data be better
  displayed in another way? **Discuss.**

- What data, from your other subjects, have you seen displayed on a chart or table
  or graph? Where, in your school, have you seen data displayed? **Discuss.**

- Make a collection of graphs and tables and charts from the newspaper or
  magazines. Look at each of these carefully. How easy are they to read? **Discuss.**

DRAWING PIE CHARTS

Example   A dairy sold four flavours of ice-cream: Strawberry, Vanilla, Banana Chip and Chocolate. This list shows the ice-creams sold in one day.

Vanilla	8
Banana Chip	14
Chocolate	23
Strawberry	55

To draw a pie chart for this we must first calculate the angles. We do this as follows:

There are 360° in a pie chart.
There were 100 ice-creams sold.

Fraction of the pie chart for Vanilla $= \frac{8}{100}$

Angle for Vanilla $= \frac{8}{100} \times 360°$
$= 29°$ (to the nearest degree)

Fraction of the pie chart for Banana Chip $= \frac{14}{100}$

Angle for Banana Chip $= \frac{14}{100} \times 360°$
$= 50°$ (to the nearest degree)

Fraction of the pie chart for Chocolate $= \frac{23}{100}$

Angle for Chocolate $= \frac{23}{100} \times 360°$
$= 83°$ (to the nearest degree)

Fraction of the pie chart for Strawberry $= \frac{55}{100}$

Angle for Strawberry $= \frac{55}{100} \times 360°$
$= 198°$

The drawing of the **pie chart** is shown in the following diagrams. The steps taken are given after the diagrams.

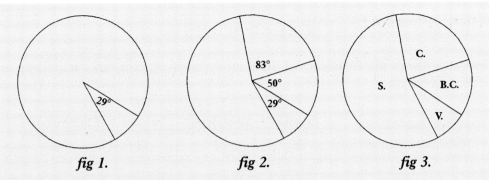

fig 1.   *fig 2.*   *fig 3.*

Step 1   Draw a circle using the compass.
Draw in any radius.
Place the base line of your protractor on this radius.
Measure and draw an angle of 29°.
This is shown in *fig 1*.

Step 2   Now draw angles of 50° and 83°. The remaining angle in the diagram
should be 198°. This is shown in *fig 2*.

Step 3   Complete the pie chart by writing a description in each section. This is
shown in *fig 3*. The pie chart should be given a title. What would be a
suitable title for this pie chart?

DISCUSSION EXERCISE 18:1

The number of ice-creams sold on another day is shown. A total of 197 were sold.

Angle of pie chart for Vanilla $= \frac{27}{197} \times 360°$
$= 49°$ to the nearest degree

Vanilla	27
Banana Chip	15
Chocolate	51
Strawberry	104

Angle of pie chart for Banana Chip $= \frac{15}{197} \times 360°$
$= 27°$ to the nearest degree

Angle of pie chart for Chocolate $= \frac{51}{197} \times 360°$
$= 93°$ to the nearest degree

Angle of pie chart for Strawberry $= \frac{104}{197} \times 360°$
$= 190°$ to the nearest degree

This time the angles 49°, 27°, 93°, 190° do not add up to 360°. Why not? **Discuss.**

How should the pie chart be drawn? **Discuss.**

EXERCISE 18:2

1. This table shows the frequency of different types of experiments carried out in a Science Laboratory.

Type of experiment	Biology	Chemistry	Physics	Electronics
Number carried out	30	27	24	9

Copy and complete:

(a) Total number of experiments carried out = $\cdots$

(b) Fraction of Biology experiments = $\frac{\cdots}{\cdots}$

(c) Angle of pie chart for Biology experiments = $\cdots$ degrees

(d) Fraction of Chemistry experiments = $\frac{\cdots}{\cdots}$

(e) Angle of pie chart for Chemistry experiments = $\cdots$ degrees

(f) Fraction of Physics experiments = $\frac{\cdots}{\cdots}$

(g) Angle of pie chart for Physics experiments = $\cdots$ degrees

(h) Fraction of Electronics experiments = $\frac{\cdots}{\cdots}$

(i) Angle of pie chart for Electronics experiments = $\cdots$ degrees

Draw a pie chart to illustrate the data in the table.

2. This table shows the number of litres of wine produced by a vineyard in one season. The figures have been rounded to the nearest thousand litres.

Type	Still White	Still Red	Sparkling	Fortified
Litres	42000	4000	8000	6000

Copy and complete:

(a) Total production of all types of wine = $\cdots$ litres.

(b) Fraction of Still White = $\dfrac{\cdots}{\cdots}$

(c) Angle of pie chart for Still White = $\cdots$ degrees.

(d) Fraction of Still Red = $\dfrac{\cdots}{\cdots}$

(e) Angle of pie chart for Still Red = $\cdots$ degrees.

(f) Fraction of Sparkling = $\dfrac{\cdots}{\cdots}$

(g) Angle of pie chart for Sparkling = $\cdots$ degrees.

(h) Fraction of Fortified = $\dfrac{\cdots}{\cdots}$

(i) Angle of pie chart for Fortified = $\cdots$ degrees.

Now draw the pie chart.

3.

Contributions of selected foods to energy intake   *kcals per person per day*

	1987
Liquid wholemilk	158
Meat and meat products	321
Butter	64
Margarine	119
Packet sugar	120
Potatoes	88
Bread	285

Source: Key Data 1990   *From: National Food Survey, 1987*

(a) Find the total number of kilocalories per person per day for the 7 types of food mentioned in the table.

(b) What fraction of these kilocalories is obtained from each of these?
    liquid wholemilk   meat and meat products
    butter and margarine   packet sugar
    potatoes   bread

(c) Work out the angles for a pie chart that shows the 6 food categories given in (b). Do these angles add to 360°? If not, why not?

(d) Decide what to do about the problem found in (c).
Draw a pie chart to show the kilocalories obtained from the 6 food categories given in (b).

4.

Organisations for young people

United Kingdom — Thousands

Duke of Edinburgh's Award Awards gained	1971	1987
Bronze	18	20
Silver	7	8
Gold	3	4

Source: Key Data 1990

(a) To the nearest thousand, how many Duke of Edinburgh's Awards were gained altogether in 1987?

(b) Draw a pie chart to show the different types of awards gained in 1987.

5.

Reading of national newspapers:

Great Britain

	Percentage of adults reading each paper in 1987	
	Males	Females
Sunday newspapers		
News of the World	30	27
Sunday Mirror	22	19
The People	20	17
Sunday Express	14	13
The Mail on Sunday	12	11
The Sunday Times	9	7
The Observer	6	5
Sunday Telegraph	5	4
Any Sunday newspaper [4]	76	71

4 Includes the above newspapers plus *The Sunday Post* and *Sunday Mail.*

From: *Social Trends 1989*

Source: Key Data 1990

(a) What percentage of the male population read a Sunday newspaper?

(b) What percentage of the female population did not read a Sunday newspaper?

(c) Why is a pie chart not a suitable way of displaying this data?

6. Collect data and draw pie charts for **one** of the following:

(a) Time you spend on chores around the house on a Saturday.

(b) Time you spend on various leisure activities during a weekend.

(c) Types of advertisements during 2 hours of TV. Put the advertisements into just four or five different categories. You could graph the time spent or the actual number of advertisements.

Review 1

Day	Sat.	Sun.	Mon.
No. of videos	130	34	76

This table shows the number of videos
hired from The Video Box each day during
a Bank Holiday weekend.

(a) How many videos were hired altogether during this weekend?

(b) What fraction of these videos were hired on Saturday?

(c) What fraction were hired on Sunday?

(d) What fraction were hired on Monday?

(e) What size angle, on a pie chart, will represent the videos hired on each of these days?

(f) Draw a pie chart to illustrate the data given in the table.

Review 2

Participation in the most popular[1] sporting activities
Great Britain   Percentages

	1986
Percentage engaging in each activity in the 4 weeks before inter-view (most popular quarter)	
Walking — 2 miles or more [2]	23
Swimming (Indoor)	11
(Outdoor)	7
Snooker/billiards/pool	11
Darts	7
Keep fit/yoga	4
Golf	4
Fishing	3
Football	3
Squash	3
Cycling	3
Tennis	3

Source: Key Data 1990

1 Activities are listed in descending order of participation rates for all adults aged 16 or over in the most popular quarter for each activity in 1986.
2 Includes rambling and hiking.

Source: General Household Survey

From: Social Trends, 1989, Table 10.13

(a) Assuming that no one participated in more than one of these sports during this 4 week period, find the percentage of the population who did not participate in the given sports.

(b) Draw a pie chart to illustrate the data.
You will need a section for those who did not participate in the given sports. Call this section "Others or None".

(c) Do you think the assumption we made in (a) was realistic?
Give reasons for your answer.

INVESTIGATION 18:3

MISLEADING PIE CHARTS

The 39% section of this pie chart appears to take up more than 39% of the complete pie chart. Why?

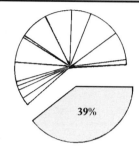

Find other misleading pie charts.
Newspapers are a good source.

Write a sentence or two about each misleading pie chart you find. Try to decide if they were intended to be misleading. If you think they were, try to find a reason why they were drawn in this way.

PRACTICAL EXERCISE 18:4

Carry out a survey. Graph the data collected on a pie chart.
You may like to refer back to **page 319 for the steps you should take to conduct a survey.**

Some suggestions for suitable surveys follow.
You may wish to do a survey on something not mentioned.
If you do choose something else, make sure the data collected can be displayed on a pie chart.

Suggested Surveys

1. **Favourite type of music of the students in your class. Have categories such as jazz, country and western, etc.**

2. **Left-handed? Right-handed? Ambidexterous?**
   Survey the students in a year group in your school.

3. **Favourite pudding of the students in your class.**

4. **Number of people in the households of students.**
   Survey the students in your class.

5. **Favourite winter sport played.**
   Survey the students in a year group.

6. **Number of pets owned by the students in your class.**

7. **The T.V. viewing habits of the students in your class.**
   This could be the time spent watching T.V. or the type of programme watched.

SCATTER GRAPHS

On a **scatter graph** we are able to display two aspects of data at the same time. For instance, we could display both the height and weight of some students.

Sometimes scatter graphs are called **scatter diagrams** or **scattergrams.**

Example The length and width of the top 10 leaves of a pot plant were measured to the nearest millimetre. The results are given in the table.

Leaf number	1	2	3	4	5	6	7	8	9	10
Length (mm)	79	70	67	73	56	61	58	78	78	54
Width (mm)	32	29	28	30	25	26	25	32	29	26

The scatter graph is drawn by plotting the points (79, 32), (70, 29), (67, 28) and so on. Each point may be plotted with a dot (●) or a cross (×). The scatter graph below shows each point plotted with a cross.

Scatter graph of Leaf width/Leaf length

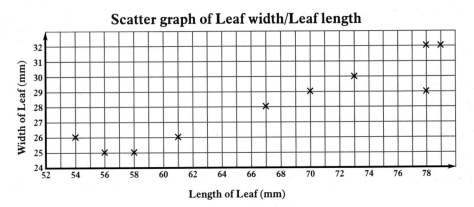

Length of Leaf (mm)

DISCUSSION EXERCISE 18:5

Length of shot-put throw (metres)	18·4	14·7	13·2	15·1	17·2
Time for 400m (seconds)	62	59	63	57	63

This table shows the results of five students who entered both the shot-put event and the 400m event at an athletics meeting.
These results are to be displayed on a scatter graph.
The six members of a group each drew up a different set of axes for the scatter graph.
These are shown below.

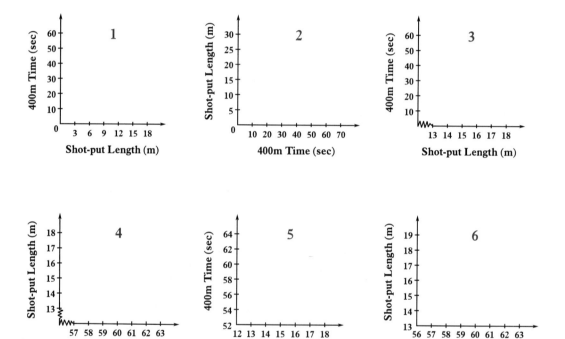

What do you think the jagged line means on the axes in 3 and 4? **Discuss.**

Are all of these sets of axes suitable for graphing the data?
Is one of these sets of axes more suitable than the others? **Discuss.**

Shoe size	3	4	5	4	3	4	2
Dress size	8	10	9	10	12	11	8

The data given in this table is to be displayed on a scatter diagram.
Could this data be displayed equally well on either of the two following sets of axes?

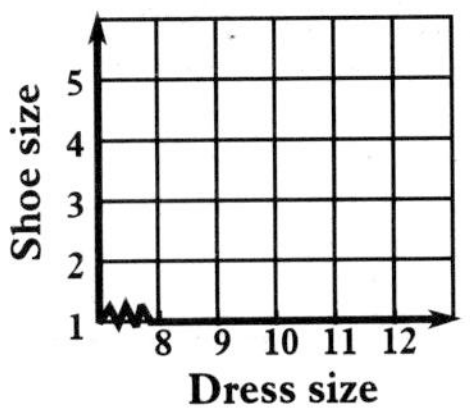

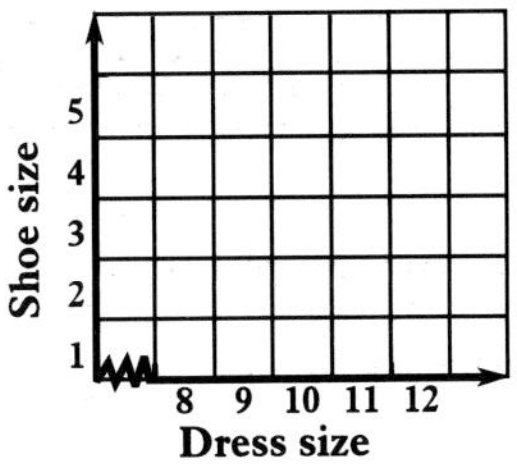

How would you graph the 2nd and 4th pairs of data (both 4, 10) on each of these sets of axes?
Is this problem likely to arise when you are graphing continuous data such as in the first table of this exercise? **Discuss.**

•

What do you think this scatter graph might represent? **Discuss.**
Make up a suitable title for this graph. **Discuss.**

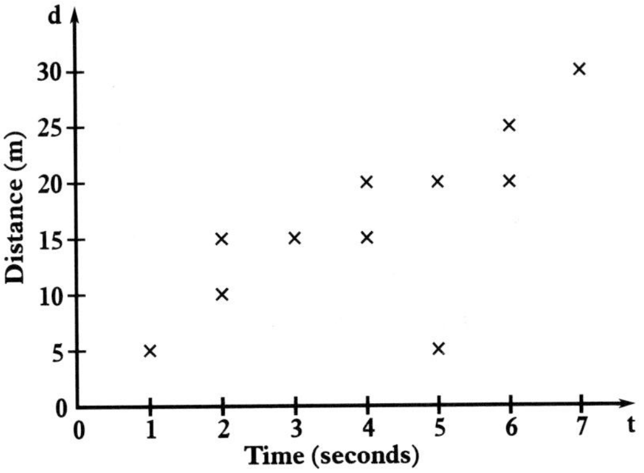

EXERCISE 18:6

1.

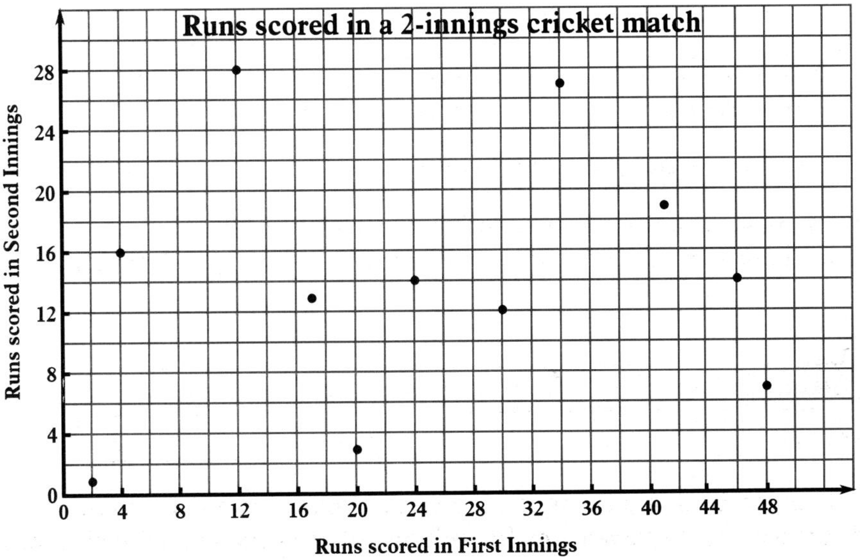

This scatter graph shows the number of runs scored by each player in a cricket team, in each of the two innings of a match.

(a) How many runs did the player who scored 20 in the first innings get in the second innings?

(b) What did the player who scored 13 in the second innings score in the first innings?

(c) How many runs did the player who scored the highest in the first innings get in the second innings?

(d) How many runs did the player who scored the highest in the second innings get in the first innings?

(e) "Players who scored well in the first innings also scored well in the second innings." Is this statement true?

2. This table shows the handspan and the length of the thumb of 8 students.

Student	Ann	Roger	Meena	Jamie	Kojo	Sue	Jason	Aba
Handspan (mm)	184	196	176	203	192	196	211	205
Thumb length (mm)	55	57	51	58	62	54	62	65

(a) Would you expect there to be a relationship between thumb length and handspan?

(b) Draw a scatter graph to show the handspan and the length of the thumb of these students. Have a sensible range of values on each axis.
Does the scatter graph show that students with longer thumbs tend to have greater handspans?

3. Gillian tossed a red and a white die together 15 times. The following table shows Gillian's results.

White die result	4	3	2	4	6	3	5	1	5	5	4	3	6	6	2
Red die result	1	6	6	2	5	2	3	3	6	5	1	2	4	5	1

(a) Which number came up on the red die when 1 came up on the white die?

(b) Which number came up on the white die when 4 came up on the red die?

(c) Would you expect a high number on the red die if a high number occurred on the white die?

(d) Draw a scatter diagram to illustrate Gillian's results. Does the scatter diagram support your answer to (c)?

Review Ali gathered data from the female students in his class.
The following table shows the foot length and height of each student.

Foot length (mm)	203	207	223	196	214	239	222	230	225	231	200	238	198
Height (cm)	160	152	164	149	155	171	156	154	160	162	149	170	155

(a) How tall is the student whose foot length is 230mm?

(b) What is the foot length of the tallest student?

(c) Do you think that students with long feet will also be tall?

(d) Draw a scatter graph for the data.
Does the scatter graph support the answer you gave for (c)?

CORRELATION

Trends can sometimes be seen clearly from scatter graphs.

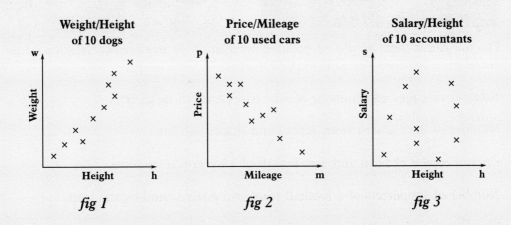

fig 1   *fig 2*   *fig 3*

fig 1 shows that the taller a dog is, the heavier it is likely to be.
fig 2 shows that the higher the mileage on a used car, the lower the price is likely to be.
fig 3 shows no trend at all. There doesn't seem to be any relationship between the height of an accountant and the salary of the accountant.

The word **correlation** is used when we talk about relationships.

For **positive correlation**, the points must be clustered around a line that slopes upwards. For instance, *fig 1* shows positive correlation between the height and weight of the dogs.

For **negative correlation**, the points must be clustered around a line that slopes downwards.
For instance, *fig 2* shows negative correlation between the mileage on a used car and its price.

If there is neither positive nor negative correlation we say there is **no correlation**. For instance, *fig 3* shows no correlation between an accountant's height and the accountant's salary.

DISCUSSION EXERCISE 18:7

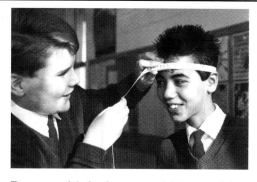 

Do you think there would be positive correlation or negative correlation or no correlation between the following? **Discuss.**

Number of pages and number of advertisements in magazines.

Number of days absent from school and marks in tests.

Circumference of head and arm length of 13-year-old students.

Number of supporters of a football team and goals scored by the team.

Number of boys and number of girls in families.

Years of education and income.

Length and weight of cats.

Amount of money people earn and the time they spend watching T.V.

Maths. mark and height of students from one year group.

Income of households and number of people in the households.

Height and number of leaves of pot plants.

Age and amount of pocket money received.

Number of rooms and number of windows in houses.

Time spent on homework and time spent watching T.V.

- Think of some pairs of variables which would be likely to have positive correlation, some that would be likely to have negative correlation and some that would be likely to have no correlation. **Discuss.**

PRACTICAL EXERCISE 18:8

1. Gather data on one or more of the following.
   Design an observation sheet for the collection of the data.
   Organise the data onto a scatter graph.
   Analyse the data. Be sure to mention correlation in your analysis.

   Weight and diameter of a variety of sports balls. (Include a golf ball, a tennis ball, a snooker ball, a netball, a soccer ball, a table tennis ball.)

   Number of photographs and number of advertisements in magazines.

   Pulse rate and time taken to run 100 metres.

   Length of arm and handspan of students.

   Armspan and distance a cricket ball can be thrown.

   The numbers obtained on a black die and a red die when they are tossed together.

2. Conduct a survey on one of the following.
   Organise the data onto a scatter diagram.
   Analyse the data, mentioning correlation.

   Number of rooms and number of windows in houses.

   Number of boys and number of girls in families.

   Age in months and number of consecutive push ups.

   Shoe size and number of people in the household of
   students.

   Pulse rate and breathing rate of a number of students.

3. Design and carry out an experiment of your choice or a survey of your choice.
   The data you collect should be able to be graphed on a scatter graph.

FOR YOUR INTEREST

Discuss one or more of the following statements fully.

Pie charts should be used more often by businesses to display data.

If we drew scatter graphs more often we might discover lots of
relationships we didn't know existed.

The data displayed on a scatter graph can also be well displayed in other ways.

Present a summary of your discussion to the rest of the class.
This summary could be presented as a talk or a mock interview or a debate. If
you choose to present the summary as a talk, make it visually interesting by
using tables and/or graphs.

DISCOVER, DISCUSS, DO

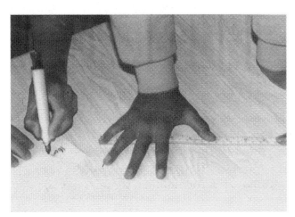 

● 1. Write down possible values you could get if you counted the number of library books on shelves.
   What if you were finding the number of chairs in classrooms?

  2. Write down possible values you could get if you measured someone's handspan.
   What if you took the temperature of water in an experiment?

   The data in **1.** could be called **counting data**. The data in **2.** could be called **measurement data**.
   Think of more examples of counting and measurement data. **Discuss.**

● Make a list of data you could collect about one of the following.

> the weather
> a city
> a farm
> medical research

Divide your list into counting data and measurement data.

DISCRETE and CONTINUOUS DATA

Discrete data can take only **particular values.**
For example, if we collected data about the number of students in classrooms, we may have 26, 27, 30, 35 etc. but not $33\frac{1}{2}$, $27\frac{1}{4}$ etc. because it is not possible to have fractional numbers of people.
Usually discrete data values are whole numbers but sometimes they do include some fractions. An example would be shoe sizes which could be 3, $3\frac{1}{2}$, 4, etc. Still only particular values are possible. You can't have a shoe size of $3\frac{1}{4}$ or $4\frac{4}{5}$ for instance. Examples of discrete data are given in the table below.

Data which can take **any value within a given range** is called **continuous data.** An example would be the length of a shoe, since this length could take any value between approximately 15cm and 30cm. For instance, the length of a shoe might be 15·6cm or 17·25cm or 29·831cm etc. Examples of continuous data are given in the table below.

DATA	
DISCRETE	**CONTINUOUS**
Shoe size	Length of a foot
School roll	Temperature at midnight
Tracks on a record	Time taken to do homework
Salary of a teacher	January rainfall at Southampton

EXERCISE 19:1

1. **State whether the following data is discrete or continuous.**

   (a) Number of students in classes

   (b) Number of sweets in bags

   (c) Length of wool in jerseys

   (d) The population of China's provinces

   (e) Length of the thumbs of the students in your class

(f)   Weight of the suitcases on an aeroplane

(g)   Number of suitcases on an aeroplane

(h)   Time at which the bell rings

(i)   Age at which women marry

(j)   The temperatures at midday during the past month

(k)   The amount of money earned babysitting in the evenings

(l)   Number of apples on trees

(m) Number of cars at car dealers

(n)   Weight of wool in sheep's fleeces

(o)   Number of votes cast in elections

(p)   Time taken to travel to school

(q)   Number of lambs born on farms

2. Write down 3 further examples of discrete data and 3 further examples of continuous data.

Review Is the following data discrete or continuous?

(a)   Weight of letters in a postbag

(b)   Number of passengers on buses

(c)   Age of students when they leave school

(d)   Daily rainfall

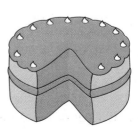

(e)   Amount of money made at cake stalls

READING FREQUENCY DIAGRAMS for CONTINUOUS DATA

Continuous data is graphed on a **frequency diagram**.

Example

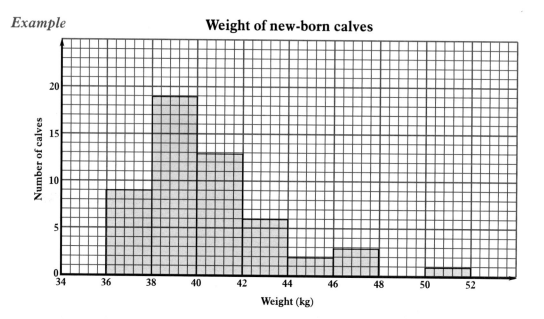

Weight of new-born calves

The horizontal axis gives the weight, in kg, of the calves. These calves have weights between 36kg and 52kg.

The first shaded "bar" of this histogram is for weights between 36kg and 38kg. We read this bar as "9 calves have weights between 36kg and 38kg".

The next shaded "bar" is for weights between 38kg and 40kg. We read this bar as "19 calves have weights between 38kg and 40kg".

There is a problem. If we had a calf with a weight of 38kg, would we include it in the 36kg to 38kg category or the 38kg to 40kg category? We cannot include it in both categories. If we did, it would be counted twice.

When we talk about the 36kg to 38kg category we include all those calves with weights between 36kg and 38kg and also those with a weight of 36kg but *not* those with a weight of 38kg.

Similarly, the 38kg to 40kg category includes all those calves with weights between 38kg and 40kg and also those with a weight of 38kg, but *not* those with a weight of 40kg.

Categories are usually called **class intervals.**
If a calf is to be included in the class interval 36kg to 38kg, its weight is at least 36kg but below 38kg.

Worked Example Use the graph from the previous example to find the following.

      (a) the number of calves which weighed less than 42kg

      (b) the number of calves which weighed at least 46kg

      (c) the total number of calves that were weighed

Answer (a) This includes all of the calves with weights from 36kg to 42kg i.e. the first 3 class intervals of the graph. Altogether there are 9 + 19 + 13 = 41 calves which weigh less than 42kg.

     (b) We need to find the number of calves which weighed 46kg or more. These are represented by the last 3 class intervals of this graph. Altogether there are 3 + 0 + 1 = 4 calves which weigh at least 46kg.

     (c) Total number weighed = 9 + 19 + 13 + 6 + 2 + 3 + 1
                             = 53

EXERCISE 19:2

1.

This frequency diagram shows the time taken to complete the school's cross-country course.

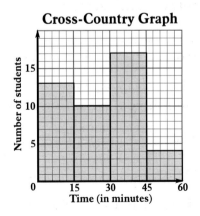

Cross-Country Graph

How many students   (a) completed this cross-country course

                          (b) completed the course in under 30 minutes

                          (c) took at least 45 minutes to complete the course?

2. This graph shows the ages of the teachers at Seaview School.

   (a) How many teachers at this school were younger than 40?

   (b) How many were at least 50?

   (c) How many were in their 20's?

   (d) Is this statement true or false? "Most of the teachers were in their 40's".

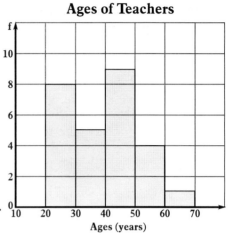

Ages of Teachers

3.

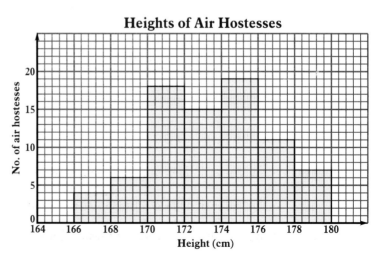

Lengths of nails

Tony's father asked him to find all the "2 inch" nails that were in the tool box. The frequency diagram gives the length (in mm) of the nails that Tony decided his father wanted.

(a) How many of these nails were at least 51mm long?

(b) How many were shorter than 50mm?

(c) How many nails did Tony find altogether?

4.

This frequency diagram shows the heights of the air hostesses who took part in Jason's survey.

Heights of Air Hostesses

(a) How many air hostesses did Jason survey altogether?

(b) How many of these air hostesses were less than 168cm tall?

(c) How many were shorter than 176cm?

(d) How many were 178cm or taller?

(e) One of the conclusions that Jason made was "Most air hostesses were at least 172cm tall". Was this conclusion correct for this data?

(f) Another of Jason's conclusions was "The shortest air hostess was 166cm". Can this conclusion be made from the graph?

Review

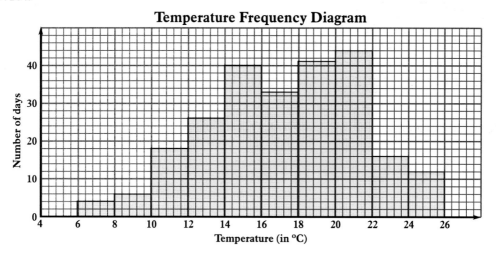

Temperature Frequency Diagram

The maximum daily temperature was recorded on a number of days. The results are shown on this graph.

(a) On how many days was the maximum daily temperature recorded?

(b) "The highest temperature recorded on any day was 26°C". Can this claim be made from this graph?

(c) On how many days was the maximum daily temperature in the 20's?

(d) On how many days was it less than 20°C?

(e) On how many days was it at least 12°C?

349

FREQUENCY TABLES for CONTINUOUS DATA. DRAWING FREQUENCY DIAGRAMS

These tables all show the same information. They show the length of the thumb on the right hand of the students in a class.

TABLE 1

Length (mm)		frequency
at least	below	
30	35	2
35	40	2
40	45	4
45	50	9
50	55	10
55	60	2

TABLE 2

Class interval (*l* is in mm)	frequency
$30 \le l < 35$	2
$35 \le l < 40$	2
$40 \le l < 45$	4
$45 \le l < 50$	9
$50 \le l < 55$	10
$55 \le l < 60$	2

TABLE 3

Length (in mm)	f
30–	2
35–	2
40–	4
45–	9
50–	10
55–60	2

TABLE 4

Length (mm)	30–	35–	40–	45–	50–	55–60
Frequency	2	2	4	9	10	2

We read $30 \le l < 35$ as "*l* is at least 30 but below 35" or as "*l* lies between 30 and 35 and may be equal to 30".

The information above is shown below, graphed on a frequency diagram.

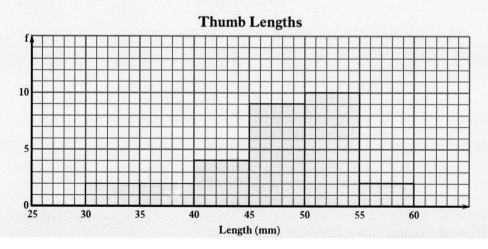

Thumb Lengths

Remember If we have to choose which class intervals to have, use these guidelines.

1. Have between 6 and 15 class intervals.

2. Make all class intervals the same width.

Example

6·4	6·1	6·7	7·1	6·0	6·5	6·4	6·2	6·4	6·3	6·1	6·8	6·7	
6·2	6·5	6·0	6·7	6·9	6·8	7·3	6·1	6·0	6·4	6·4	6·5	6·1	
6·8	6·4	6·5	6·4	7·3	6·0	6·1	6·1	6·5	6·8	6·9	6·2	7·0	
6·0	6·2	6·2	6·9	6·3	6·4	6·7	6·8	6·2	6·7	6·4	6·1	6·5	

EARTHQUAKE!!

This data gives the size of some of the recent strong earthquakes in the South Pacific.
The data on the first two lines has been recorded on the tally chart below.

Magnitude	Tally	Frequency
6·0–	JHt II	
6·2–	III	
6·4–	JHt III	
6·6–	III	
6·8–	III	
7·0–	I	
7·2–7·4	I	

EXERCISE 19:3

1.

Time taken (min.)	0 –	1–	2–	3–	4 –	5–	6 –	7–8
Number of students	39	54	123	347	29	42	21	16

This frequency table gives the time taken for students to evacuate the school during a fire drill.

(a) How many students evacuated the school in under 3 minutes?

(b) How many students took at least 5 minutes to evacuate?

(c) Once all the students were out of the school, a count was made. How many students were counted?

2.

Weight Loss (in kg)	0–	2–	4 –	6 –	8 –	10–	12–	14 –	16 and over
Frequency	4	3	7	12	10	5	3	10	2

This table gives the weight lost by the members of the local "Fatloss" club during November and December.

(a) How many members lost less than 4kg?

(b) How many lost at least 10kg?

(c) How many lost less than 10kg?

(d) Can you tell from this table if there was anyone who didn't lose any weight during November and December?

(e) How many members were there in this "Fatloss" club?

(f) Why isn't it sensible to draw a frequency diagram for this data?

3. These figures give the time, in minutes, that 50 athletes took to complete a cross country course.

30 37 43 55 52 47 49 36 44 40 41 49 52 53 39 41 46

42 50 49 39 53 54 57 43 59 34 38 40 42 48 53 50 52

37 36 45 53 48 42 52 39 41 46 50 52 38 58 57 46

(a) What was the least time taken?

(b) What was the greatest time taken?

(c) Copy and complete this tally chart and frequency table for the data.

Class interval (t is time, in min)	Tally	f
$30 \leq t < 35$		
$35 \leq t < 40$		
$40 \leq t < 45$		
$45 \leq t < 50$		
$50 \leq t < 55$		
$55 \leq t < 60$		

(d) Draw a frequency diagram for this data.

4.

Ages of Females		
Age	**Wales**	**Northern Ireland**
0 –	91000	67000
5 –	88000	65000
10–	84000	62000
15–	105000	67000
20–	113000	64000
25–	109000	60000
30–	89000	53000
35–	94000	48000
40–	97000	48000
45–	80000	42000
50–	77000	39000
55–	78000	38000
60–	83000	37000
65–	84000	36000
70–	68000	29000
75–	60000	25000
80–	42000	16000
85–90	29000	10000

This table gives the number of females, to the nearest thousand, in Wales and Northern Ireland.

(a) Draw a frequency diagram to illustrate the ages of females in Wales. Draw another frequency diagram to illustrate the ages of females in Northern Ireland.
Write a sentence or two about any differences or similarities in the shape of the two frequency diagrams.

(b) Regroup the data into class intervals 0–, 10–, 20–, etc.
The first part of this regrouping is shown for the females in Wales.

Age	Females in Wales
0–	91000 + 88000 = 179000
10–	84000 + 105000 = 189000
20–	113000 + 109000 = 222000
30–	89000 + 94000 = 183000

Copy this and complete the regrouping for the females in Wales. Also make a similar frequency table for the females in Northern Ireland.

(c) Draw two more frequency diagrams; one for the regrouped data for the females in Wales and the other for the regrouped data for the females in Northern Ireland.

Do these graphs show the same differences or similarities as the graphs drawn in (a)?

5. Decide on suitable class intervals to use for the following lists of data.
Remember to have between 6 and 15 class intervals.
Remember to have the class intervals the same width.

(a) This data is the time, in minutes, it took for 60 students to jog or run around the park.

```
22  16  21  24  23  15  17  19  32  28  22  27  34  18  22
33  25  31  17  27  19  25  34  21  15  29  16  30  24  18
24  34  24  20  15  26  28  21  31  32  24  24  16  30  27
16  19  27  31  31  26  26  28  22  22  30  20  17  17  33
```

(b) This data gives the weight, in grams, of the books on a shelf in the library.

```
742    241    332    478   1245    832    746    291    160    635
1042    368    760    590    742    834    564   1340    824    683
174    960    236    746    328    387    823    894    910   1043
712    521    972    834    424    927    591    242    741    230
846   1320   1010    204    819    367    724    621    631    198
```

(c) This data gives the handspan, in mm, of some 13-year-old girls.

```
171  182  202  164  198  211  164  173  177  173  192  205  232
223  189  186  191  194  197  205  231  207  169  173  184  209
176  181  207  164  196  203  221  238  160  169  184  207  197
188  164  219  199  222  203  198  196  191  172  168  199  206
```

Review 1 This frequency diagram shows the injury time played in the football games last season, on the local pitch.

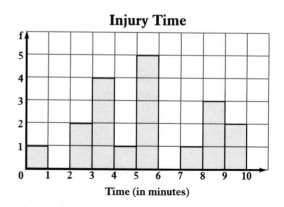

Injury Time

Time (in minutes)

(a) How many of these games had injury time played of less than 5 minutes?

(b) How many had at least 6 minutes injury time?

(c) How many games were played on this pitch last season?

(d) Can you tell from this frequency diagram the number of games in which there was no injury time played?

Review 2 The following data gives the weight (in kg) carried by the horses in the last three races at a County Racing Club's winter meeting.

56	55	55	55	54	54	52·5	51	51
57	57	57	57	57	57	57	57	57
57	57	54·5	54·5	54·5	54·5	54·5	54·5	57
56·5	55	55	55	54	54	54	53·5	53
53	53	52·5	52·5	52·5	52	51·5	51	51

(a) Use a tally chart to sort the data, then copy and complete this frequency table.

Weight (kg)	51–	52–	53–	54–	55–	56–	57–58
Frequency							

(b) Draw a graph for the data.

SURVEYS

The tally chart for the **collection of continuous data** must have class intervals. These should all be the same width. That is, the tally chart must have equal class intervals.

Example   Simon thought he had short arms. He decided to collect data on the length of the right arm of other students of his age. He designed the following tally chart for the collection of his data.

LENGTH of ARM of 13-year-old boys			
Length (cm) at least	below	Tally	Frequency
44	46		
46	48		
48	50		
50	52		
52	54		
54	56		
56	58		

DISCUSSION EXERCISE 19:4

In the previous example, Simon made the following decisions before he wrote up his tally chart: he was going to measure in cm

he was going to measure underarm, from the armpit to the wrist

he was only going to measure the arms of boys

Why did Simon make these decisions?

What other decisions would Simon have to make?

Discuss with your neighbour or group or class.

The data should be **organised** by graphing it on a frequency diagram.

Always — have frequency on the vertical axis

— label the axes

— show the scale that is used on both axes

— give your graph a suitable title.

The way the data is **analysed** will depend on the reason for collecting it.

For instance, if Simon (in the previous example) was just interested to know the arm length of other boys of his age he would probably write conclusions such as

"The range of arm lengths was . . ."

"More boys had arm length between . . . cm and . . . cm than between any other values" etc.

However, if Simon was collecting the data because he wanted to test the statement "I have shorter arms that most other boys of my age" he would probably write a conclusion such as "Since about 80% of boys of my age have arms that are longer than mine, I conclude that I have got short arms".

PRACTICAL EXERCISE 19:5

Carry out a survey that involves the collection of continuous data. Organise and analyse your data. Look back at **page 319** for the steps you should take to conduct a survey.

Choose a topic that interests you. You may choose from the suggestions that follow or you may collect data about a hobby or a sport or some other activity in which you are interested.

You may wish to make and test a statement.

Suggested survey topics

1. Height (in cm) of 12-year-old girls (or boys) in your school. You could use a different year group if you wished.

2. Playing time for the tracks on the L.P.s or C.D.s that you, or your friends, or your family own.

3. Handspan of the students in your class.

4. Distance the students in your class travel to get to school.

5. Temperature at some shady place in your school grounds.
   Collect the data at the same time each day.
   Collect data for at least 20 days.

6. Time you take to move between classes during each classroom change in one particular week.

7. Collect data from an experiment in one of your other subjects.

8. Collect a number of frequency diagrams from newspapers and magazines.
   Analyse the information on them.

INVESTIGATION 19:6

MISLEADING FREQUENCY DIAGRAMS

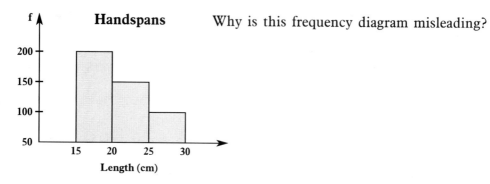

Why is this frequency diagram misleading?

Investigate other misleading ways of drawing frequency diagrams.

You could make a collection of frequency diagrams from the newspaper or magazines to illustrate your investigation.

FOR YOUR INTEREST

Manufacturers, scientists, advertisers, the media, publishers, store managers, and schools might display data on a frequency diagram.

Discuss one of the following statements in relation to these people or organisations.

A frequency diagram can be used to persuade people.

Frequency diagrams should always be used in reports.

Frequency diagrams are not used often enough.

Make a summary of your discussion.

DISCOVER, DISCUSS, DO

- *"It is probable that Georgina will watch a video next weekend."*

Craig claimed that this meant that there was a very good chance of Georgina watching a video next weekend.

Sasha challenged Craig — "But Craig, what do you mean by a very good chance?"

Craig replied "I mean that Georgina will be just about certain to watch a video next weekend."

Sasha said "Do you mean there is a 1 in 100 chance that Georgina will not watch a video?"

"Well, I wouldn't put the chance of her not watching a video quite that low; maybe 1 chance in 10," Craig replied.

Sasha then said "You mean 90 chances in 100 that she will."

"About that," Craig replied.

Which words or phrases used by Sasha or Craig have a very precise meaning in mathematics? **Discuss.**

How might other people interpret the statement: "It is probable that Georgina will watch a video next weekend"? **Discuss.**

- Write down some statements which contain one or more of the words or phrases in the following box. **Discuss.**

1 in 5 chance	likely	certain to happen	highly probable
will never happen	even chance	probability of $\frac{1}{4}$	less than even chance

- Sasha was tossing two coins together.

Craig said "There is a 1 in 3 chance, that is probability of $\frac{1}{3}$, that on the next toss you will get two heads."

"I disagree with you," Sasha said. "I think there is a 1 in 4 chance, that is probability of $\frac{1}{4}$, that the next toss will be two heads."

Craig argued strongly that he was right. Sasha argued equally strongly that she was right. What arguments might each have used? Who was right? **Discuss.**

- Sasha and Craig are going on holiday to Majorca with their parents. Their holiday begins as follows:

They travel by train to Gatwick Airport.
They fly from Gatwick to Majorca.
They hire a car and drive to the Hotel Playa.

Write some statements about things that could have happened to this family, from the time they left their home to the time they book into the hotel. **Discuss** the probability of these things happening.

Continue Sasha's and Craig's holiday for them. Write down a statement about each thing they do and the things that happen to them. **Discuss** the probability of these things happening.

POSSIBLE OUTCOMES for TWO EVENTS

Outcomes may be given as a **list**, in a **table** or on a **diagram**.

Example   When two coins are tossed together, the possible outcomes may be shown in a list as HH, HT, TH, TT.
    HH means a head on the first coin and a head on the second coin.
    HT means a head on the first coin and a tail on the second coin.
    TH means a tail on the first coin and a head on the second coin.
    TT means a tail on the first coin and a tail on the second coin.

or in a table as

1st coin		2nd coin H	2nd coin T
	H	HH	HT
	T	TH	TT

or on a diagram as

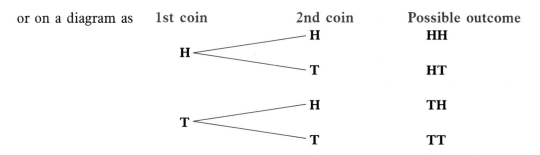

1st coin	2nd coin	Possible outcome
H	H	HH
	T	HT
T	H	TH
	T	TT

EXERCISE 20:1

1. In a co-ed. class, one student presents the daily puzzle at the beginning of a maths. lesson. This same student, or another, gives the solution at the end of the lesson.

   Complete the following list of possible outcomes for the gender of the students involved with the daily puzzle. (B stands for boy, G stands for girl.) GG, GB, . . .

2. Each day, when Dale gets home from school, his mother is listening to the radio. The only stations she listens to are Radio 1, Radio 2, Radio 3 and Radio 4.

   Make a list of all the possible outcomes for the radio stations that Dale's mother could be listening to when Dale gets home from school today and tomorrow.

3. Two dice are tossed together.
   Complete the following list of possible outcomes.

   1, 1   1, 2   1, 3   1, 4   1, 5   1, 6
   2, 1   2, 2   . . .

4. A coin and a die are tossed together.

   Copy and complete this table which shows the possible outcomes.

		die					
		1	2	3	4	5	6
coin	H		H2				
	T					T5	

5. Peter, Jake and Barry took Chantelle, Deirdre and Lisa to a disco. During the evening, each boy danced with each girl.

   Make a table to show all the possible outcomes of which boy had the first dance with which girl.

6. Some red and some black counters are placed in a bag.
   One counter is drawn at random and then replaced in the bag. Another counter is then drawn.

   Make a table to show the possible outcomes for the colours of the two counters drawn.

7. The Jacks, Queens and Kings are taken from a pack of cards. These are shuffled. One card is drawn at random.

   The card is replaced and another drawn.

   Copy and complete the following diagram to show all the possible outcomes.

1st card	2nd card	Possible outcome

```
      1st card          2nd card         Possible outcome

                            J                  JJ
          J                 Q                  JQ
                            K                  JK


          Q


          K
```

Review 1 Each of the 5 letters in the word MATHS is written on a small card.
These 5 cards are then placed in a bag.
One card is chosen, at random, from the bag. This card is replaced in the bag.
A second card is then chosen, at random.

Make a list of the possible outcomes for the letters that were on these two cards.

Review 2

Two dice are thrown together. The numbers obtained are added together.

Copy and complete this table to show all the possible outcomes.

		Second die					
		1	2	3	4	5	6
First die	1	2	3	4	5	6	7
	2	3	4	5			
	3						
	4						
	5						
	6						

Review 3 In a competition there are three horses; Flash, Blackie and Angel. The first two sections of this competition are dressage and cross-country.

Copy and complete this diagram to show all the possible outcomes for the winner of the first two sections of this competition.

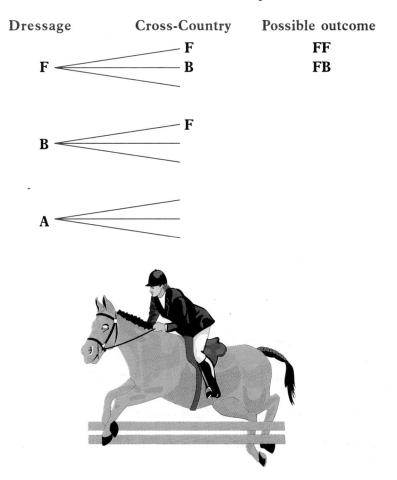

Dressage	Cross-Country	Possible outcome
	F	FF
F	B	FB
B	F	
A		

CALCULATING PROBABILITY

Remember: we calculate the probability of an event occurring by using the following formula.

For equally likely outcomes,

$$\textbf{Probability of an event} = \frac{\textbf{Number of favourable outcomes}}{\textbf{Number of possible outcomes}}$$

We must find all the **possible outcomes** and from these select the **favourable outcomes**. We may use a listing, a table or a diagram to show all the possible outcomes.

Worked Example 1 Find the probability that, in a 2-child family, both children are girls.

Answer All the possible outcomes can be found by drawing a diagram as follows:

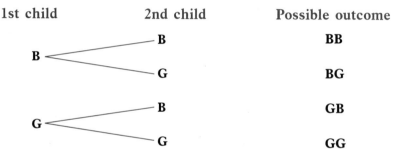

From the diagram we see that there are four possible outcomes;
BB, BG, GB, GG.
Only one of these outcomes is favourable; GG.

Then, P (both girls) = $\frac{1}{4}$

Worked Example 2 A die and a coin are tossed together. Find the probability that we get a head and a number greater than 4.

Answer All the possible outcomes can be written as a list as follows:
H1   H2   H3   H4   H5   H6   T1   T2   T3   T4   T5   T6

There are 12 possible outcomes.
There are two favourable outcomes; H5, H6.

Then, P (H and number greater than 4) = $\frac{2}{12}$ or $\frac{1}{6}$

Worked Example 3 Two dice are tossed and the numbers obtained are added together.
Find the probability of getting (a) a total of 7
(b) a total of at least 11.

Answer All the possible outcomes can be given in a table as shown.

		Second die					
		1	2	3	4	5	6
First die	1	2	3	4	5	6	7
	2	3	4	5	6	7	8
	3	4	5	6	7	8	9
	4	5	6	7	8	9	10
	5	6	7	8	9	10	11
	6	7	8	9	10	11	12

The number of possible equally likely outcomes is 36.
(a) Of all the possible outcomes, six of them are 7. There are six favourable outcomes.

$$P(7) = \tfrac{6}{36} \text{ or } \tfrac{1}{6}$$

(b) Favourable outcomes are 11 and 12. 11 occurs twice and 12 occurs once. There are three favourable outcomes.

$$P(\text{at least } 11) = \tfrac{3}{36} \text{ or } \tfrac{1}{12}$$

EXERCISE 20:2

1. Families with two children are studied. One of these families is chosen for further study.
    Find the probability that in this chosen family
    (a) the children will both be boys
    (b) one child will be a boy and one a girl
    (c) at least one of the children will be a girl
    (d) not more than one of the children will be a boy.

    (Use the possible outcomes given in *Worked Example 1.*)

2. A coin is tossed and a die is rolled. Find the probability of getting
    (a) a tail and a 3
    (b) a tail and an even number
    (c) a head and a number greater than 2
    (d) a head and a multiple of 2
    (e) a tail and a number less than 7
    (f) a head and a number greater than 6.

    (Use the possible outcomes given in *Worked Example 2.*)

3. Two dice are tossed and the numbers obtained are added.
   Find the probability of getting a total of

   (a) 2   (b) 5   (c) 9   (d) 12   (e) 1.

   (Use the possible outcomes given in **Worked Example 3.**)

4. For the example given in **question 3** find the probability of getting the following totals.

   (a) less than 7   (b) at least 7   (c) more than 7

   (d) exactly 8   (e) at least 8   (f) less than 8

   (g) more than 8

5. (a) What is the most likely total to get when two dice are tossed?

   (b) What is the least likely total?

6.

A spinner is attached to the centre of a circular card as shown. The card is divided into thirds.
The spinner is spun twice and the two numbers obtained are added together.

Copy and complete the table to show all the possible outcomes.

	2nd spin		
	2	4	7
1st spin 2			
4			
7			

Find   (a) P (6)   (b) P (14)   (c) P (7)

(d) P (even number)   (e) P (multiple of 3)   (f) P (at least 8)

(g) P (less than 8)   (h) P (more than 7)   (i) P (less than 7)

(j) P (prime number).

Review 1 Two coins are tossed together.
Write down all the possible equally likely outcomes.

Find   (a) P (TT)   (b) P (just one H)   (c) P (at least one T).

Review 2 Three counters are put into a bag. One is green, one is white and the other is black. A counter is drawn at random and its colour noted. The counter is then put back in the bag.
Another counter is then drawn at random and its colour noted.

Write down all the possible equally likely outcomes for the colour of the two counters. You could use a table or a diagram to help.

Find (a) P (both black)   (b) P (same colour)

(c) P (different colours)   (d) P (just one is black)

(e) P (at least one is black)   (f) P (neither is black).

EXHAUSTIVE EVENTS

Exhaustive events account for all possible outcomes.

The list HH, HT, TH, TT gives all the possible outcomes when two coins are tossed. We say the events HH, HT, TH, TT are exhaustive since they account for (or exhaust) all the possibilities. No other outcomes are possible.

If events are exhaustive, it is certain that one of them will happen.

Example Consider the events "an even number", "an odd number" when a die is tossed.
Favourable outcomes for the event "an even number" are 2, 4, 6.
Favourable outcomes for the event "an odd number" are 1, 3, 5.
When a die is tossed the only possible outcomes are 1, 2, 3, 4, 5 or 6.
The events "an even number", "an odd number", account for all these possible outcomes. Hence we say the events "an even number", "an odd number", are exhaustive.

Example Consider the events "a prime number", "an even number" when a die is tossed.
Favourable outcomes for the event "a prime number" are 2, 3, 5.
Favourable outcomes for the event "an even number" are 2, 4, 6.
The events "a prime number", "an even number" are not exhaustive since they do not account for all the possible outcomes. They do not account for the possible outcome of 1.

DISCUSSION EXERCISE 20:3

- Are the following pairs of events exhaustive? (Each refers to the tossing of a die.) **Discuss.**

  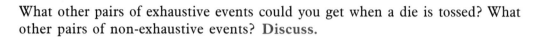

  "a prime number", "an odd number"
  "a multiple of 3", "an even number"
  "a multiple of 2", "an odd number"
  "a number less than 4", "a number greater than 3"

  What other pairs of exhaustive events could you get when a die is tossed? What other pairs of non-exhaustive events? **Discuss.**

- Write down pairs of exhaustive events and pairs of non-exhaustive events that you could get when a card is drawn from a pack. **Discuss.**

- **Discuss** exhaustive and non-exhaustive events which relate to a game of football or some other game or to things you do on a school day.

MUTUALLY EXCLUSIVE EVENTS

Example   When this spinner is spun it could stop in the section marked 1 or 2 or 3 or 4 or 5 or 6 or 7 or 8.

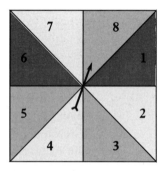

Let the event "stops on an odd number" be event A.
Let the event "stops on the 2" be event B. The events A and B cannot happen at the same time. We say that event A and event B are mutually exclusive.

Now suppose that event A is "stops on an odd number" and event B is "stops on a multiple of 3." In this case, events A and B can happen at the same time. This would be so if the spinner stopped in the section marked 3 since 3 is both an odd number and a multiple of 3. In this case, the event A and the event B are not mutually exclusive.

Events which cannot happen at the same time are called **mutually exclusive events.**

EXERCISE 20:4

State whether or not the following events A and B are mutually exclusive.

1. A die is tossed.
   Event A : tossing an even number
   Event B : tossing an odd number

2. Two coins are tossed.
   Event A : two heads
   Event B : one head and one tail

3. A die is tossed.
   Event A : a number greater than 4
   Event B : an odd number

4. Two coins are tossed.
   Event A : two heads
   Event B : at least one head

5. A card is drawn from a full pack.
   Event A : a spade
   Event B : an ace

6. A day dawns.
   Event A : it is a fine day
   Event B : it is windy

7. A sheep has lambs.
   Event A : the lambs are twins
   Event B : the lambs are triplets

8. Two students are chosen at random.
   Event A : one student wears glasses
   Event B : one student is tall

9. A counter is drawn from a box containing red, blue and white counters.
   Event A : a red counter
   Event B : not a red counter

Review 1 A die is tossed.
   Event A : a number less than 4
   Event B : the number 4

Review 2 Salina goes shopping.
   Event A : Salina goes shopping with Kate
   Event B : Salina goes shopping with Shannon

DISCUSSION EXERCISE 20:5

• Think of pairs of events which are mutually exclusive. **Discuss.**
  Think of pairs of events which are not mutually exclusive. **Discuss.**

• A card is drawn from a pack.
  Event A : an ace   **Event B :** the king of spades
  What might **event C** be if the three events A, B and C are mutually exclusive?
  Discuss.
  What might **event C** be if the three events A, B and C are not mutually
  exclusive? **Discuss.**

DISCUSSION EXERCISE 20:6

A coin is tossed. Are the outcomes "Head", "Tail" mutually exclusive? Are they exhaustive?

What is   P (H)?
What is   P (T)?
What is   P (H) + P (T)?

Two coins are tossed together. Are the outcomes HH, HT, TH, TT mutually exclusive? Are they exhaustive?

What is   P (HH)?
What is   P (HT)?
What is   P (TH)?
What is   P (TT)?
What is   P (HH) + P (HT) + P (TH) + P (TT)?

When do probabilities of outcomes add up to 1? **Discuss.** As part of your discussion use the words "mutually exclusive."

PROBABILITY of an EVENT NOT HAPPENING

Consider tossing a die.
The possible outcomes are 1, 2, 3, 4, 5, 6. There are six possible outcomes.

Consider the event "tossing a 3".
There is just one favourable outcome; getting a 3. Then $P(3) = \frac{1}{6}$

Now consider the event "not tossing a 3".
There are 5 favourable outcomes; getting 1, 2, 4, 5 or 6. Then $P(\text{not } 3) = \frac{5}{6}$

Notice that if we add together the probabilities of the two events "3" and "not 3" we get answer of 1. This is to be expected since these two events account for all the possible mutually exclusive outcomes. One of these two events is certain to happen.

Also notice that $P(\text{not } 3) = 1 - P(3)$ and $P(3) = 1 - P(\text{not } 3)$

For any event:

Probability of the event not happening = 1 – Probability of the event happening

or

Probability of the event happening = 1 – Probability of the event not happening

Worked Example A box contains 100 counters. Seven of these are green. The rest are either red or white. The box is tipped over and all the counters, except one, spill onto the floor.
What is the probability that the counter remaining in the box is not a green counter?

Answer $P(G) = \frac{7}{100}$ $P(\text{not } G) = 1 - \frac{7}{100}$

$$= \frac{93}{100}$$

EXERCISE 20:7

1. The probability of Yeorgi getting a hole in one at mini golf is $\frac{2}{5}$. What is the probability that he will not get a hole in one?

2. Elfie has a telephone answering machine. If the probability of a caller not leaving a message on the machine is 0.3, find the probability of a caller leaving a message.

3. If the probability that a novice jumper hits the top rail is 0.65, what is the probability that this jumper does not hit the top rail?

4. The probability of a pack of crisps not being underweight is 0.95. What is the probability of a pack being underweight?

5. In a box of chalk, 10 pieces are white, 5 are yellow and 3 are red. Emma chooses one piece at random. Find the probability that this stick is (a) yellow
                                                                                (b) not yellow.

6. Derek has a number of different coloured felt-tip pens in a special case. There are 2 red, 3 purple, 1 green, 5 blue, 1 yellow and 2 black felt-tip pens in Derek's case. He takes one out at random. Find the probability that the one he took out is (a) blue
                                                                                                                                               (b) not blue.

7. Ali did a survey on how often his school bus was late. The data he collected showed that the bus was early, or on time, 83 times out of 95.
From the results of his survey, Ali estimated the probability of this bus being late the next time he caught it.
What answer should Ali get?

Review 1 The probability that a car, calling at a service station, needs oil is 0·12. What is the probability that a car, calling at this service station, does not need oil?

Review 2 Of 50 chocolates in a box, 20 contain a nut. One chocolate is chosen at random from this box.
Find the probability that this chocolate   (a)   contains a nut
                                         (b)   does not contain a nut.

EXPECTED NUMBER

We can use probability to estimate the **expected number** of times an event is likely to occur.

Worked Example   If I throw a die 180 times, how many sixes am I likely to get?

Answer   On any one throw $P(6) = \frac{1}{6}$

On 180 throws, I expect to get $180 \times \frac{1}{6}$ sixes i.e. 30 sixes.

Worked Example   The probability that a box of chocolates is underweight is 0·03. Of 1500 boxes of chocolates, how many do you expect to be not underweight?

Answer P (underweight) $= 0·03$

P (not underweight) $= 0·97$

Number expected to be not underweight $= 1500 \times 0·97$

$= 1455$

EXERCISE 20:8

1. The probability of Jack hitting the bull's eye with a dart is $\frac{1}{20}$. How many times does Jack expect to hit the bull's eye if he throws 200 darts?

2. The probability that Ari makes no mistakes in a Maths. Aural Test is 0·4. During next year, Ari will do 20 of these tests. In how many of these, do you expect Ari to make no mistakes?

3. The probability of a golfer sinking a putt is 0·18. How many putts would you expect this golfer to sink in her next 150 attempts?

4. The probability of a horse falling at the Double Jump is $\frac{1}{20}$. This jump is jumped by 140 horses during the jumping season. How many of these horses will be expected to fall at the Double Jump?

5. The probability of a novice swimmer getting cramp in a distance race is $\frac{1}{6}$. How many of the 18 novice swimmers in a long distance race would you expect not to get cramp?

6. The probability of Mrs Hanlin's class working on coursework during any one maths. lesson is 0·25. During how many of the next 60 maths. lessons do you expect that Mrs Hanlin's class will not be working on coursework?

7. The probability of passing a driving test at the first attempt is $\frac{2}{3}$. Of 60 people attempting the test for the first time, how many would you expect to fail?

8. Three out of every ten flights arriving at an airport are late. Of 300 flights arriving at this airport, how many do you expect to be late?

9. Jason is late for school on 3 days out of 10.

   (a) What is the probability that Jason is late for school?

   (b) In the next 50 school days, how many times do you expect Jason to be late?

10. A die is tossed 300 times.
    On how many of these tosses would you expect to get a six?

11. Two coins are tossed together 60 times.
    On how many of these tosses would you expect to get two heads?

Review 1 The probability that all tows will be operating at a ski-resort is 0·85. This ski season, this resort hopes to open on 120 days. On how many days this season do you expect all the tows will be operating?

Review 2 (a) Write down all the possible digits for the last digit of a car's number plate.

        (b) What is the probability that the last digit is an 8?

        (c) Of 5000 number plates, how many would you expect to have 8 as the last digit?

Review 3 The probability of a day in April being wet is $\frac{2}{5}$.
How many days in April are likely not to be wet?

GAMES 20:9

**These are games of skill, not games of chance.
You need never lose these games!**

THE COLOUR GAME: a game for 2 players

Players take it in turn to colour in either one or two of the squares on this grid. If a player chooses to colour in two squares they must be joined by at least one edge; (the two squares coloured in red on the diagram are not allowed at one turn). The winner is the player who colours in the last square.

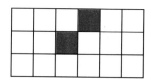

continued . . .

. . . *from previous page*

COUNTER GAME: a game for 2 players

● ● ● ● ● ● ●   ● ● ● ● ●

Begin with two piles of counters; (there may be any number of counters in the piles). The two players take it in turn to remove either one counter from one pile or one counter from each pile.
The winner is the player who removes the last counter.

PRACTICAL EXERCISE 20:10

1. Design and make two different spinners which have a probability of $\frac{1}{3}$ of stopping in each section.

2. Invent a game which uses a playing board, dice and counters.
   Write the rules for the game clearly and concisely.
   Play each of the games invented by the groups in your class and award marks to each.
   Marks should be given for the originality of the game, the construction, clarity of the instructions and for how interesting your group found the game.

FOR YOUR INTEREST

Discuss one or more of the following statements. Find examples which support your point of view.

A probability gives all the information you need about the likelihood of an event occurring.

Probabilities are the best way to inform the public about the likelihood of events occurring.

Probability should be used when planning for future events.

You could write a summary of your discussion.

You could join with another group and debate one of the statements. If you do this, one group should present arguments *for* the statement and the other group present arguments *against* the statement.

1. Two cards are drawn from a pack. The first card is replaced in the pack before the second card is drawn.

   Copy and complete this table to show the possible outcomes for the suits of the cards drawn.

		Second card			
		H	S	D	C
First card	H	HH			
	S	SH			
	D		DS		DC
	C			CD	

2. Which of the following is discrete data and which is continuous data?

   (a) time of arrival of trains at Victoria Station

   (b) length of trains

   (c) number of passengers on trains

   (d) distance between Victoria and Waterloo Stations

3. In a game two coins, one a 20p coin and the other a 10p coin, are dropped onto a large round mat. This mat is divided into thirds as shown in the diagram.

   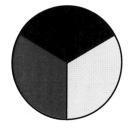

   Copy and complete the following list of possible outcomes for the colour of the region on which the coins could fall. (R stands for red, G for grey, B for black. RG means the 20p falls on the red and the 10p falls on the grey. GR means the 20p falls on the grey and the 10p falls on the red.) RR, RG, RB, GR, . . .

4.

Age	0–	10–	20–	30–	40–	50–	60–	70–80
Frequency	3	2	5	4	6	4	3	1

   Draw a frequency diagram for this data.
   Make up a title for your graph.

5. Copy and complete this diagram to show the gender of the children in 2-child families.

Oldest child	Youngest child	Possible outcome

G —< G   GG
         B

B —< G
     B

6. Which of the following data would be suitable for graphing on a scatter diagram?

(a) Distance travelled to school.

(b) Distance travelled and time taken to get to school.

(c) Time spent fishing and the number of fish caught.

(d) Results of tossing a die 15 times.

(e) Height and length of foot of 13-year olds.

(f) Maths. and Science marks of Year 3 students.

(g) Height and weight of different species of animals.

7. A card is drawn from a full 52 card pack.
Which of the following pairs of events are exhaustive?

(a) a red card, a black card

(b) a diamond, a heart

(c) a face card, not a face card

8. The probability of a fisherman catching an under-sized lobster is 0·08. If under-sized lobsters are caught, they must be thrown back to sea.

Find the probability that a lobster is not thrown back to sea.

9.

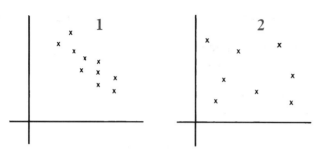

(a) Which of these graphs shows no correlation?

(b) Which shows positive correlation?

(c) Which shows negative correlation?

10. Vincent was doing a survey on the number of doors in cars. To collect his data he stood at the entrance to the carpark of Aintree racecourse, on Grand National day. After he had collected his data, he organised it on the following frequency table.

Number of doors	2	3	4	5
Frequency	82	124	492	22

(a) How many cars did Vincent include in his survey?

(b) How many degrees on a pie chart will represent the 3-door cars?

(c) Draw a pie chart to represent the data.

11. This graph shows the weight of the luggage of the people on a coach tour.

(a) How many had luggage that weighed less than 20kg?

(b) How many people were on this coach tour?

(c) Is the following statement true? "Most people's luggage weighed between 15 and 20kg."

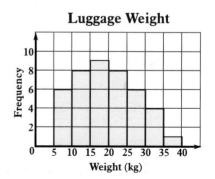

378

12. In which of the following are the events A and B mutually exclusive?

   (a) Event A : John goes to the football match
        Event B : Jessie goes to the football match

   (b) Event A : a diamond is drawn from a pack of cards
        Event B : a picture card is drawn from a pack of cards

   (c) Event A : a prime number is obtained when a die is tossed
        Event B : a six is obtained when a die is tossed

13.

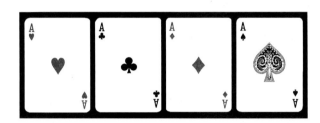

The four aces are taken from a pack of cards.
One ace is drawn at random from these four aces.
The card is then put back with the other aces and another ace is drawn.
Write down all the possible outcomes for these two events.

Find   (a) P (both spades)   (b) P (both black)   (c) P (no hearts)

        (d) P (different suits)   (e) P (different colours).

14. (a) Would you expect there to be positive correlation, negative correlation or no correlation between the time people spend reading and the time they spend watching television?

    (b) Jody gathered the following data from ten students in her class. Each of these students recorded the time (to the nearest hour) they spent reading and the time they spent watching T.V. during one weekend.

Student	C.A.	R.S.	A.M.	Z.D.	N.M.	F.G.	A.G.	D.H.	M.A.	D.P.
No. of hours watching TV	10	3	8	5	1	13	6	14	12	4
No. of hours reading	2	7	4	4	10	3	7	1	1	11

What sort of graph should you display this data on to look for correlation?

Draw a graph to check the correlation.

15. Mrs Jones timed all the phone calls her sons made during the last month. This list
    gives the times in minutes and seconds (e.g. 4·12 stands for 4 minutes and 12 seconds).

6·24	5·12	3·04	6·26	5·01	3·52	4·14	7·19	6·34	2·05
5·40	4·48	5·17	2·59	3·48	2·00	1·46	0·48	6·06	0·50
2·45	6·00	3·01	4·28	3·36	1·02	7·48	2·44	2·00	3·40
3·50	1·28	0·45	3·54	5·00	4·47	7·41	6·05	6·34	5·20
4·40	2·32	3·49	2·00	4·09	3·48	5·20	2·47	5·10	1·40
6·05	5·10	7·09	5·42	5·04	6·42	7·52	6·09	4·06	5·42
5·32	0·50	4·50	3·48	4·25	4·40	7·10	0·55	6·10	

(a) Copy and complete this frequency table.

Length of Call (min)		Tally	Frequency
at least	below		
0	1		
1	2		
2	3		
3	4		
4	5		
5	6		
6	7		
7	8		

(b) Draw a frequency diagram for this data.

16. Four full packs of cards (52 cards in each) are shuffled together. A card is chosen
    at random, then put back and the pack shuffled again. This is done 260 times.
    How many picture cards (Aces, Kings, Queens and Jacks) do you expect there to
    have been in the 260 cards chosen?

17. Sandra decided to collect data to see if there was
    a relationship between the circumference of a
    person's wrist and the length of a person's hand.

    Describe how Sandra could collect this data. As
    part of your description, design a table for the
    collection of this data.

    Sandra decided to graph the data on a scatter graph.
    Explain why this is sensible. Mention correlation as part of your explanation.

INDEX